HANDYMAN
CLUB OF AMERICA

Tools & Techniques

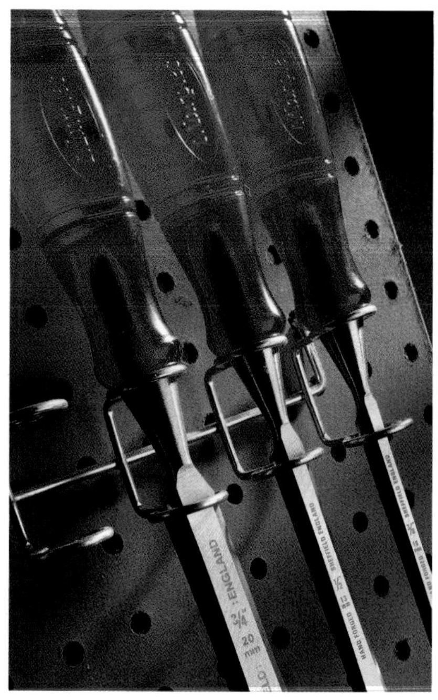

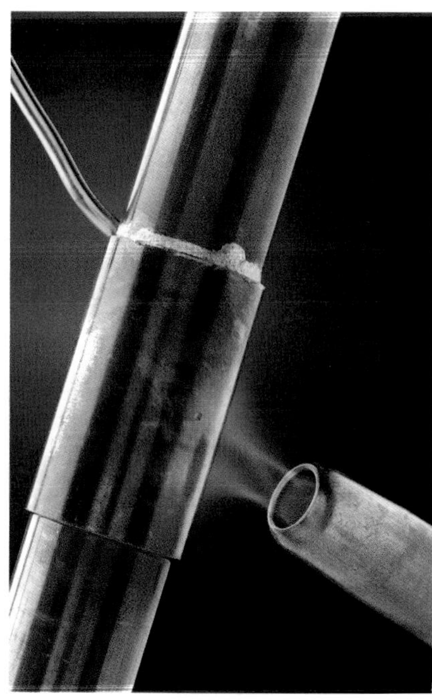

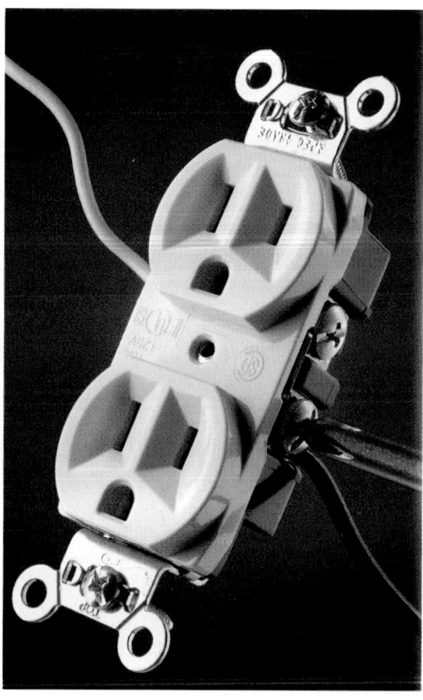

Handyman Club Library™

Handyman Club of America
Minnetonka, Minnesota

Tools & Techniques

Printed in 2011.

CREDITS

Tom Carpenter
Creative Director

Jen Weaverling
Managing Editor

Wendy Holdman
Book Design and Production

Dan Cary
Contributing Editor, Photo Production Coordinator

Chris Marshall
Editorial Coordinator

Steve Boman, Paul Currie, Mark Johanson
Writers

Steve Anderson
Contributing Writer

Mark Macemon
Lead Photographer

Ralph Karlen
Photography

John Nadeau
Technical Advisor and Builder

Craig Claeys
Contributing Illustrator

Charlie Swenson
Technical Consultant

ISBN 13: 978-1-58159-489-8

2 3 4 5 6 7 8 / 15 14 13 12 11

Handyman Club of America
12301 Whitewater Drive
Minnetonka, Minnesota 55343
www.handymanclub.com

TABLE OF CONTENTS

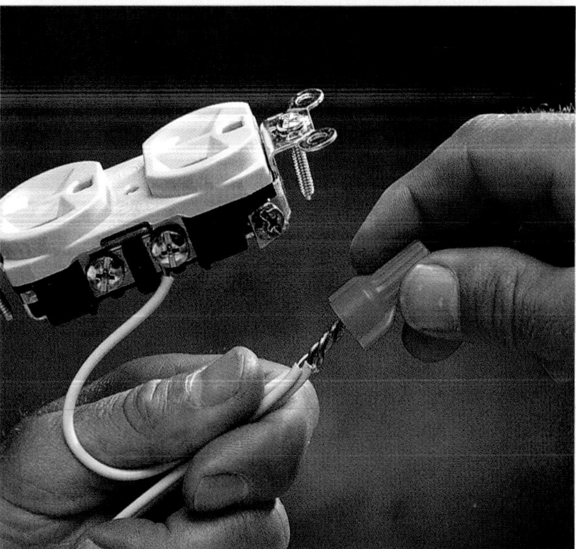

Introduction

If you were allowed only one home reference book in your library, this might well be the volume to choose. From tool use and basic woodworking tips to plumbing, wiring and metalworking, you'll find a little bit of everything in the fully-packed pages that follow.

The information to be found in this book is not here by accident. Over the years, we've learned a lot about the Members of the Handyman Club of America—partly because many of us who worked to make this book are Club Members ourselves. We've attempted the same projects, faced the same problems and challenges, and asked the same questions.

The first section of this book deals with a subject that's close to all our hearts: the workshop. The workshop is both a source of pride and a welcoming retreat for the handyman. Our search to make it harder-working, more efficient and more comfortable is a never-ending quest. The workshop information you'll find here covers a wide range of topics: from good advice about organizing your too-limited shop space to tips for laying out projects quickly and accurately, to sound skill-building and helpful hints for using just about every tool you own.

The second section of this book deals with plumbing. In this brief but very complete treatment, you'll discover the basics of handling the most common plumbing materials: You'll also find plenty of useful information to help with the plumbing projects you're most likely to take on.

And finally, this book concludes with a section on wiring that will help take the fear out of doing electrical projects and repairs. We've included all the basics you need to know about cable, making connections, and handling wiring materials safely.

Whether you're a weekend handyman or an experienced tradesman, you'll learn many new and useful things about your workshop and your home simply by taking the time to examine and read this book—we think you'll agree that it's time well spent.

IMPORTANT NOTICE

For your safety, caution and good judgment should be used when following instructions described in this book. Take into consideration your level of skill and the safety precautions related to the tools and materials shown. Neither the publisher, North American Membership Group Inc., nor any of its affiliates can assume responsibility for any damage to property or persons as a result of the misuse of the information provided. Consult your local building department for information on permits, codes, regulations and laws that may apply to your project.

Workshop

General Workshop

A workshop is constantly evolving. It begins with the selection of a space: half of a double garage, a room in the basement or, if possible, a separate outbuilding. Preparing the space for use as a workshop takes some work and planning. In almost all cases, you'll need to increase the electrical service to the area by adding dedicated 20 amp lines for your major tools, and perhaps 240 volt service for a state-of-the art table saw, radial-arm saw or shaper. You'll need to assess the ventilation and perhaps add a window or a vent fan. If possible, a built-in dust collection system should be installed before you start setting up the working shop. A finishing area (perhaps a spray booth) and storage needs should also be addressed.

Add tools over time. First, a few essential tools like a table saw or radial-arm saw, a drill press, and an assortment of hand tools and portable power tools. As you gain more experience and your interests become more defined, additional tools like a router and router table, and specialty tools such as a lathe or shaper, are thrown into the mix. Meanwhile, your supply of hardware, jigs and building materials will continue to grow (and will require efficient storage).

Whether your workshop is a drop-down worksurface in the laundry room or a gleaming, 2,000 square foot shrine, you'll need to develop and follow good tool maintenance and shop upkeep practices.

POWER TOOLS YOU'LL NEED (BY EXPERIENCE LEVEL)

Beginner

- Circular saw with combination blade
- Jig saw
- Power sander, pad-type
- Small workbench or set-up table
- Corded drill (reversible with variable speed)
- Cordless drill/driver with basic bits and accessories
- Shop vacuum

Intermediate

Add:

- Reciprocating saw
- Table saw
- Power miter saw
- Hammer drill
- Drill press
- Belt sander
- Random-orbit sander
- Router & router table
- Bench grinder
- Dust collection system
- Tool sharpening center
- Scroll saw
- Biscuit joiner

Advanced

Add:

- Jointer
- Air compressor and air tools
- Power planer
- Sanding station
- Band saw
- Sliding compound miter saw
- Lathe
- Spray booth and HVLP sprayer
- Shaper
- Welding equipment

TYPICAL GARAGE WORKSHOP LAYOUT (DOUBLE GARAGE)

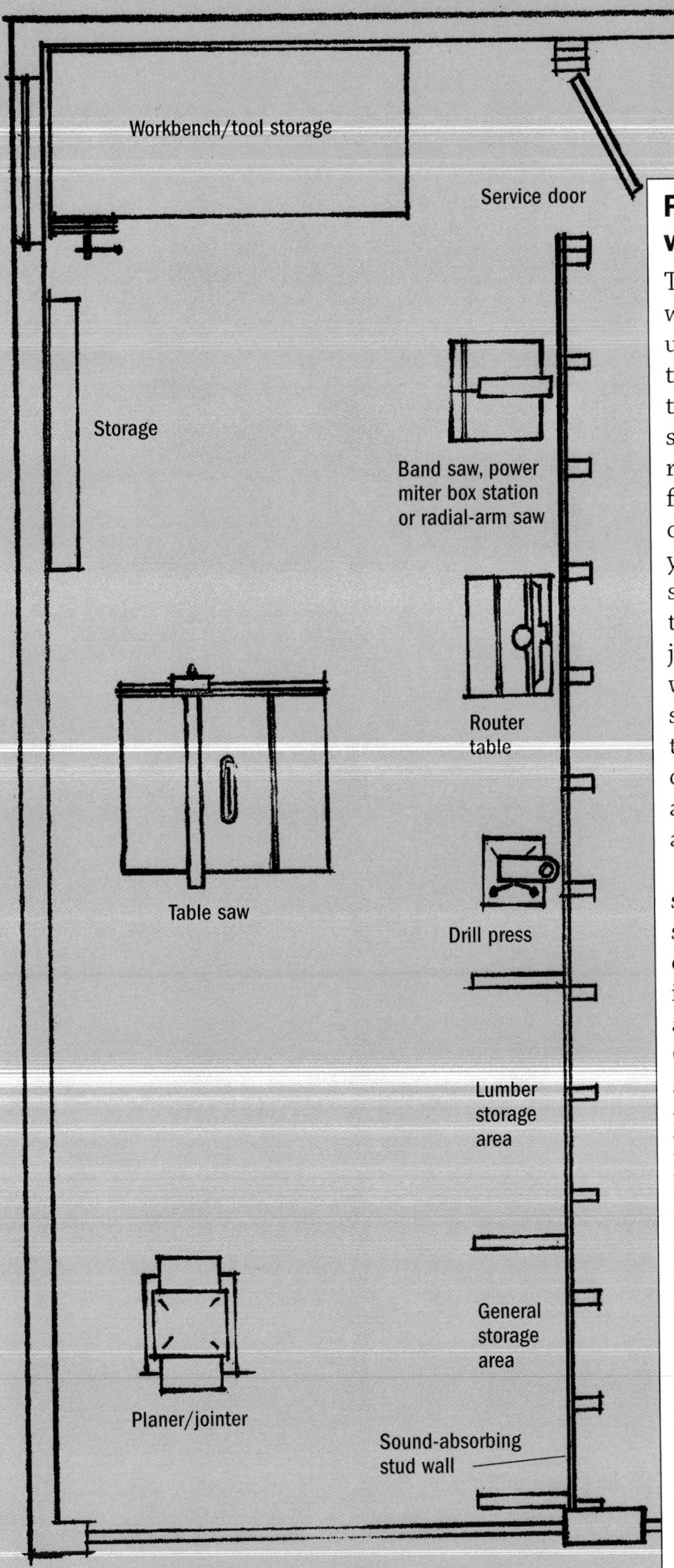

Planning & setting up your workshop: Start with a sketch

There's no single best way to set up your workshop. Since every handyman has unique interests, needs and resources, the trick to constructing a workshop that works for you is to learn to understand your needs and to maximize your resources. Start with your shop space—for most of us, a room in the basement or part of a garage. Draw a sketch of your shop area as it exists. Take measurements and include your main shop tools and work or storage areas. Often, just the simple exercise of sketching will reveal inefficiencies in the layout or suggest better arrangements. Be sure to include power sources, windows and doors in the drawing, as well as lights and any built-in fixtures, like shelving and wall cabinets.

Once you've drawn your existing shop, make a wish list of tools, accessories and systems you'd like to add over the next few years, including finishing booths, dust collection systems and lumber storage or drying areas. Compare that list to your current shop space. Can everything possibly fit? If not, you may want to amend your wish list, or look for ways to replace single-purpose tools with multi-purpose work areas that conserve space. For example, consider replacing your old radial-arm saw with a sliding compound miter saw, or perhaps you might replace one or two of your larger stationary tools with smaller benchtop versions. Pay attention to the space around tools as you plan, making sure to allow enough room to use each tool effectively and safely. Refer to your plan on a regular basis, and update it as your needs and circumstances change.

SAFETY EQUIPMENT

Create an emergency area

The workshop is perhaps the most accident-prone area of your home. Sharp blades, heavy objects, dangerous chemicals and flammable materials are just a few of the factors that increase the risk of accidents in the shop. While good housekeeping, respect for your tools and common sense will go a long way toward reducing the risk of accidents, you should still be prepared in the event an accident occurs. Designate part of your shop as an emergency center. Equip it with a fully stocked first aid kit, fire extinguisher and telephone with emergency numbers clearly posted.

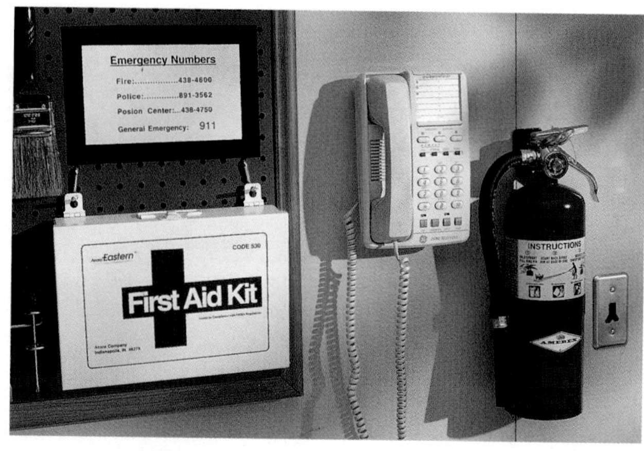

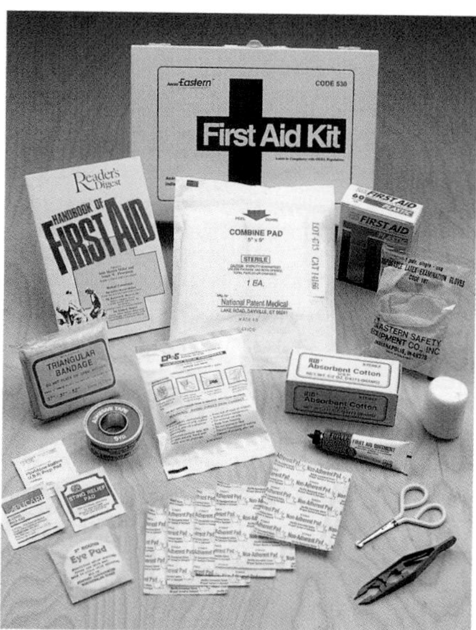

A well-equipped first aid kit should contain (as a minimum) plenty of gauze and bandages, antiseptic first aid ointment, latex gloves, a cold compress, rubbing alcohol swabs, a disinfectant such as iodine, and a first aid guidebook.

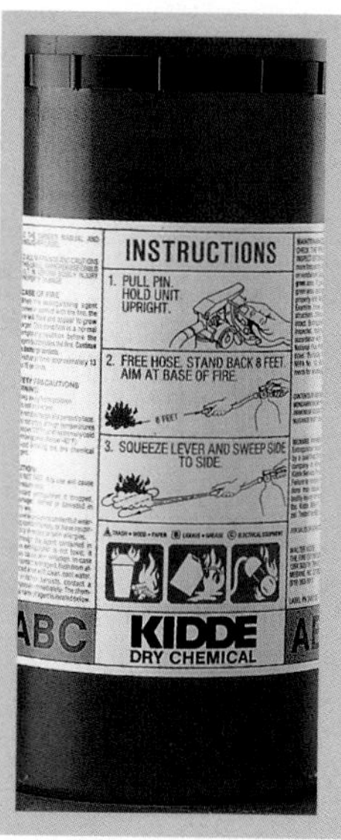

THE ABC'S OF FIRE EXTINGUISHERS

Fire extinguishers are rated by their ability to combat fires of varying causes. An extinguisher rated "A" is effective against trash, wood and paper fires. "B" will extinguish flammable liquid and grease fires. "C" can be used on electrical fires. For the workshop, choose a dry chemical extinguisher with an "ABC" rating.

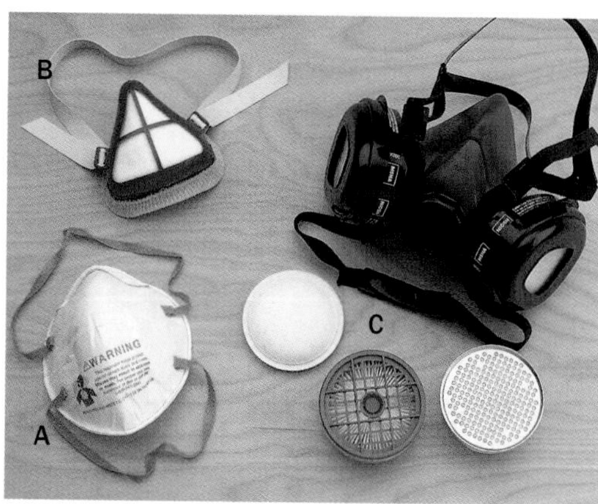

Protect against dust and fumes. A particle mask (A) is a disposable item to be worn when doing general shop work. A dust mask (B) has replaceable filters and flexible facepiece to keep out finer particles, like sawdust and insulation fibers. A respirator (C) can be fitted with filters and cartridges to protect against fumes and very fine particles, especially when working with chemicals.

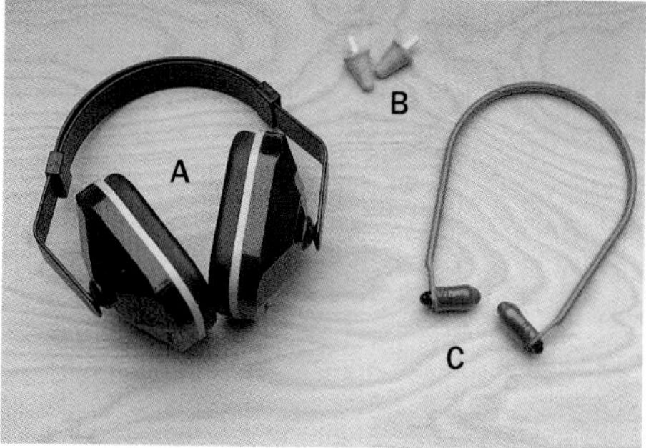

Protect your hearing when operating power tools or performing other loud activities. Ear muffs (A) offer the best protection, followed by expandable foam earplugs (B) and corded ear inserts (C).

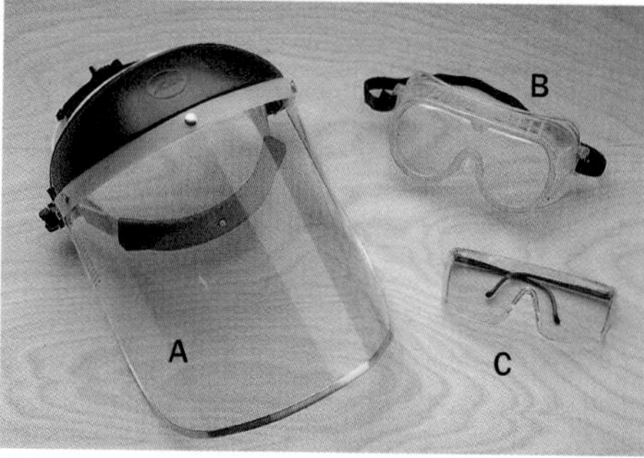

Eye protection should be worn at all times in the workshop. A face shield (A) is worn when doing very hazardous work, such as operating a lathe. Safety goggles (B) and glasses (C) should have shatterproof polycarbonate lenses.

WORKSHOP FIRST AID TIPS

Note: None of these treatments should be considered a substitute for medical attention. They are intended as guidelines on how to react to workshop mishaps. Whenever anyone is injured, contact a doctor as soon as possible.

SITUATION	TREATMENT
Deep gash/excessive bleeding	1. Maintain firm pressure on the wound with a clean cloth. 2. Dress with a gauze bandage. 3. If bleeding persists, and wound is a non-fracture, elevate the affected area so it is above the heart.
Deep puncture wound	1. Clean wound with soap and water. 2. Loosely cover wound with gauze bandage. 3. Apply insulated ice bag or cold compress to reduce swelling, relieve pain and impair absorption of toxins. 4. Be aware that internal bleeding may occur.
Stab wound/embedded object	1. Leave the embedded object in place. Do NOT remove it. 2. Apply a clean cloth or gauze pad to the area around the wound. 3. Prevent movement of the object by wrapping it with gauze.
Amputation	1. Maintain constant pressure with a clean cloth. 2. Carefully wrap severed item in gauze that has been moistened with either water or saline solution. 3. Place severed item in a sealed plastic bag. 4. Place this bag into a larger bag containing water and ice (never let severed part come in direct contact with ice).
Burn	1. If the burn is more severe than first-degree (skin that is red or slightly swollen) it should not be treated at home. See a doctor immediately. 2. For minor burns, immerse the affected area in cold water for five minutes. Gently apply a cold, wet cloth to areas that are unable to be immersed. Change the cloth frequently.
Electric shock	1. Quickly and safely break victim's contact with affecting current (disconnect plug or shut off breaker). 2. ALL electrical burns should be considered severe. Internal tissue may be affected more severely than the minor damage appearing on the skin. 911 should be called immediately if the electrical shock has caused any of the following: erratic heartbeat, severe jolt, abnormal tingling, unconsciousness (momentary or prolonged), muscle spasms or aches, fatigue, headaches or a visible burn.
Chemicals in eyes	1. Do not rub or irritate the affected eye. 2. Flush with warm water.

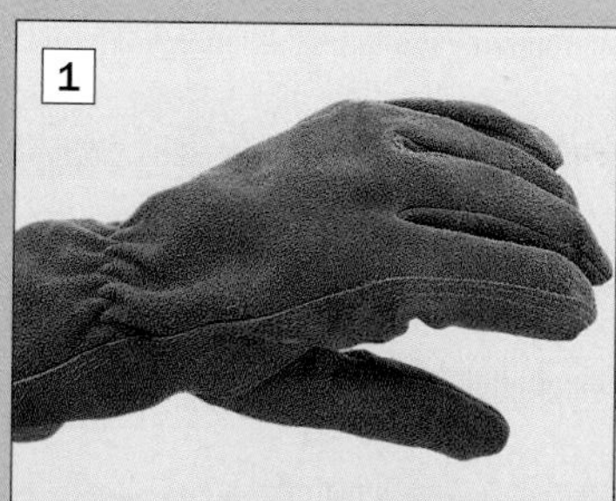

GET A GRIP ON GLOVE SELECTION

Always wear the proper glove for the task at hand. Maintain a supply of good-condition gloves of the following types, and add special purpose gloves as needed.

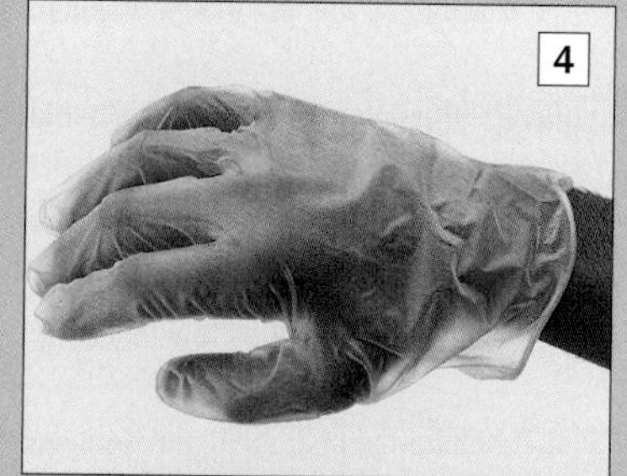

1 Heavy work gloves for handling building materials and general interior and exterior wear

2 Jersey or heavy cotton gloves for yardwork and general wear

3 Rubber-dipped masonry gloves for working with concrete and mortar

4 Disposable plastic gloves for painting and light finishing and for handling hardwoods, like cherry, that are sensitive to oils in skin

5 Neoprene rubber gloves for working with caustic chemicals, such as chemical paint stripper, and for working around electrical current

6 Household-type rubber gloves for painting and finishing and for working with cleansers

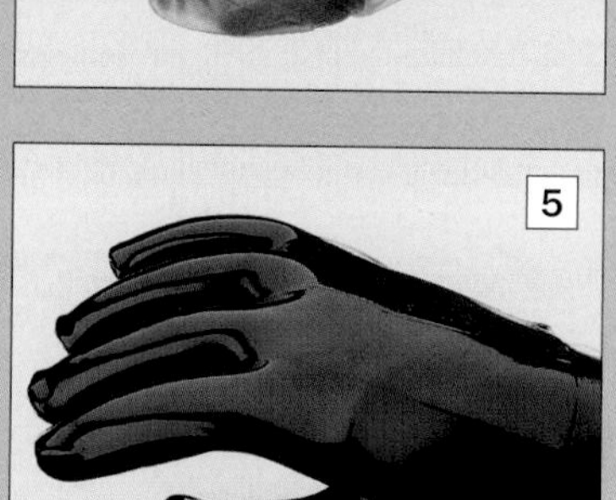

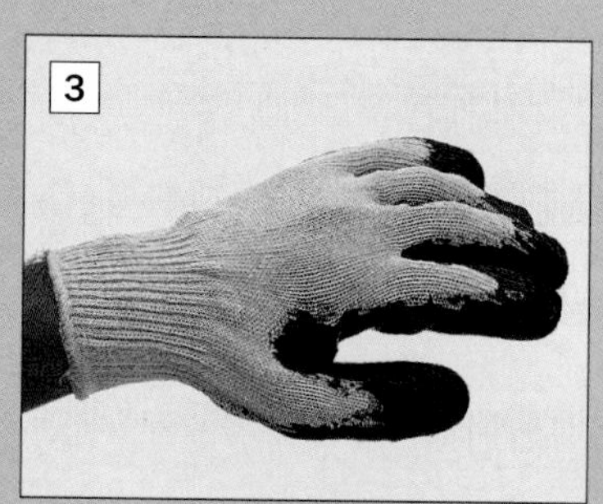

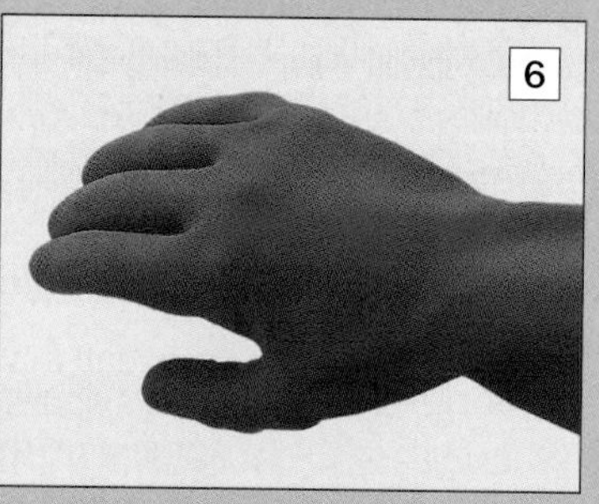

Remove-to-lock keys protect against unauthorized or unsupervised tool use

Many power tools, particularly stationary tools, come equipped with a removable lock key that is inserted into the ON/OFF switch of the tool. The tool cannot be turned on if the key is not in place. Store the lock keys in a convenient place that's out of sight from the tool.

EXTENSION CORD RATINGS

To make certain that your power tools run safely and at peak performance, use only extension cords that are rated to handle the amperage of the tool.

CORD LENGTH	GAUGE	MAXIMUM AMPS
25 ft.	18	10
25 ft.	16	13
25 ft.	14	15
50 ft.	18	5
50 ft.	16	10
50 ft.	14	15
75 ft.	18	5
75 ft.	16	10
75 ft.	14	15
100 ft.	16	5
100 ft.	12	15
125 ft.	16	5
125 ft.	12	15
150 ft.	16	5
150 ft.	12	13

TIPS FOR DUST COLLECTION & DUST COLLECTION SYSTEMS

Dust from workshop activities poses many threats to safety and to producing good results. It is a fire hazard, a health hazard when breathed in, and a general irritant. It is responsible for ruining countless carefully applied finishes, and if uncontrolled it will shorten the life span of your power tools. A good dust collection system is a must in any workshop. It can be as simple as a shop vac with a dust filter used locally, but the best solution is to construct a network of hoses connected permanently to your stationary shop tools and powered by a quality dust collector.

A tool vac is a relatively new entry in the dust collection field. It's similar to a shop vac in size and power. Tools are connected to the power source through a receptacle mounted on the tool vac. This allows the vac to shut on and off automatically as the tool is used.

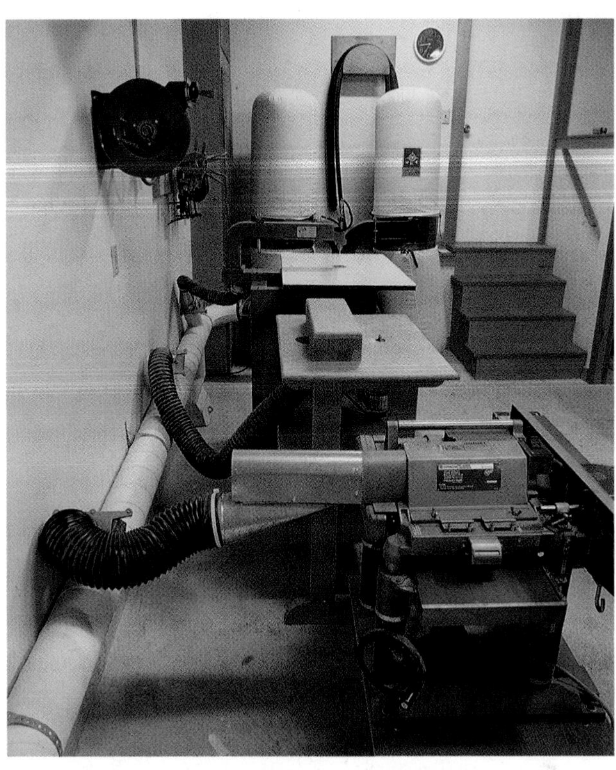

The two-stage dust collector in the background of this workshop photo is connected to all of the stationary power tools in the shop with dedicated 4-in. or larger hoses mounted to the walls and positioned to be out of the way when work is taking place.

How to ground a dust collection system

1 Due to the dangers of sparking caused by static electricity, a dust collection system should be electrically grounded so the built-up electricity can escape. Attach a strand of bare copper wire to the metal cabinet of each stationary tool in the dust collection system (assumes that tools are grounded through the power supply system). Drill a small guide hole into the hose port near the tool and feed the wire into the hole.

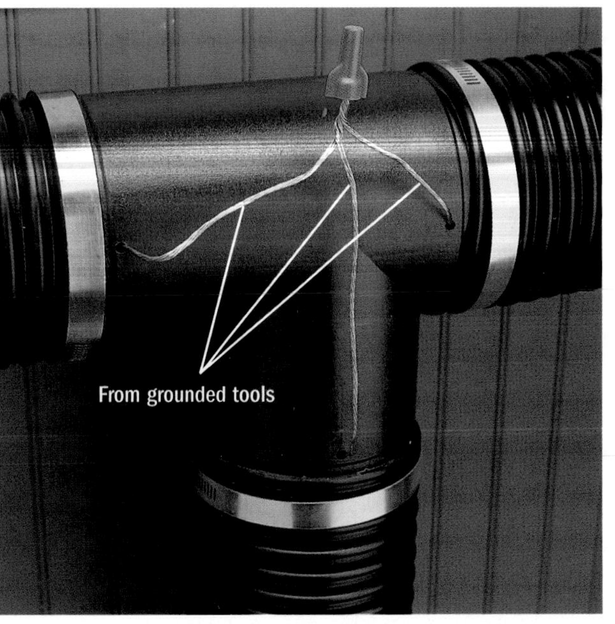

2 Drill exit holes at hole connectors and pigtail ground wires together with a wire nut. You may need to caulk around the wire openings to maintain the vacuum seal.

KEEP YOUR SHOP CLEAN AND COMFORTABLE

Perforated hardboard (pegboard) is the wallpaper of the workshop. In addition to general pegboard hooks, you can purchase whole systems of hanging devices in many sizes and configurations to effectively support and organize specific tools. Use tempered hardboard if available.

A shop magnet finds and rescues screws, washers, drill bits and other small metal parts that have a way of disappearing into the nearest heap of sawdust or shavings as soon as you turn your back.

A roll-around cabinet, like this mechanic's parts cabinet, is a great shop furnishing for storing hand tools, saw blades, drill bits, hardware and other small tools that need to be kept organized. By rolling the cabinet to your work area, you'll save a lot of trips back and forth across your shop retrieving tools or putting them away again.

Wall-mounted clamp racks protect your clamps and keep them organized and accessible. A few lengths of scrap lumber and some ingenuity are all it takes to devise your own clamp storage system. Cut notches to hold heavier bar and pipe clamps. Smaller clamps can simply be tightened onto your rack or hung from a cord.

Cushioned mats or even carpet scraps strategically placed will help minimize fatigue on your feet, legs and back regardless of the floor type.

GENERAL TIPS FOR SHOP TOOL MAINTENANCE

Identify your shop tools. Every handyman knows that borrowed tools often end up on permanent loan. Keep tabs on your shop tools by engraving your name or initials into the tool casing with a rotary tool or carving tool. In addition to reminding your friends and family members where the tool came from, identification marks may help you recover your tools in the event of a robbery.

Keep blades clean and sharp. Some people enjoy the art of coaxing a razor-sharp blade onto knives and chisels, but for most of us it's just another shop chore that's easily ignored—especially with less glamorous tools, like the pruning shears being sharpened with a grinding bit and rotary tool above. To help make sure the sharpening and tool maintenance actually happen, dedicate one day or weekend every year to tool maintenance, including sharpening.

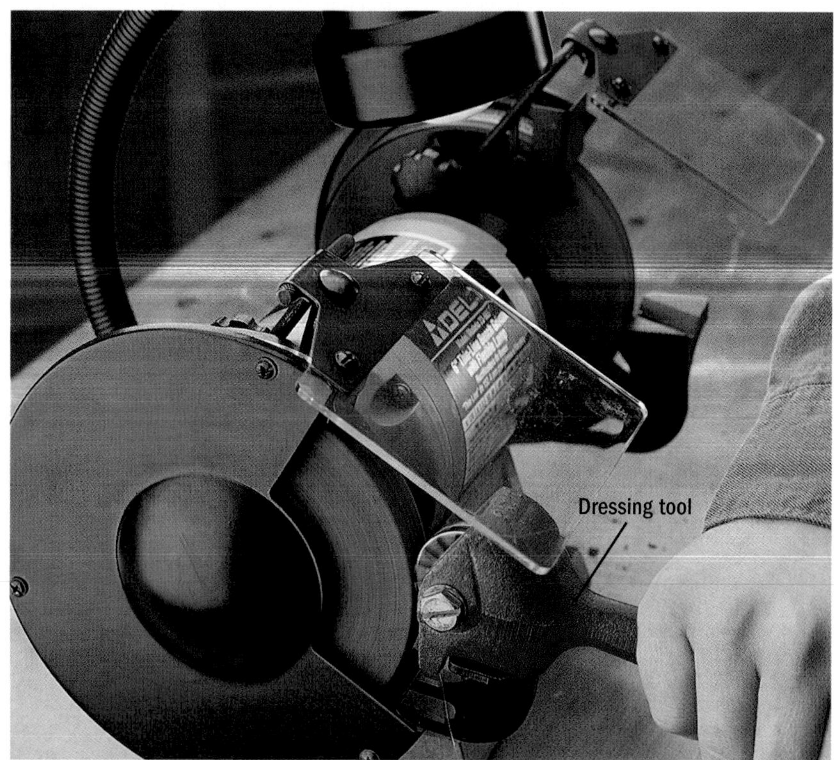

The bench grinder is one of the most important tools in any shop for keeping other tools up and running at peak performance levels. But it too requires occasional maintenance. Over time, the grinding wheel or wheels build up resins and other gunk that settle into the grit of the wheel, where they harden each time you use the grinder. If you notice that your wheel has a brown, burnished appearance, it's time to dress the wheel. This procedure can be accomplished with a dressing tool, like the one shown at right, or simply with a stick made of silicone carbide. Simply apply the dressing tool or carbide stick to the spinning grinding wheel and inspect the wheel visually until the surface is clean and fully restored.

WOODWORKING WOODS

Choosing the best wood species for your project goes a long way toward ensuring success. Different species naturally lend themselves better to the types of machining required for a project, as well as the overall look. For example, project parts that incorporate decorative edge profiles may be easier to shape using soft wood, but ultimately harder, more straight-grained wood will stand up better over time. Cost and local availability are also important determining factors. When choosing wood, pay particular attention to the tone of the wood when a finish is applied. To get a good idea what the finished color will be, simply dampen a small section of a planed board with mineral spirits or rubbing alcohol.

Walnut has rich, dark tones when topcoated. Grain is relatively straight. Moderately easy to work. Moderate to expensive. Species shown is black walnut.

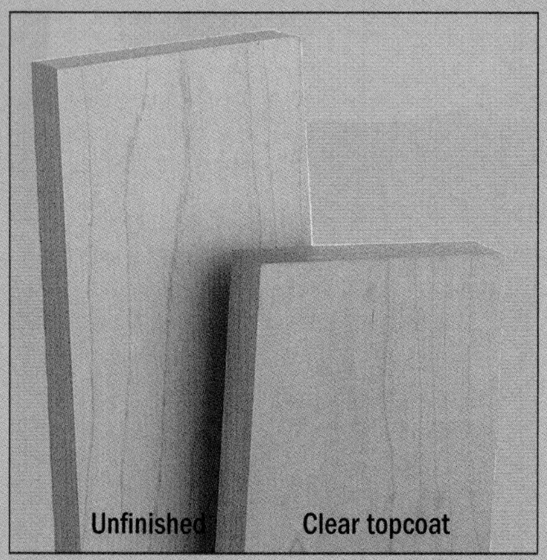

Maple is a light-colored hardwood with straight, tight grain. Hardness makes it durable, but somewhat difficult to work. Inexpensive to moderate. Species shown is hard maple.

Ash is a readily available, inexpensive hardwood. Its color and grain are not distinguishing, but it can be finished to replicate more expensive hardwoods.

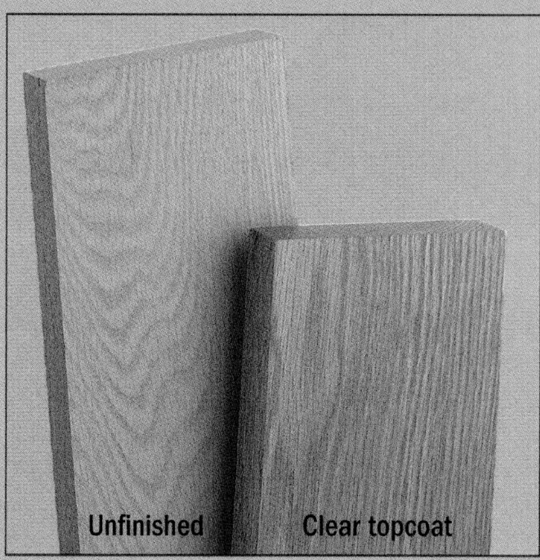

Red oak is one of the more inexpensive and prevalent wood species in today's marketplace. Has dramatic grain figure and warm red color. Fairly easy to work.

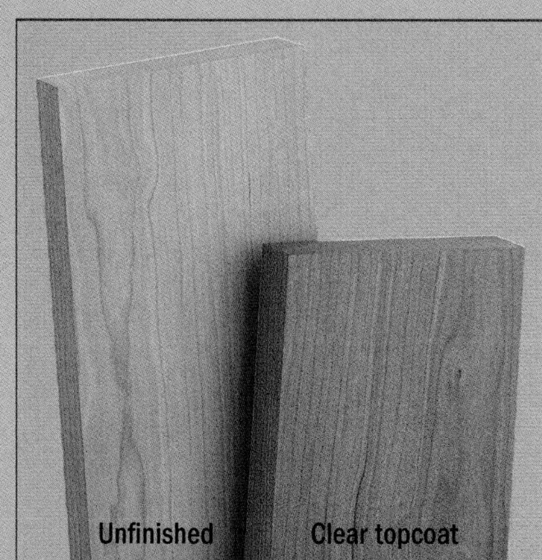

Cherry has a deep, reddish brown color when finished (color varies greatly between heartwood and sapwood). It is hard and tends to be brittle. Occasionally splotchy when finished. Moderate to expensive. Species shown is black cherry.

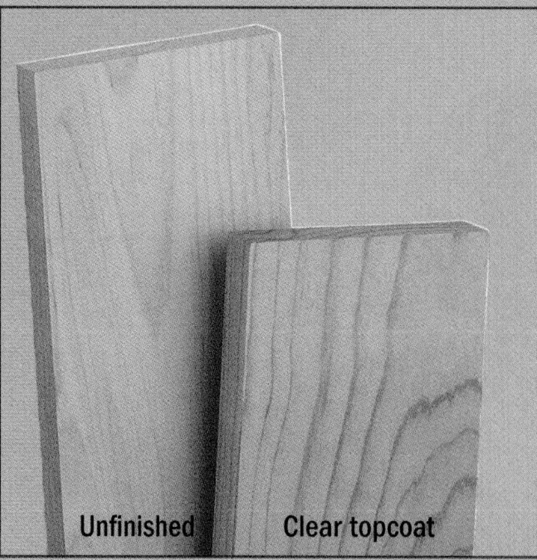

Pine is a very general species term used to refer to most coniferous softwood. It ranges from white to yellow according to species. Generally easy to work with strong grain patterns. Inexpensive to moderate. Species shown is ponderosa pine.

White oak is a versatile hardwood with a distinctive appearance. Used extensively in furniture-building, as well as in boatbuilding. It is moderate in price (quartersawn tends to be higher cost). Moderate workability.

PLYWOOD GRADES & CHARACTERISTICS

Plywood is generally graded according to the veneer on both the front and back panels, as well as the exposure durability type. For example, Exterior C-D plywood would have one side conforming to the "C" grade, and the other side conforming to the "D" grade, with an "Exterior" exposure rating. The following charts explain American Plywood Association veneer grades, along with exposure durability types.

VENEER GRADE	CHARACTERISTICS
N	A smooth, natural-finish select heartwood or sapwood veneer that is free of open defects. It will not allow more than six repairs (wood only) per 4 × 8-ft. panel. Well matched for both grain and color.
A	A smooth, paintable veneer that does not permit more than 18 neat repairs per sheet. In less demanding applications, it may be used with a natural finish.
B	A solid surface veneer that allows shims, circular repair plugs and tight knots up to 1 in. Repairs of some minor splits permitted.
C-Plugged	An upgraded "C" veneer that limits splits to ⅛-in. width, and does not permit knotholes or borer holes in excess of ¼ × ½. Some broken grain allowed. Synthetic repairs permitted.
C	A veneer with tight knots to 1½ in. Can have knotholes up to 1 in. across the grain, or up to 1½ in. if the total width of knots and knotholes is within specified limits. Wood or synthetic repairs are okay. Permits discoloration and sanding defects that do not impair its strength, while limiting splits and stitches.
D	Allows knots and knotholes to 2½-in. width across the grain within specified limits. Permits limited splits and stitches. This grade is limited to interior or Exposure 1 panels*

**Exposure Ratings are:*

Exterior: fully waterproof bond designed for applications subject to permanent exposure to moisture.

Exposure 1: fully waterproof bond, but not intended for permanent exposure to weather or moisture.

Exposure 2: interior type with intermediate glue. Intended for protected construction applications where slight exposure to moisture can be expected.

Interior: designed exclusively for interior applications.

GRADE STAMPS

APA
RATED SHEATHING
32/16 15/32 INCH
SIZED FOR SPACING
EXPOSURE 1
000
NRB 108

Plywood grade stamps indicate the actual thickness of the material (sometimes to within 1⁄32 in.). The stamp also indicates whether the plywood is exterior rated.

Dimension lumber is rated by species, general quality (lower numbers indicate higher quality) and the mill where the lumber originated.

NOMINAL VS. ACTUAL BOARD SIZES

NOMINAL SIZE	ACTUAL SIZE
1 × 1	¾ × ¾
1 × 2	¾ × 1½
1 × 3	¾ × 2½
1 × 4	¾ × 3½
1 × 6	¾ × 5¼
1 × 8	¾ × 7¼
1 × 10	¾ × 9¼
1 × 12	¾ × 11¼
2 × 2	1½ × 1½
2 × 3	1½ × 2½
2 × 4	1½ × 3½
2 × 6	1½ × 5¼
2 × 8	1½ × 7¼
2 × 10	1½ × 9¼
2 × 12	1½ × 11¼

SHOP FURNISHINGS YOU CAN BUILD

Workbench/set-up table

The workbench/set-up table project shown here is the kind of workshop furnishing that may not get a lot of attention, but would be sorely missed if you were forced to do without it.

To build this workbench/set-up table, start by cutting the legs, rails and stretchers to length from 2 × 4 stock. Group the eight legs into four pairs, and attach the rails at the top and 8 in. up from the bottoms of the legs. Use wood glue and drive 3-in. deck screws through the rails and into the leg pairs, making sure everything is square. Then, fasten the bottom stretchers to the inside edges of the leg pairs, with their ends flush against the lower rails. Fasten the top stretchers on the outside edges of the leg pairs, overlapping the ends of the top rails. Cut and glue the two subtop panels together, and attach them to the top rails and stretchers, then cut and glue the worksurface to the subtop assembly. After the glue has dried, you may want to trim around the edges of the worksurface with a router and piloted roundover or flush-cutting bit. Finally, cut and attach the shelf to the lower rails and stretchers with 1½-in. deck screws.

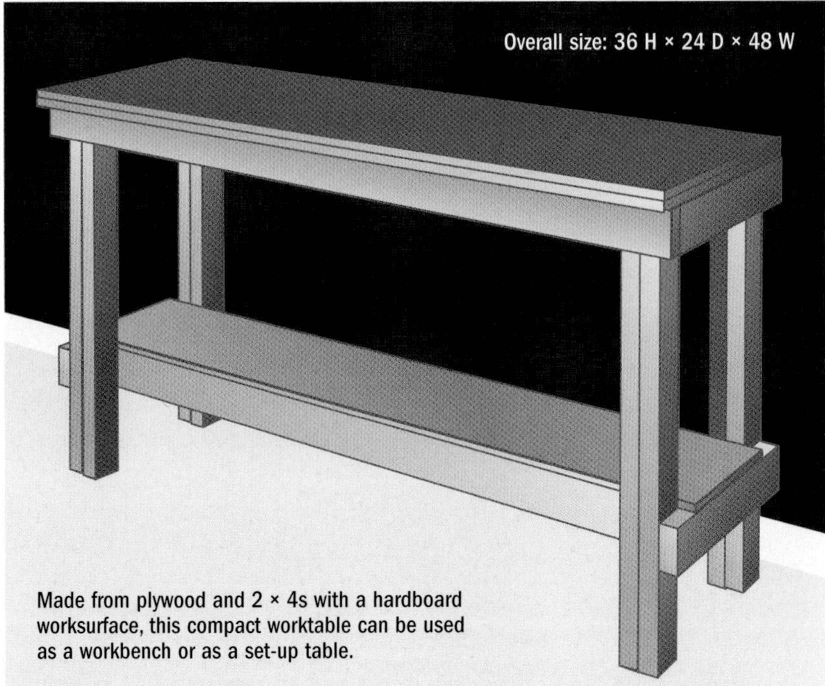

Made from plywood and 2 × 4s with a hardboard worksurface, this compact worktable can be used as a workbench or as a set-up table.

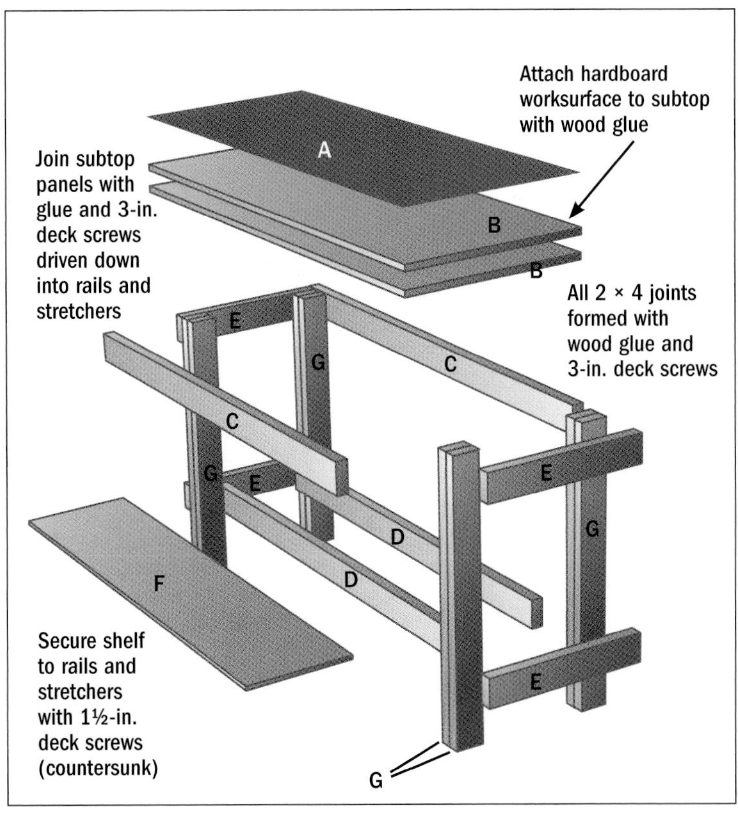

WORKBENCH/SET-UP TABLE CUTTING LIST

KEY	NO.	PART	SIZE	MATERIAL
A	1	Worksurface	¼ × 24 × 48	Hardboard
B	2	Subtop	¾ × 24 × 48	Plywood
C	2	Stretcher (top)	1½ × 3½ × 48	Pine 2 × 4
D	2	Stretcher (bottom)	1½ × 3½ × 45	Pine 2 × 4
E	4	Side rails	1½ × 3½ × 19	Pine 2 × 4
F	1	Shelf	¾ × 12 × 48	Plywood
G	8	Legs	1½ × 3½ × 34¼	Pine 2 × 4

Materials:

(6) 2 × 4 × 8 ft. pine studs

(3) ¾ × 2 × 4 ft. plywood handy panels OR two ¾ × 4 × 8 ft, sheets plywood

(1) ¼ × 2 × 4 ft. tempered hardboard handy panel

Wood glue, deck screws (1½ , 3 in.)

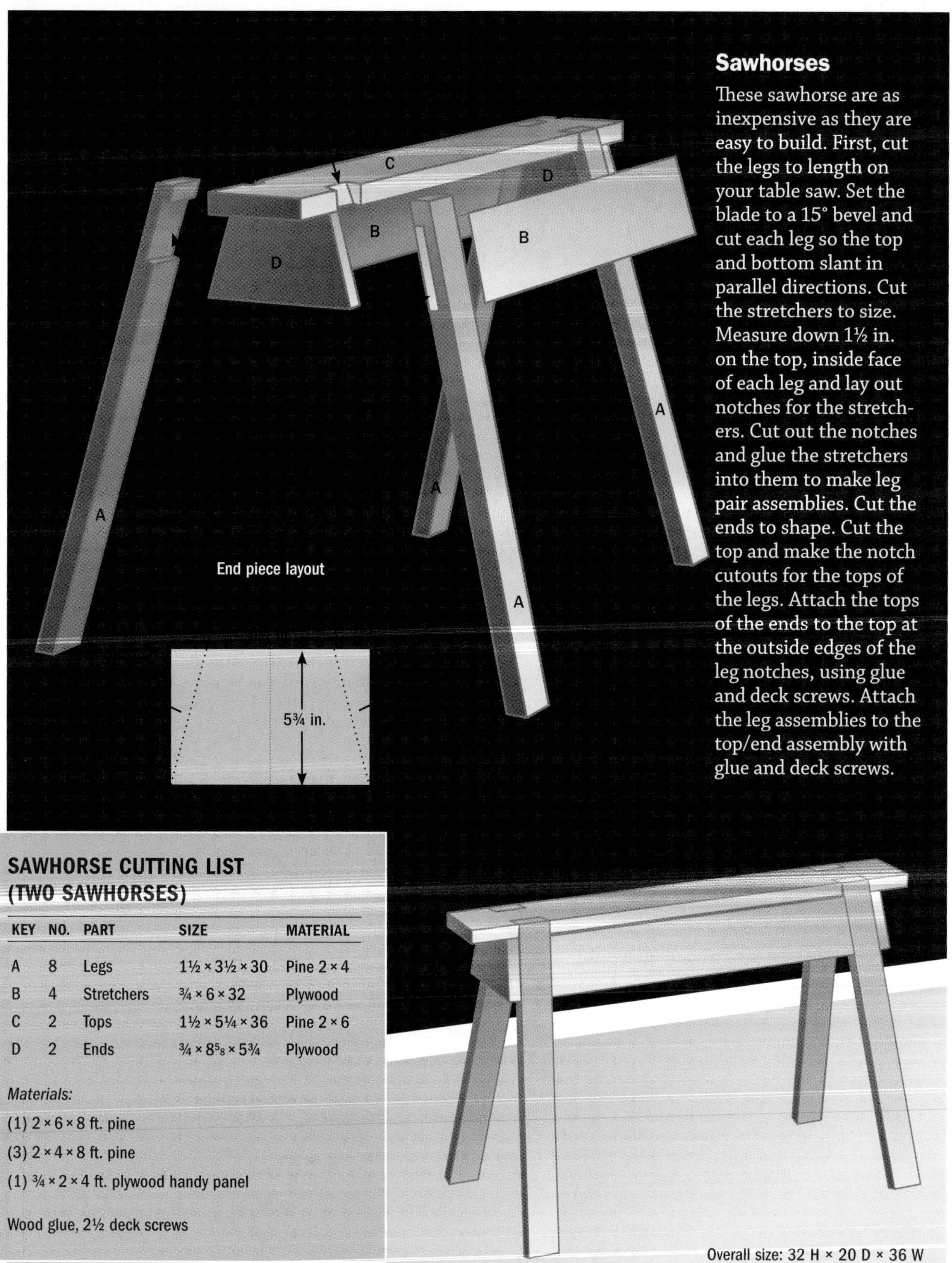

Sawhorses

These sawhorse are as inexpensive as they are easy to build. First, cut the legs to length on your table saw. Set the blade to a 15° bevel and cut each leg so the top and bottom slant in parallel directions. Cut the stretchers to size. Measure down 1½ in. on the top, inside face of each leg and lay out notches for the stretchers. Cut out the notches and glue the stretchers into them to make leg pair assemblies. Cut the ends to shape. Cut the top and make the notch cutouts for the tops of the legs. Attach the tops of the ends to the top at the outside edges of the leg notches, using glue and deck screws. Attach the leg assemblies to the top/end assembly with glue and deck screws.

SAWHORSE CUTTING LIST (TWO SAWHORSES)

KEY	NO.	PART	SIZE	MATERIAL
A	8	Legs	1½ × 3½ × 30	Pine 2 × 4
B	4	Stretchers	¾ × 6 × 32	Plywood
C	2	Tops	1½ × 5¼ × 36	Pine 2 × 6
D	2	Ends	¾ × 8⅝ × 5¾	Plywood

Materials:

(1) 2 × 6 × 8 ft. pine

(3) 2 × 4 × 8 ft. pine

(1) ¾ × 2 × 4 ft. plywood handy panel

Wood glue, 2½ deck screws

Measuring, Marking & Layout

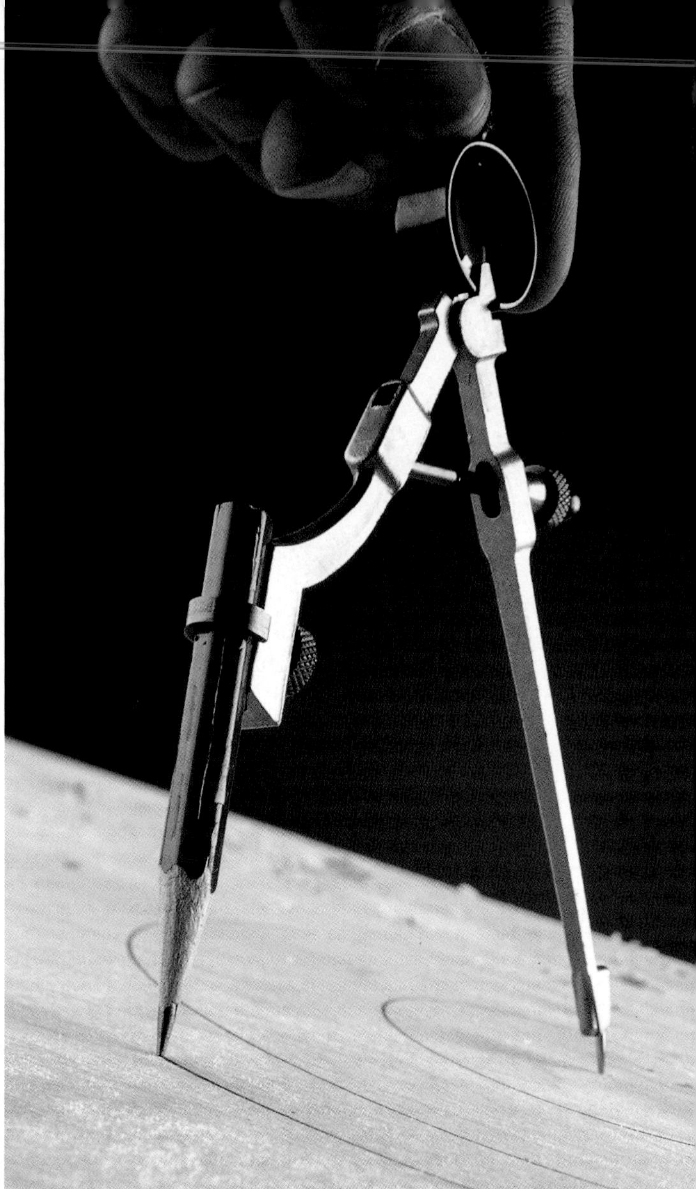

Successful workshop projects start with careful, accurate measuring, marking and layout. The most critical elements in these steps of the process are good planning, accurate measuring and using sharp marking tools that create readable lines. The level of precision needed varies according to the intricacy and complexity of your project. Rough carpentry (for example, putting up stud walls or installing floor underlayment or roof decking) requires a certain amount of care, but generally you can achieve satisfactory results using tape measures, framing squares and a lumber pencil as a marking tool. Trim carpentry (installing moldings and decorative trim) requires a higher degree of accuracy, so you'll want to involve steel rules, levels and angle gauges in the process. A good sharp pencil will usually give you marking lines of acceptable accuracy. Fine woodworking carries the highest standard of accuracy. You'll want to use marking gauges, compasses and any of a wide selection of specialty measuring tools to create well-made projects. Generally, a marking knife or a scratch awl is the marking tool of choice for fine woodworking.

In this chapter you'll find a wealth of tips and tool information to help you get professional measuring, marking and layout results as quickly and efficiently as possible.

TAPE MEASURE TIPS

To obtain accurate readings from a tape measure, start measuring at the 1-in. mark. The end hook on a tape measure often has some play in it, which can alter measurements slightly. And even a secure hook may be bent or caught against a splinter or bump. Don't forget to subtract one inch from the final reading. Steel rules are generally more accurate than tape measures, but they too can become worn or nicked—for best results, sight from the 1-in. mark on any measuring device.

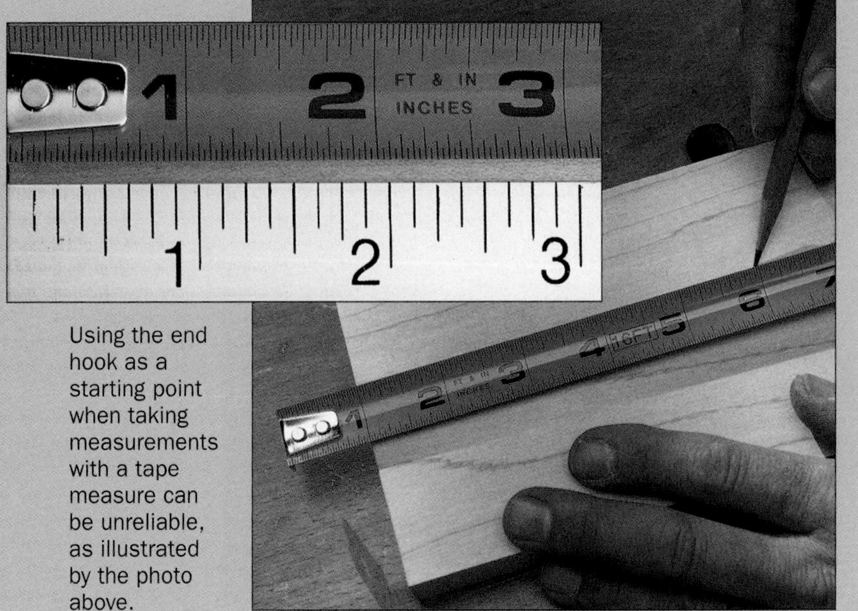

Using the end hook as a starting point when taking measurements with a tape measure can be unreliable, as illustrated by the photo above.

Rating marking tools: Four degrees of accuracy

Choosing the best marking tool for your project is a matter of weighing the amount of tolerance you're willing to accept against the readability of the lines you scribe—as well as the ease and speed with which the tool can be used. *Marking knives* create highly accurate lines because the flat blade rides flush against a straightedge and cuts through wood fibers and grain contours that can cause a pencil to waver. They're the tool of choice for most fine woodworking projects. *Scratch awls* also cut through fibers and grain, but the round shaft causes the point to be offset slightly from the straightedge. Lines scored with a scratch awl are easier to see because they're wider, which is especially helpful when marking softwoods. *Pencils* are popular marking tools for rough carpentry and some woodworking tasks. A regular pencil sharpened to a fine point will create a fairly precise, readable line. Lumber pencils require less frequent sharpening and create dark, highly readable lines.

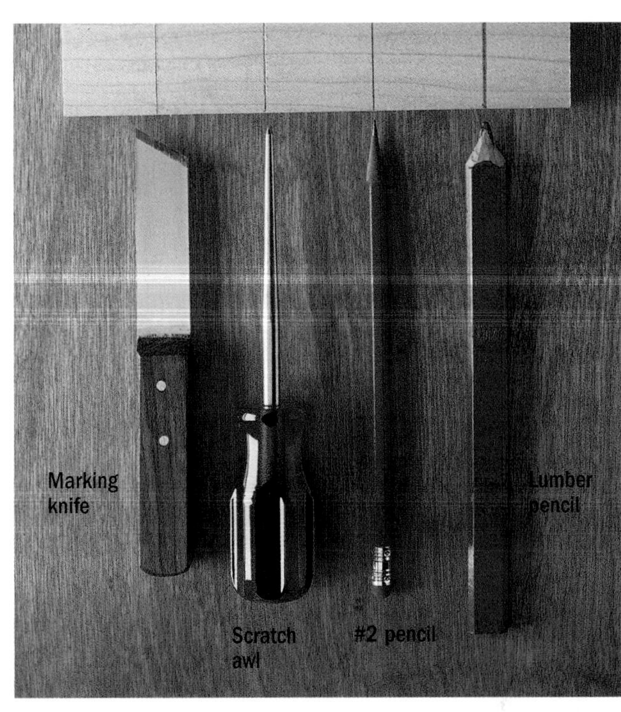

MEASURING, MARKING & LAYOUT

TIPS FOR SCRIBING & LAYING OUT

Use a white pencil to mark dark-colored wood, like hardboard or walnut.

Attach medium-grit sandpaper to your toolbox to make a convenient and safe sharpener for lumber pencils.

Use a grease pencil to mark metal, plastic and other materials that can't be marked clearly with a pencil.

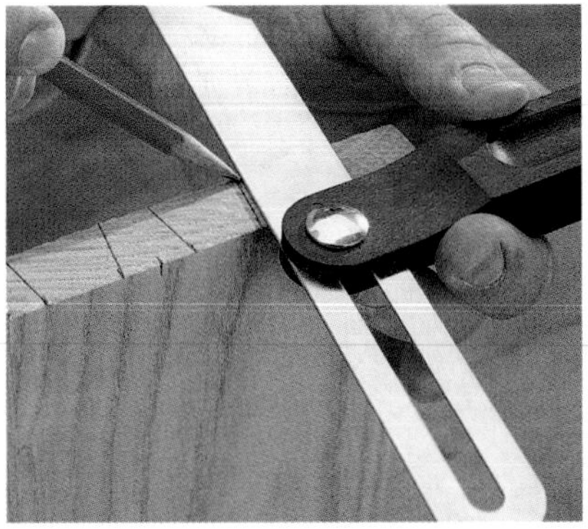

Use a sliding T-bevel to transfer angles to your workpiece.

Transfer grid drawings to your workpiece by drawing a scaled grid, then re-creating the pattern using the grid as a reference.

Make a sturdy template from hardboard or another durable material when making multiple parts with the same profile.

THREE WAYS TO SCRIBE PARALLEL LINES

Rough carpentry: To create a fast and reasonably accurate line parallel to the edge of a board, use your fingers as a marking gauge. Hold a pencil firmly at the desired mark and glide your hand along the length of the board, using your bent knuckles as an edge guide.

Trim carpentry: A much more accurate parallel line can be transferred with a combination square and a pencil. Measure the distance you need, place the square against the edge of the board, and glide the square and the pencil together along the length of the cut.

Woodworking: The most accurate parallel lines can be drawn with a marking gauge. Measure the distance and firmly glide the tool the length of the cut.

A quick note on the speed square

Created for use in roof construction, *speed squares* allow you to mark angles quickly and accurately in any workshop or construction situation. By pivoting the speed square against one edge of the workpiece, you can mark cutting lines angled by degree or by slope. The slope angles can be found by sighting along the row of numbers labeled *Common numbers.* These numbers represent the number of inches of slope per foot when the pivot end of the square is pressed against the edge of the board and the Common number is aligned on the same edge of the workpiece as the pivot. The degree marks are used in the same manner. Be sure to mark lines along the *marking edge* of the speed square. In the photo to the right, a 2 × 4 is being marked for a 25° cut.

TWO OPTIONS FOR TRACING A WALL CONTOUR

When installing built-in cabinets or wall shelving, you may need to trim the end of a shelf, countertop or trim piece to follow the line of a wall that's out of square. Rather than relying on trial-and-error to get the workpiece to fit snugly into an out-of-square corner, transfer the contour of the wall to make a cutting line on the workpiece.

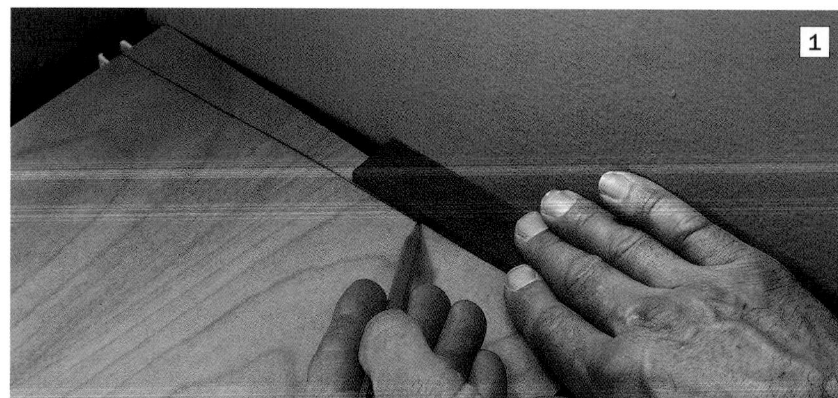

1. Using a spacer. Cut a small, square piece of scrap hardboard and set the end of the board against the walls. Press the scrap-wood spacer against the wall, and drag it along the profile of the wall, following with a pencil as you go.

2. Using a compass. Simply set the compass so the legs are about an inch apart, then follow the wall profile with the point, tracing along with the pencil in the other compass leg to make cutting lines.

HOW TO FIND MITER ANGLES FOR BASE MOLDING

1 To determine the correct length and cutting angle for base moldings, first lay masking tape on the floor at the corner. Use a scrap piece of molding to extend a line beyond the corner for each wall.

2 Press the blade of a sliding T-bevel against one wall and adjust the blade angle so the handle of the tool runs through the point where the lines on the masking tape intersect. Trace the line for reference, then transfer the angle of the T-bevel to your miter box. You can also use the baseboard outlines to measure the length for each trim piece.

An easy way to divide evenly

When you need to divide a board into equal sections, don't worry about performing elaborate mathematical calculations (such as dividing a 7¾-in.-wide board into four equal portions). Instead, just lay a ruler on the board and angle it until it measures a distance easily divisible by the number of cuts. Make certain one edge of the ruler is on the "0" mark. In the example to the left, the ruler is angled so that the 12 in. mark touches the far edge of the board. Dividing the board into four pieces is easy: Just mark the board at inches 3, 6 and 9. Repeat the procedure farther down the board and use the marks to draw parallel cutting lines on the board.

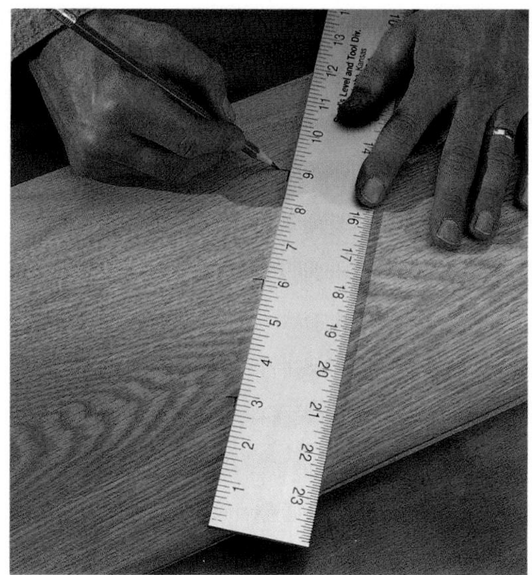

Use a marking gauge

Mortise cuts must be extremely precise. To mark the cuts properly, use a marking gauge, available at good hardware stores. As with any marking tool, hold it firm and steady.

Build a center-marking jig

Build a simple center-marking jig with a scrap piece of 2 × 4 and doweling. The gauge can be as wide as you like. Just be certain that the dowels are an equal distance from the center pencil hole. On the reverse side of the jig, insert two dowels 1 in. from the center hole. This side will allow you to find the center on narrow pieces up to 1⅝ in. wide. When using the jig, angle it so both dowels are pressing firmly against the side of the board you are marking.

Find the center of a circle

Clamp a combination square or other straightedge to a framing square. The edge of the straightedge should be flush with the inside corner of the square where the two legs meet. Position the framing square so each leg is at a flush tangent to the workpiece, then trace the edge of the straightedge past the center of the workpiece at two or more spots. The point where the lines meet is the centerpoint.

Two ways to draw shallow arcs

Creating a regular arc requires tricky calculations or an elaborate jig, right? Not necessarily. A trio of nails and a strip of wood will do the job. Tack one nail at each endpoint of the arc, and tack the third nail at the apex of the arc, spaced evenly between the endpoints. Cut a thin strip of plywood or hardboard that's at least a few inches longer than the length of the arc. Bend the strip between the nails as shown in the above, right photo. Trace along the inside edge of the strip to draw your shallow arc. A variation of this method is simply to insert the wood strip between the jaws of a pipe clamp and tighten the clamp until the strip bows to form an arc of the radius you're seeking (See photo, above left). This method is not as accurate, but it won't leave any nail holes in the workpiece.

Make a simple trammel for drawing circles

A trammel is a marking device that pivots around a centerpoint to create a circle. You can buy fancy milled steel woodworking trammels, or you can make your own with a thin strip of hardboard. Just drive a nail through one end of the strip, then measure out from the nail toward the other end an amount equal to the radius of the circle. Mark a centerpoint for drilling a pencil guide hole at that point (usually, ⅜ in. dia.). Tack the nail at the center of the workpiece, insert the pencil into the guide hole, then make a single revolution around the nail with the pencil to draw the circle.

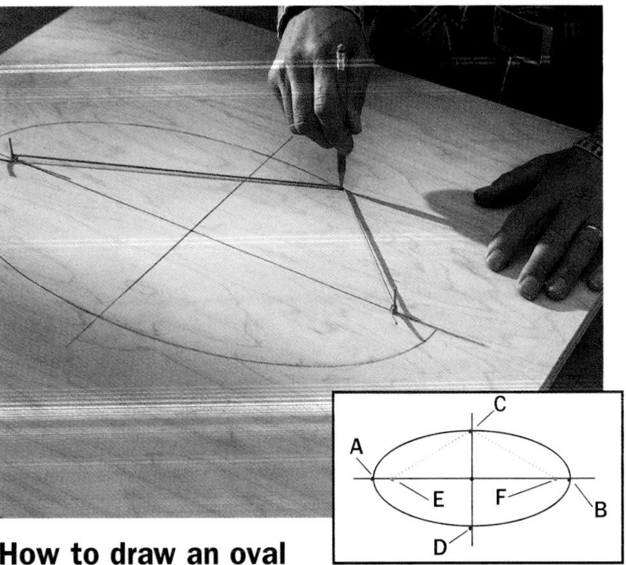

How to draw an oval

Draw perpendicular lines to mark the length and width of the oval. Measuring out from the point of intersection, mark endpoints for the length (A, B) and the width (C, D). Set a compass or trammel to draw an arc that's half as long as the length of the oval. With the point of the compass or trammel at one endpoint for the oval width (C or D), scribe hash marks on the length line (points E, F). Tack nails at points E and F. Tie a string to the nails so the amount of string between the nails is the same as the distance from A to F. Pull the string taut with a pencil tip and trace the oval.

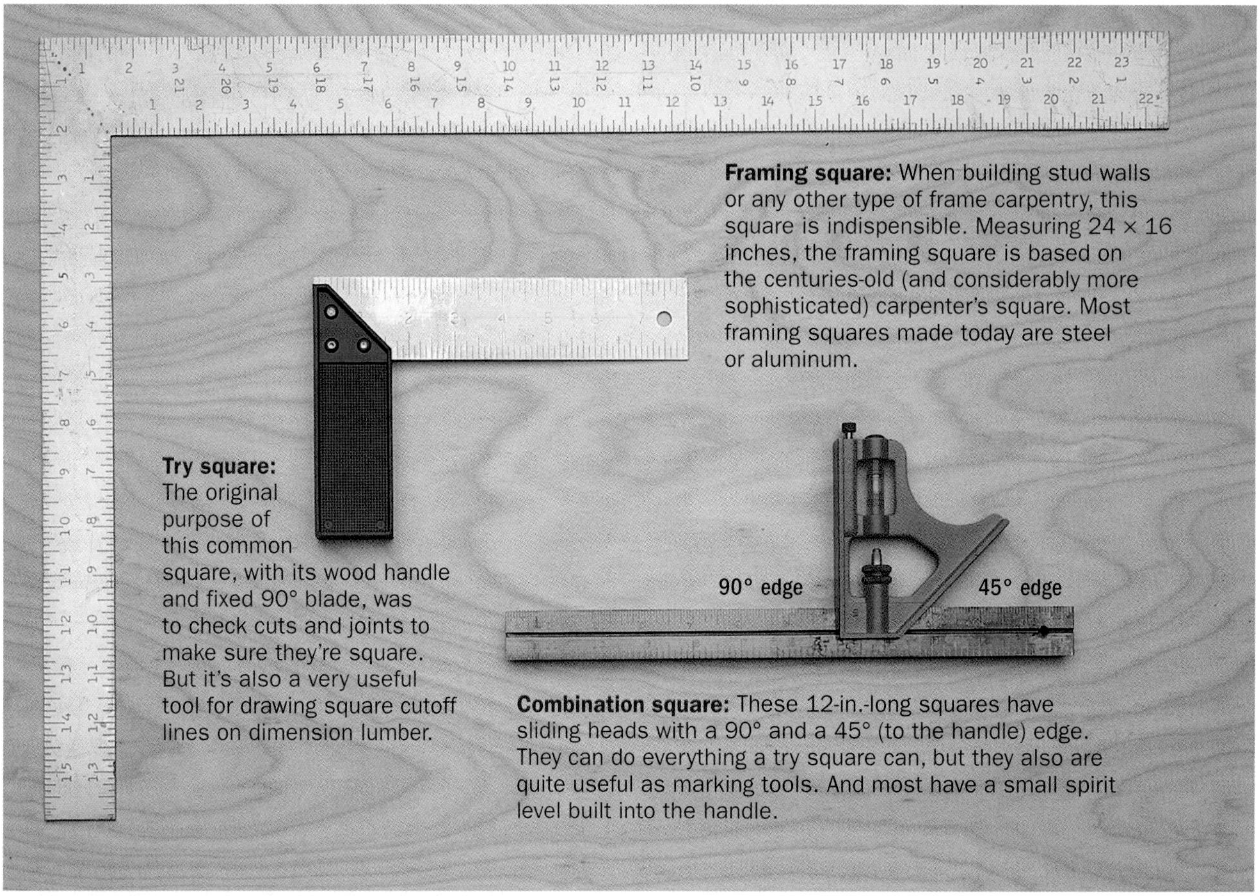

Framing square: When building stud walls or any other type of frame carpentry, this square is indispensible. Measuring 24 × 16 inches, the framing square is based on the centuries-old (and considerably more sophisticated) carpenter's square. Most framing squares made today are steel or aluminum.

Try square: The original purpose of this common square, with its wood handle and fixed 90° blade, was to check cuts and joints to make sure they're square. But it's also a very useful tool for drawing square cutoff lines on dimension lumber.

90° edge

45° edge

Combination square: These 12-in.-long squares have sliding heads with a 90° and a 45° (to the handle) edge. They can do everything a try square can, but they also are quite useful as marking tools. And most have a small spirit level built into the handle.

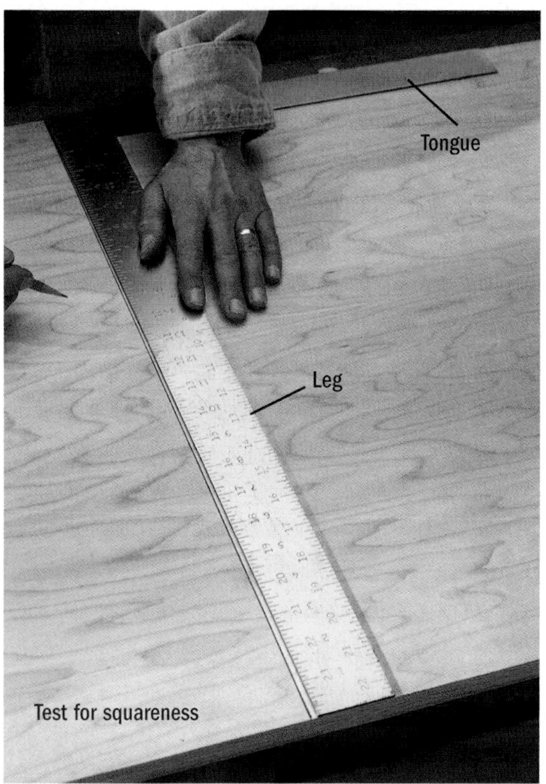

Test for squareness

Getting back to square one

Over time, even the highest quality steel squares can fall out of square. To test if your steel square is still accurate, align the tongue of the square with the edge of a wide board and trace a line along one side of the leg. Flip the square over and check to see if the leg is still parallel to the line. If not, the square is out of square. You may be able to correct the problem with a steel punch and a hammer. If the square's inside angle is less than 90°, punch a small depression near the square's inside corner. Check the angle, and continue to punch small depressions near the inside corner until the angle is correct. If the inside angle is more than 90°, punch small depressions on the outside corner of the square.

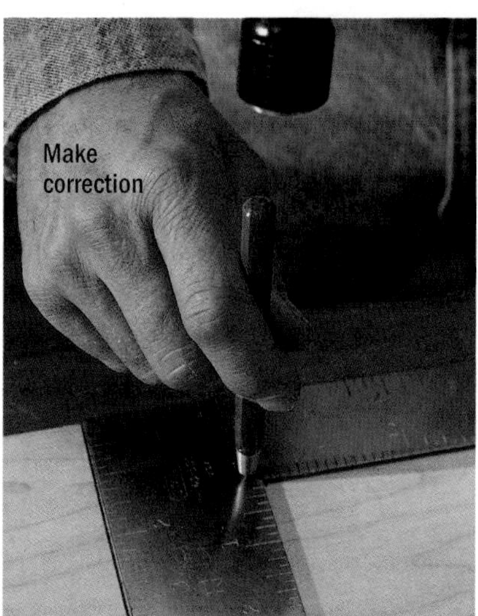
Make correction

Measure the diagonals to test frames & casework for square

Drawers, frames, cabinet carcases, tabletops . . . any workshop project that depends on square corners should be tested repeatedly while it's under construction to make sure that it's still in square. A quick and reliable way is to measure the distance between outside corners on opposing sides of the project. If the measurements are equal, the project is square. If not, you'll need to make adjustments. If your project is a glued-up box or frame, as shown to the right, make adjustments by pushing or pulling on one clamp, while keeping the other steady.

IS YOUR LEVEL LEVEL?

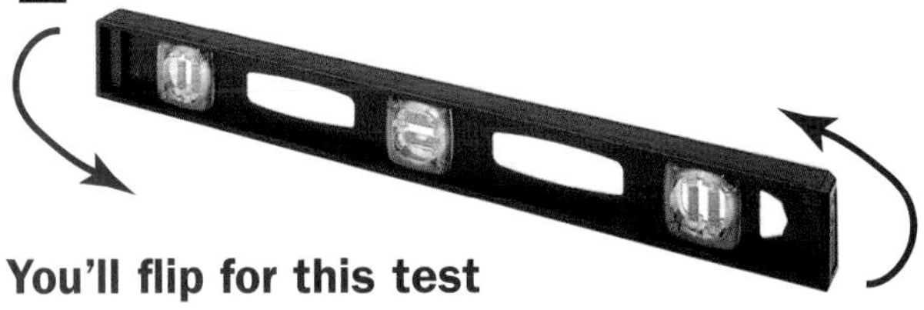

You'll flip for this test

To find out if your spirit level is truly level, set it on a smooth, flat surface (like a piece of fiberboard) and shim beneath the surface with wood shims until the bubble in the lower vial reads level. Then, flip the level and check to see if the bubble in the upper vial gives a similar reading. If not, one of the vials has fallen out of calibration. You can also perform a similar test with the end vials that are used to check for plumb.

LEVEL UP, PLUMB DOWN

Transferring a point from a floor to a ceiling (or vice versa) is an important skill to have when doing frame carpentry. To mark a point on the floor (sole plate) that's directly below a point on the ceiling (cap plate), simply suspend a plumb bob from the higher point and mark the location of the tip when the plumb bob comes to rest. To find the point directly above another point, raise a straight board from the lower point and adjust its position with a level until it's exactly plumb, then mark the higher point.

Gallery of Levels

The 4-foot level

Whether its made from mahogany, laminated wood, plastic resin or extruded aluminum, the 4-ft. level is the cornerstone of many building trades. They're used for everything from plumbing stud walls (as shown here) to leveling concrete block to installing cabinets or grading soil. No tool collection is complete without one.

The water level

The water level is an ancient device used to find level points that are far apart or separated by obstructions. The original water levels consisted of two glass vials connected by tubing. The tubing was filled with colored water and the vials attached to the two points being leveled. The height of the water in each vial would always be equal. The new-fangled electronic version of a water level shown here is used for leveling fences, grading soil and setting concrete forms. The electronic module shown to the right is set at the desired height of the project. Then, the end of the level hose (See opposite page) is raised or lowered at the fence post or form brace locations. When level is achieved, the module emits a loud buzzing noise.

The line level

Used mostly in masonry, this simple device clips onto a mason's string so the string can be leveled to establish grade or course height.

The post level

When installing fence posts, attach a post level to the post top with a rubber band, and adjust the post until the level tells you it is plumb and level.

The collection of handsaws shown above can perform just about any cutting task you're likely to encounter in your workshop. (A) 8- to 10-TPI cross-cut saw for general cutting of dimension lumber or sheet goods; (B) Backsaw for miter-cutting; (C) Hacksaw for cutting metal; (D) Wallboard saw for making cutouts in wallboard and other soft building materials; (E) Flush-cutting saw for trimming wood plugs and through tenons; (F) Dovetail saw saw pictured is smaller version called "Gentleman's saw"; (G) Japanese saw (cuts on the pull stroke) for quick trim-carpentry cutting; (H) Fret saw for making delicate scrolling cuts; (I) Coping saw for curved cuts in trim carpentry.

Team of handsaws can handle any cut

Choosing the right tool for the job is especially important when using hand-powered tools.

Guide keeps handsaws in line

This easy-to-build cutting guide will ensure straight, accurate cuts with a handsaw. Simply join two pieces of scrap plywood at a right angle, making sure the heads of the fasteners are recessed. Add a piece of scrap wood at the front of the jig to make a lip for holding the jig tightly against your workpiece.

BAND SAW & JIG SAW BLADES

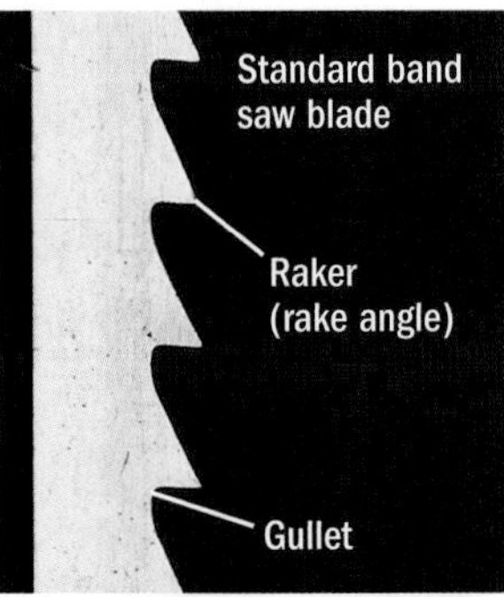

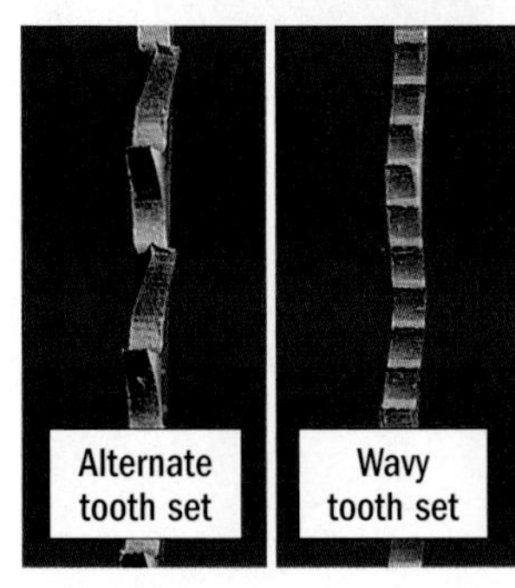

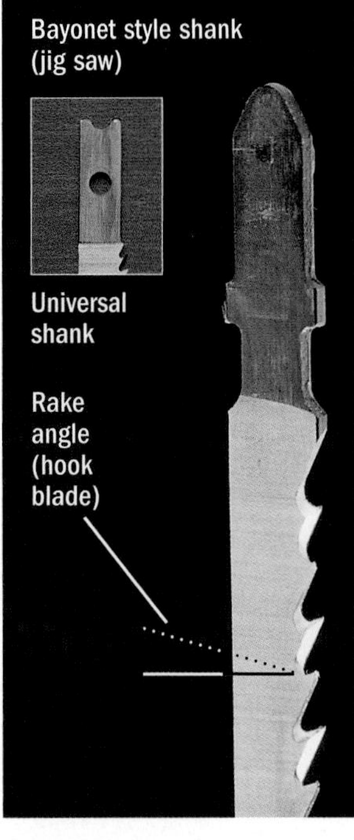

Straight blades for jig saws, band saws, scroll saws and reciprocating saws vary by number of teeth per inch (tpi), the set of the teeth, the rake angle of the teeth, and the width and thickness of the blade. The type of metal used to make the blade and the presence of carbide or other hardened steel tips affect the longevity (and the price) of the blades. Blades for some tools have numerous tooth configurations: for example, band saw blades can be purchased with *standard teeth* (above), or *skip-tooth* and *hook-tooth* configurations.

CIRCULAR SAW BLADES

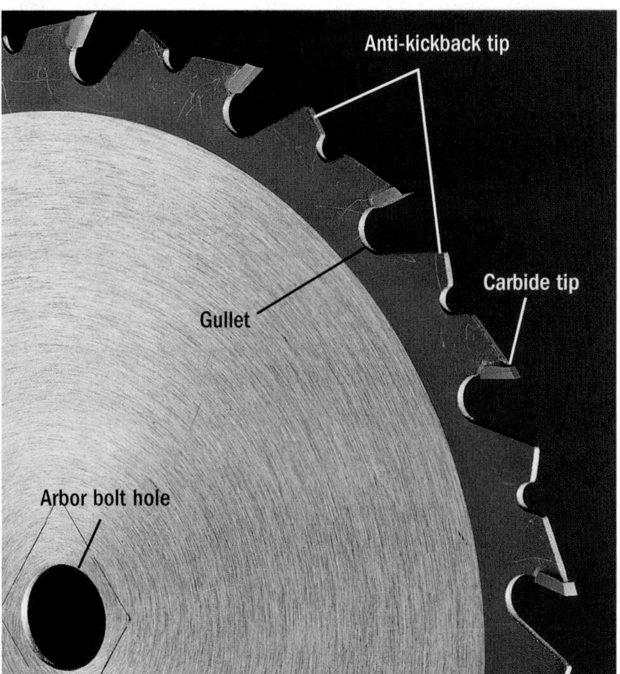

Circular saw blades are fitted onto portable circular saws, table saws, radial-arm saws and power miter saws. Select blades by matching the number of teeth per inch to the task at hand—but make sure the tpi number is for the correct blade diameter (anywhere from 3½ in. to 18 in. or so, with 7¼ in. the most common for portable circular saws, and 10 in. the most common for table saws, power miter saws and radial-arm saws).

RECIPROCATING SAW BLADE TYPES

Reciprocating saws are used to perform many different construction tasks. The size and shape of the blades used changes dramatically according to use. Keep a complete set of blades in your saw case.

A good set of reciprocating saw blades includes: (A) 6 in., 18 tpi blade for heavy metal; (B) 6 in., 10 tpi blade for general cutting; (C) 9 in., 6 tpi blade for fast cuts and general roughing in; (D) 12 in., 8 tpi blade for cutting timbers and other thick materials; (E) 6 in., 4 tpi blade for fast, rough wood-cutting; (F) 6 in., 5 tpi blade for fast, cleaner cuts; (G) 3⅝ in., 14 tpi blade for curved cuts in hard woods.

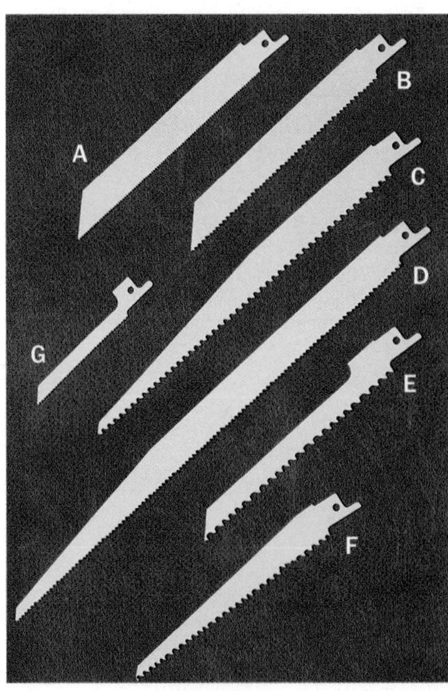

Common circular saw blade styles (right) include: (A) General purpose combination blade (good for ripping); (B) Thin-kerf anti-kickback blade (note expansion slots); (C) Roofer's blade (for portable circular saws); (D) Trim-cutting blade (for clean, relatively fast cross-cuts); (E) Carbide-tipped cross-cutting blade (good for power miter saws). Generally, more teeth per inch produce cleaner, slower cuts.

SAW BLADE SELECTION CHART

Band saw

TASK	WIDTH (IN.)	PITCH	STYLE*	SET*
Scrollwork, joinery	⅛	14 tpi	ST	AB or R
Cutting light metal	⅛	14 tpi	ST	W
Tight curves	⅛	6 tpi	SK	AB
Smooth curves	3⁄16	10 tpi	ST	AB
General purpose	¼	6-8 tpi	ST or SK	AB
Rip-cutting	¼	4-6 tpi	H	AB or R
Gen. crosscutting	⅜	8-10 tpi	ST or SK	AB or R
Fast crosscutting	⅜	4 tpi	SK	AB
Resawing	½	4 tpi	H	AB

*Key ST=standard, SK=skip-tooth, H=hook-tooth, AB=alternate-bevel, R=raker, W=wavy

Jig Saw

TASK	MATERIAL	LENGTH	PITCH
Fast, rough carpentry	Wood	4 in.	6 tpi
General purpose	Wood	4 in.	8 tpi
Smooth finish	Wood	4 in.	10 tpi
Extra-smooth finish	Wood	3 in.	12-14 tpi
Light metal	Metal	3 in.	12-14 tpi
Thick metal	Metal	3 in.	24 tpi

Circular Saw

TASK	TYPE	TPI (8¼-IN./10-IN. DIA.)
General purpose	Combination	16-36/18-50
Trim carpentry	Cross-cut	40-64/60-80
Rough carpentry	Cross-cut	34-40/40-60
Smooth cross-cutting	Cross-cut	50-64/60-80
Rip-cutting	Ripping	16-36/18-24
Plywood and particleboard	Plywood/panel	48-64/60-80
Light metal	Metal-cutting	58-64/60-72

Scroll Saw

TASK	TYPE	GAUGE	PITCH
General cutting	Scrolling	#5	15 tpi
Cutting without tear-out	Reverse-tooth fret	#7	11.5 tpi
Fine scrollwork	Scrolling	#7	12 tpi
Very tight curves	Spiral-tooth	#2	41 tpi
Fast cuts	Fret	#9	11.5 tpi

Give your blades a bath

Saw blades that aren't performing as well as you like don't necessarily need sharpening: they may just need a quick cleaning. Special pitch/resin removing compound or ordinary oven cleaner can be used to clean blades (be sure to wear gloves).

COPING BASE TRIM FOR AN INSIDE CORNER

1 Cut one mating board square, and cut the other at a 45° bevel, using a miter saw. The beveled board should be slightly longer than the finished length.

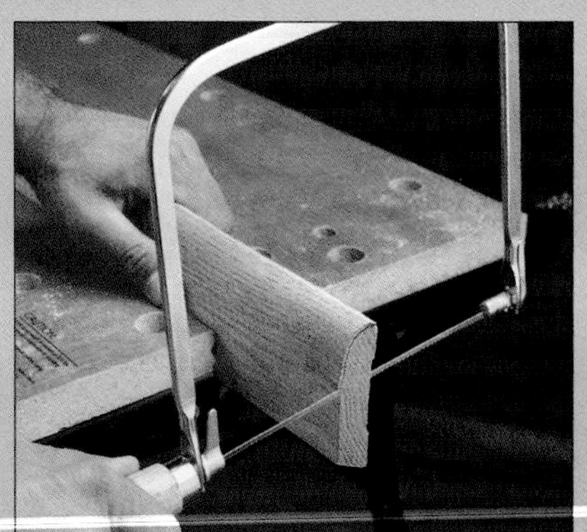

2 With the square-cut board flush in the corner, use a coping saw to trim the excess wood from the beveled end, leaving an end that's perpendicular but tapers up to follow the profile of the molding.

3 Apply the wood finish to both boards, then slip the beveled board into the corner so it overlaps the end of the square-cut board.

Make & use a straightedge

Build an 8-ft. straightedge to cut plywood and paneling with your circular saw. The straightedge shown below has a ¼-in. plywood base, and a 1 × 2 cleat (you can also use a strip of plywood) that serves as a saw guide. After assembling the straightedge, position the circular saw with the foot tight against the cleat and trim off the excess portion of the plywood base. To use the straightedge, position the trimmed edge of the plywood base flush with your cutting line and clamp the straightedge to the workpiece.

Good-side-down for cleaner cuts

Portable circular saws cut on the upward rotation of the blade. To avoid tear-out on the better face of your workpiece, turn it good-face-down when cutting.

TWO TECHNIQUES FOR MAKING PLUNGE CUTS

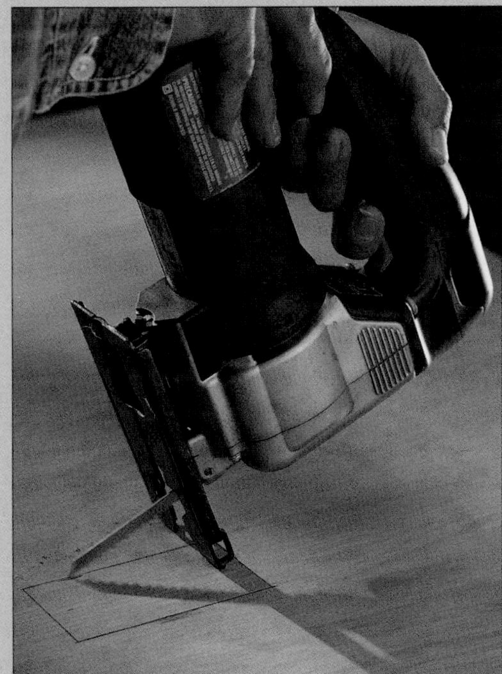

Use a jig saw: Tip the jig saw forward on the front edge of its foot. Align the tip of the blade with the cutting line, then turn on the saw and gently but firmly lower the blade into the cutting area. The blade will want to bounce, but by maintaining firm pressure on the front of the foot you can keep it under control until it enters the wood.

Use a circular saw: Place the front edge of the foot against the board, retract the blade guard and hold it in a raised position with your thumb. Turn on the saw and lower the blade into the wood, using the front of the saw foot as a fulcrum. Always wear safety goggles.

Rotary cutters use drilling action to make internal cuts

Spiral cutting tools are a cross between a jig saw or reciprocating saw and a power drill. The spiral-shaped cutting bit for the tool looks and acts like a drill bit, but, like a jig saw, it cuts straight or curved lines in building materials like drywall, tile, plaster, fiberglass and wood using different bits. A relatively new tool innovation, these compact cutters are especially useful in making internal cuts and cutouts. In the photo to the right, a spiral cutting tool is being used to cut holes for water supply pipes in a sheet of cement board.

CUTTING

MAKING CURVED CUTOUTS

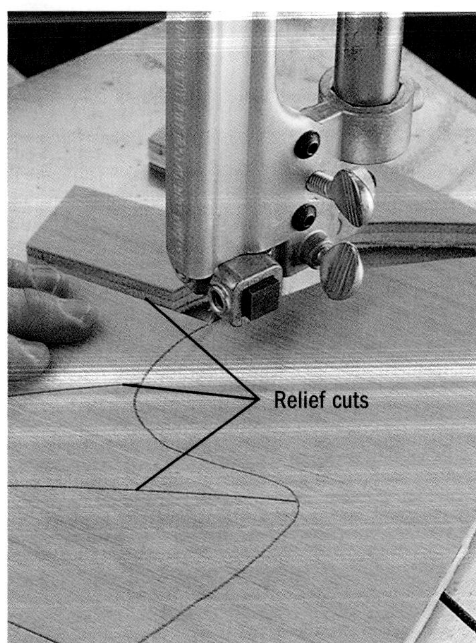

Cut a loop to make a square

Making square internal cuts can be a perplexing problem, but here's a simple solution: cut along one leg of the square, and keep cutting past the corner. Loop the saw blade back and cut the second leg.

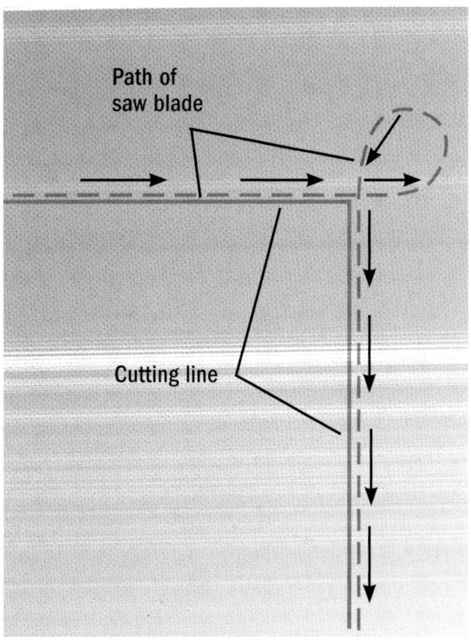

Relief cuts prevent binding

When making a curved contour cut using a jig saw, band saw or scroll saw, make relief cuts from the edge of the workpiece to the cutting line, in the waste area, so waste can be removed as you cut.

MINIMUM RADIUS CUTS FOR BAND SAW BLADES

As a general rule, you should choose the widest band saw blade that can handle the job you're doing. But because the width of the blade limits the tightness of the curves you can cut, you should choose the widest blade that can follow your tightest cutting radius.

BLADE WIDTH	SMALLEST RADIUS CUT
1/8"	3/16"
3/16"	3/8"
1/4"	5/8"
3/8"	1 1/4"
1/2"	3"
3/4"	5"
1"	8"

Cut perfect circles with a router compass

Most DIYers think of routers as primarily tools for cutting decorative profiles or perhaps an occasional dado or rabbet. But they can also be very effective tools for cutting stock to size and shape. When the right bits and techniques are used, they produce extremely clean edges that often require no sanding.

If you need to cut a square workpiece into a circular shape, a router compass is an excellent choice. Simply secure the router base to the wide end of the compass, set the adjustable center pin to the desired radius of the cut, and secure the pin at the center of the circle. For best results, make the cut in several passes of increasing depth. A single-flute straight bit or a spiral upcut bit can be used to remove large amounts of waste in the cutting area, without bogging down.

CUTTING

TIPS FOR CUTTING WITH A POWER MITER BOX

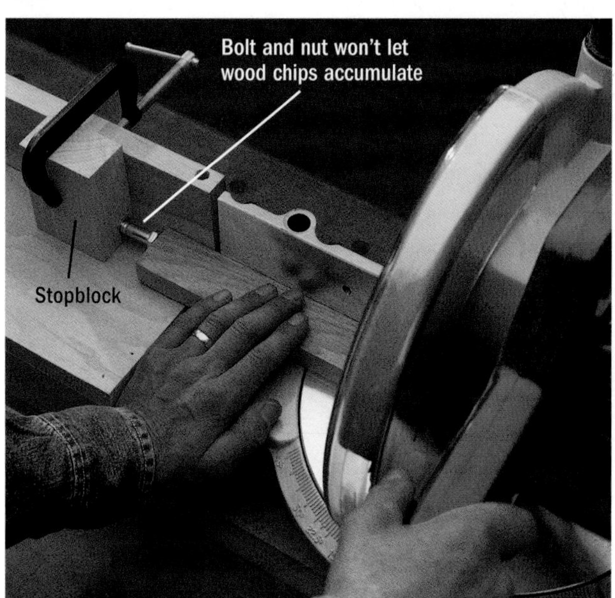

Stopblock speeds up repetitive cuts

When making repetitive cuts with a power miter saw (or radial-arm saw), clamp a stopblock to the saw fence at the desired length. A lag screw driven squarely into the edge of the stopblock creates a solid surface for aligning the workpiece, while keeping wood chips from building up between the block and workpiece.

Jig takes the math out of beveling molding

Cutting miter-bevels in crown molding often involves tricky math and very precise angles. To simplify the task, use this jig. Join a straight board about 3 in. high to a strip of ¼-in. plywood about 6 in. wide. These will be the "fence" and "table" of the jig. Place a piece of crown molding into the "L" formed by the fence and table, and adjust it until the beveled sides are flush against the fence and table. Mark the position on the table, remove the molding and attach a wood strip at the mark. This strip will hold the molding at the proper angle for bevel-cutting miters.

A jig for the jig saw

Make circular cutouts with a jig saw and trammel jig. The jig shown above is created by attaching a cradle for the saw foot in one end of a strip of plywood. Cut a guide hole in the plywood for the saw blade. Tack a nail into the jig so the distance from the nail to the saw blade equals the radius of the circle you want to cut. Then, simply drive the nail through the jig and into the center of the stock. The trammel will pivot on the nail, creating a perfect circle as you cut.

CUTTING

RESAWING STOCK ON A BAND SAW

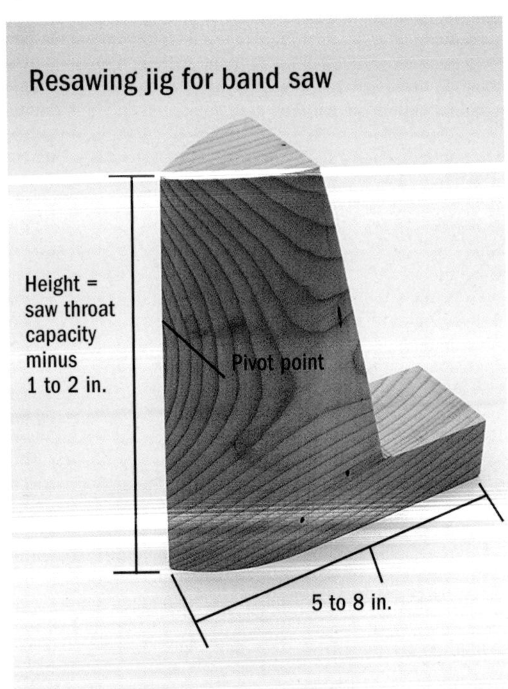

Resawing thick lumber into thinner strips for woodworking is a job best accomplished with a band saw. The simplest method is to attach a fence to the band saw table, parallel to the blade, and feed the stock through as you would when rip-cutting on a band saw. The downside to this method is that the saw blade tends to travel, following the grain of the wood, and resulting in an uneven cut that requires quite a bit of surface planing. One way to minimize the unevenness of the resaw cut is to use a jig like the one shown to the left. When clamped to the saw table so the pivot point is even with the cutting edge of the blade, the jig may be used as a guide to set the thickness of the cut. Because the pivot point is so narrow, you can adjust the feed direction of the board to compensate for blade travel, resulting in a more even cut. You'll still need to surface-plane the workpiece, but you'll waste less wood.

Relief block keeps cutoff pieces free and clear when cross-cutting

Use a relief block to prevent cut-off pieces from getting jammed between the fence and the blade when cross-cutting on the table saw. The relief block can simply be a piece of scrap wood clamped to the fence. Make sure the relief block is positioned behind the point where the workpiece will make first contact with the saw blade. Never stand directly behind the workpiece when feeding it into the blade.

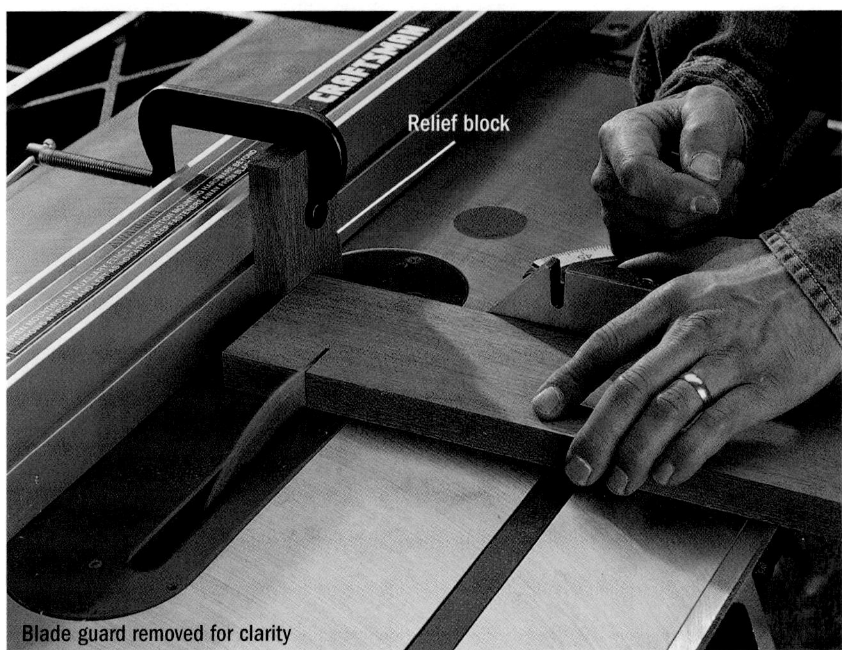

Blade guard removed for clarity

As a rule, take measurements

Don't trust the cutting scale on the table saw fence if you're making precise cuts. Instead, measure the distance from the cutting edge of the blade to the fence with a steel rule when setting up for your cut. Double-check the distance after securing the fence, and make a practice cut on scrap for added precision.

Get blade height just right

Use a combination square to set the height of a table saw blade. The bottom of the square should just be touching the tip of one of the teeth. Because tooth length is not always uniform, spin the blade by hand and make sure you're referencing off the tooth that will cut deepest (be sure to unplug the saw first).

RIPPING NARROW STRIPS

When rip-cutting a single narrow workpiece from a wider board, the narrow strip should be on the opposite side of the blade from the rip fence (left photo). This keeps the wider portion of the board between the blade and the rip fence to allow more room for your hand or a pushstick. To rip a series of narrow workpieces, set the distance between the blade and the rip fence to match the intended width of the workpieces you need. Use a narrow pushstick to guide the pieces along the rip fence (right photo).

A single part

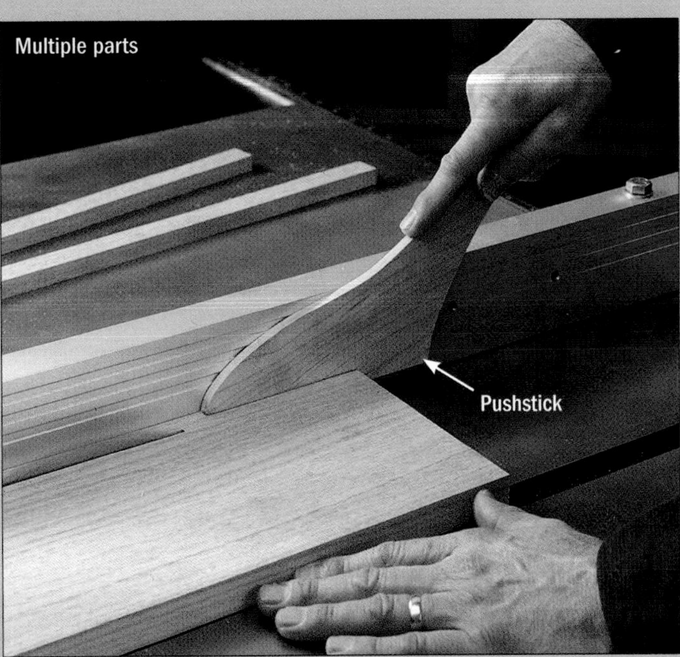

Multiple parts

Wood fences make good sense

Adding a wooden auxiliary fence to your table saw (or just about any other tool) extends the life of both your saw fence and your saw blades by eliminating damaging metal-to-metal contact. An auxiliary fence that's taller than the saw fence also creates a good surface for clamping jigs, stopblocks and hold-downs. The fence shown here is made from hard maple and attached to the metal fence with T-bolts that fit into a slot in the saw fence so no screw heads protrude.

Cross-cut sled

With tracks on the underside that ride in the miter slots, a cross-cut sled supports the workpiece so it can't pivot or shift as you feed it through the blade. You can purchase a cross-cut sled or build your own from plywood and acrylic, as shown here.

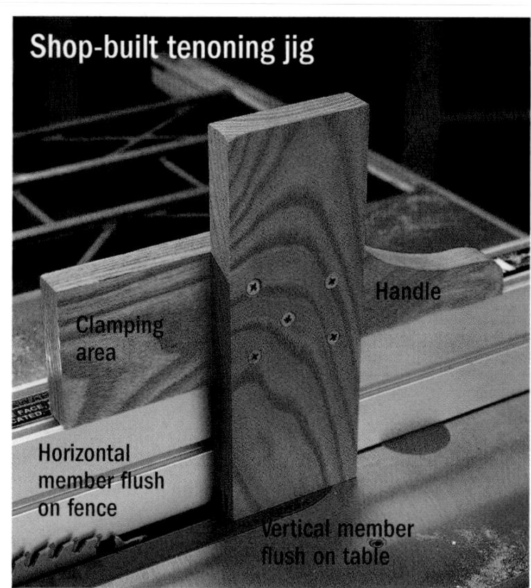

Sweet cheeks for tenons

Making the cheek cuts for tenons is clumsy and dangerous without a good tenoning jig—and the results are usually disappointing. This shop-built tenoning jig is easy to make from scrap wood and will help you produce tenons that fit on the first try. First, cut the vertical and horizontal members—the horizontal member should have a contour on the tail to create a handle, as shown above. Join the two members with wood screws, arranged so the distance from the bottom of the horizontal member to the bottom of the vertical member is equal to the height of your saw fence. Make sure the members are exactly perpendicular. To use the jig, clamp your workpiece to the jig and feed the workpiece into the blade, keeping steady pressure against the fence and the table (See photo, above right). Cut all the way through the workpiece and the jig. Always test your cuts on a scrap board before cutting your workpieces. Use your miter gauge to guide the workpiece when cutting the tenon shoulders.

TRIM WEDGE AND DOWEL ENDS WITH A FLUSH-CUTTING SAW

A flush-cutting saw with a very flexible blade is the ideal tool for trimming off the ends of tenon wedges or dowels. The saw shown above is a Japanese saw that cuts on the pull stroke.

THE "POOR MAN'S MORTISING MACHINE"

There are many methods you can use to cut mortises for mortise-and-tenon joinery. The best way is to purchase a special mortising machine or a mortising attachment for your drill press. But if you'd rather not spend the money on these expensive tools, the following method will produce clean mortises when done carefully. It's a little slower and takes some trial and error, but for the weekend woodworker who already owns a drill press, it's a good option.

1 Carefully lay out your mortise using a marking gauge or straightedge. Choose a drill bit the same diameter as the thickness of the mortise (3/8 in. is common), then remove the waste wood from the mortise by drilling overlapping holes using a depth stop.

2 Use a sharp chisel to clean up the sides of the mortise so they're flat and smooth. Make sure the flat face of the chisel is contacting the wood. Clean up the ends of the mortise with a chisel the same width as the thickness of the mortise.

TIPS FOR MINIMIZING TEAROUT

Tearout, or *chipout,* is probably the most common problem encountered when cutting and shaping parts. It occurs when wood fibers are torn away by the action of the blade or bit, leaving ragged edges with voids. When cutting with power (or hand) saws, make it a habit to arrange your workpiece so the moving saw teeth enter the good face and exit the bad (less visible) face. It is the exit side where tearout occurs, particularly when cross-cutting. If you are using a table saw, chop saw, band saw, scroll saw, hand saw, or drill, place the good face up. Circular saws and jig saws cut on the upstroke, so cut with the good face down. Tearout also can be minimized by choosing a finer-toothed blade and keeping it sharp. Feeding the work too fast can worsen tearout.

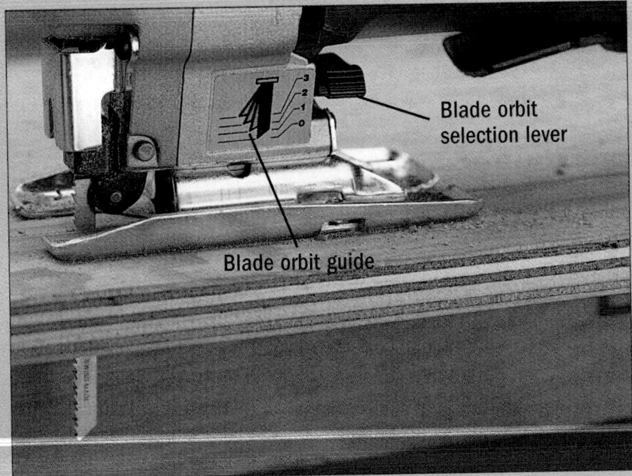

Flatten your orbit. When using a jig saw with orbital cutting action, the path of the saw blade actually makes an abbreviated arc that increases the cutting speed, but can also increase tearout. For the cleanest possible cut, set the blade to its flattest cutting plane.

Enter the better face. Tearout occurs when the blade exits, so position the workpiece so the blade enters the better face first. With circular saws, the bad face should be up; on table saws, it should be down.

Zero-clearance throat plate. To minimize tearout when cutting plywood across the grain directly on the saw table, replace the gaping factory throat plate with a shop-made plywood version. Insert small flathead screws under the corners and adjust them in or out to shim the plate up or down so it's flush with the table. Then position the rip fence over the plate (away from the blade path) and raise the spinning blade to cut a tight kerf.

Tape the cutting line. Sheet goods covered with thin veneers, melamine or laminate are prone to tearout and chipping around the blade slot opening in the throatplate. To avoid this problem, adhere a strip of masking tape along the cutting line on the bottom of the panel before you make the cut. The tape will keep the veneer, melamine or laminate from splintering or chipping. In addition, install a sharp triple-chip, crosscut or plywood blade. Saw with the "good" (untaped) face of the panel face-up on the saw table.

Cabinetmaker's chisels

Most of the wood chisels sold and owned today are bevel-edge cabinetmaker's chisels (see photo, right). Available in standard widths ranging from ¼ to 1½ in., they can handle a variety of everyday cutting tasks, including cutting mortises and paring tenons. If you're a serious woodworker who appreciates hand tools, you may want to look into a set of mortising chisels, which have thicker shanks and wider, shock-resistant handle butts. Better quality chisels are made with hardened steel that hold an edge for a long time. The main differences are in handle material, size and feel. If investing in a set of quality chisels, make sure the ones you choose feel comfortable and well balanced in your hand.

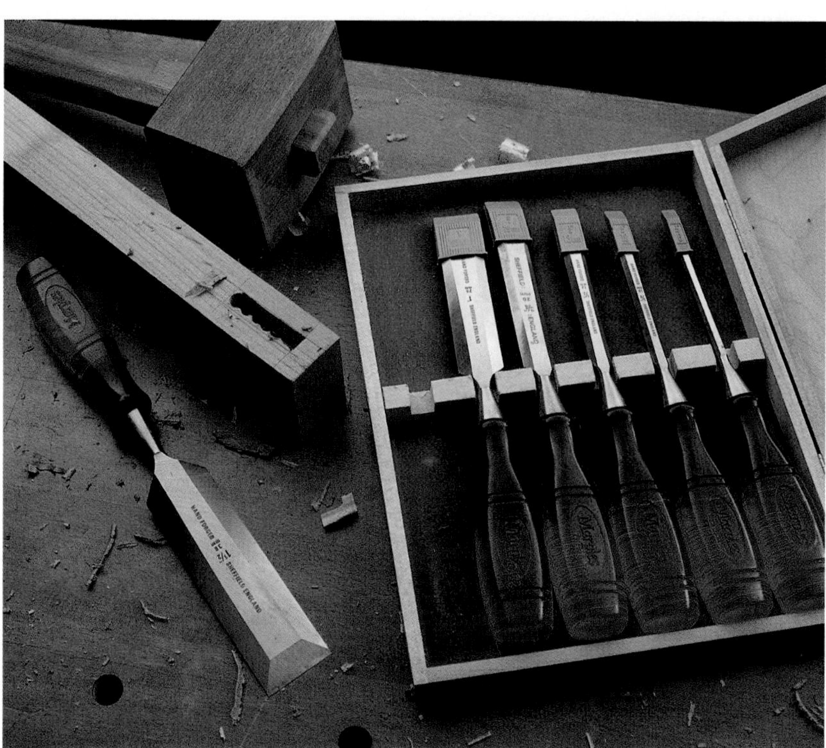

HOW TO SHARPEN CHISELS

1 A sharp blade is the key to achieving quality results with your chisels. You can use oil stones or water stones to sharpen your chisels. In this case oil stones are used. First, flatten the back of the chisel. Apply a few drops of oil to the stone and place the back of the chisel flat on the face of the stone. Work the chisel back and forth several times until the first half inch of the blade is flat.

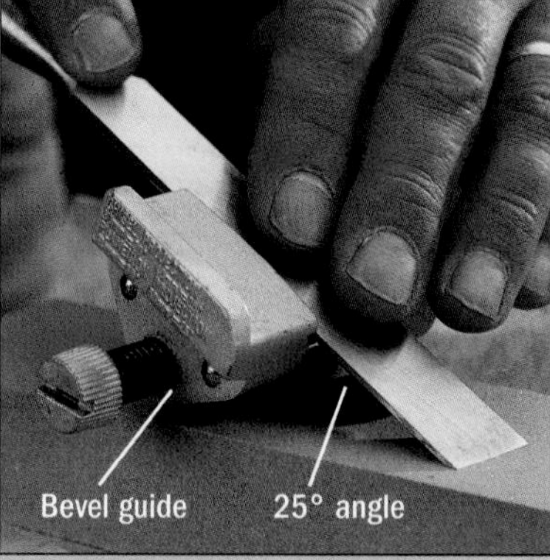

2 Wipe the stone with a clean rag, and apply more oil. Turn the blade over, and hold it at a 25° angle so the bevel is flat against the stone. Draw the tool back and forth. Here, a bevel guide is used for a precise edge angle.

3 Put a micro-edge on the blade by lifting it slightly so just the tip touches the stone. Draw the blade lightly two or three times along the stone, until a slight burr can be felt along the back of the blade. Turn the blade over, hold it flat (as in step 2) and draw it one time along the stone to remove the burr. Done properly, this will give the chisel a razor-sharp edge.

THE RIGHT WAY TO CUT HINGE MORTISES

Installing hinges (or strike plates) is a frequently encountered task for the handyman, and as often as not we rely on the trial-and-error method—with mixed results. Here's the best way to cut a hinge mortise.

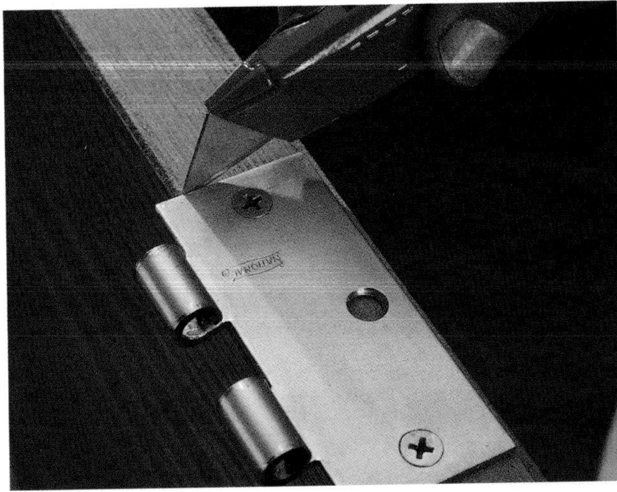

1 Remove the hinge pin (if its removable) and position the hinge leaf or strike plate on the edge of the door or on the door jamb. Tack it into place with screws, then score an outline around the plate with a utility knife. This prevents the wood from splintering past the ends of the mortise.

2 Choose a chisel that's close to the same width as the mortise. With the beveled side of the chisel facing toward the mortise, tap the butt of the chisel handle with a wood or rubber mallet. Cut into the wood to a depth equal to the thickness of the hinge leaf or strike plate. Cut along all sides of four-sided mortises.

3 With the beveled edge of the chisel tip flat against the workpiece, make a series of relief cuts in the waste wood area of the mortise. Space the cuts ⅛ to ¼ in. apart (make closer cuts in harder woods). The cuts should be equal in depth to the finished depth of the mortise.

4 Clean out the waste wood by driving the chisel against the direction of the relief cuts.To avoid digging in too deep, try to keep the beveled edge of the tip flat in the mortise. Scrape the bottom of the mortise smooth. If you need to deepen the mortise, repeat the procedure—don't simply try to make deeper scraping cuts.

HOW TO CUT BRICKS & PAVERS

1 Install a masonry blade in your circular saw. Adjust the saw blade to cut about ¼ in. deep. When cutting multiple bricks or pavers, clamp them together for gang-cutting. Draw your cutting line and score it with the masonry blade. Wear eye protection at all times.

2 Set each scored brick or paver on-edge on a semi-resilient surface (like a sheet of plywood). Position the blade of a wide brickset on the edge, aligned with the scored cutting line. Strike the brickset with a 3-lb. maul until the brick or paver cleaves along the cutting line.

Option: Use a wet saw. If your project requires that you cut more than a dozen or so bricks or pavers, think seriously about renting a wet saw for the job. Available at most rental centers, wet saws are fast and easy to operate. Simply set the brick or paver on the tool bed with the cutting line aligned with the saw blade and lower the counter-weighted blade. Do not pull down forcefully on the blade.

HOW TO CUT TILES WITH A TILE CUTTER

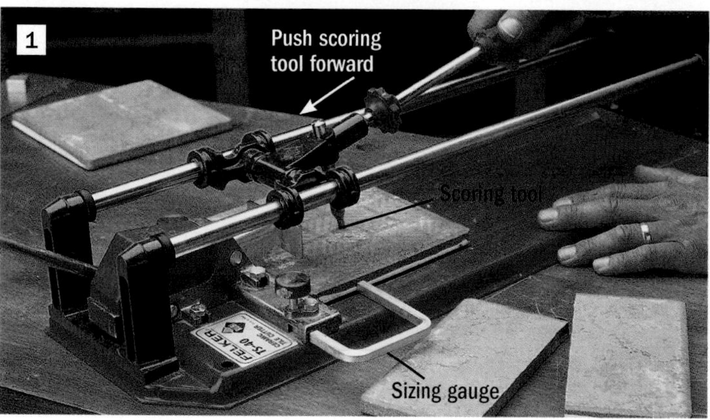

1 Set the tile on the bed of the tile cutter so the cutting line is aligned with the point of the scoring tool. Some tile cutters, like the one above, are equipped with a sizing gauge so you can set the tool to make multiple cuts that are the same width. Lighter duty cutters often cut on the pull stroke, but the rented, heavy-duty model shown here cuts on the push stroke. Press down on the lever that lowers the scoring tool and push forward, scoring the cutting line.

2 Retract the scoring tool clear of the tile, then lower the lever that controls the breaking bars. These bars exert downward pressure toward the trough in the center of the bed, causing the tile to snap along the scored line.

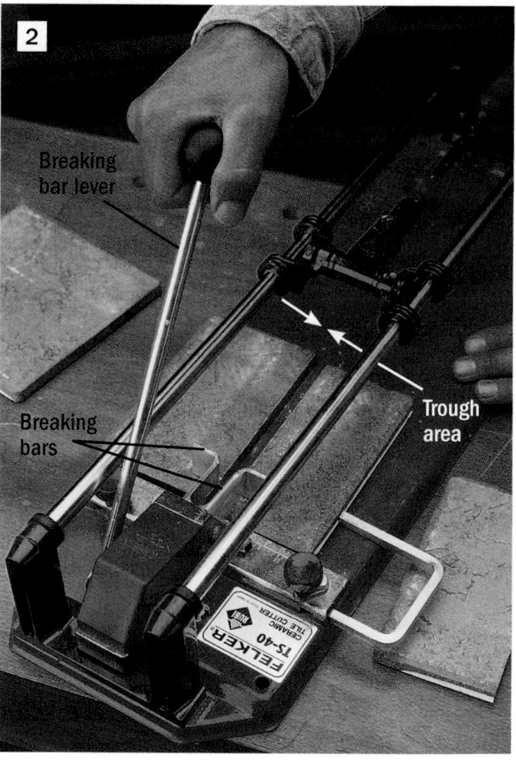

CUTTING

HOW TO CUT GLASS

1 Set the sheet of glass on a soft, non-skid surface like the rug pad shown above. Lubricate the cutting wheel with lightweight machine oil. Using a straightedge as a guide, score a cutting line with a glass cutting tool. Press down firmly on the tool—the goal is to create a score line that breaks the glass surface in a single pass. Making multiple passes will result in a filed or very rough cut.

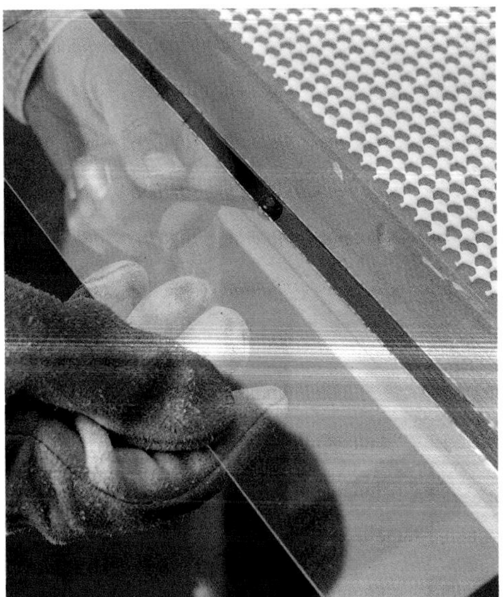

2 Slide the glass sheet to the edge of your worksurface so the scored line overhangs the edge. Wearing work gloves, apply gentle downward pressure to the waste section of glass. Then, tap lightly on the underside of the scored cutting line with the ball end of the glass cutting tool. This will cause the glass to fracture along the cutting line. Smooth the cut edge with emery paper.

GLASS DATA SHEET

TYPE	CHARACTERISTICS	USES
Sheet	Lowest cost, noticeable waviness due to thickness variations	Windows, cabinet doors, general household use
Plate	Ground and polished to a degree much flatter than sheet glass	Large display windows, table tops, glass shelves
Tempered*	High impact strength and small, relatively harmless fragments when shattered	Patio doors, French doors, skylights, overhead windows

**Both sheet glass and plate glass may be tempered*

CUTTING PLEXIGLAS

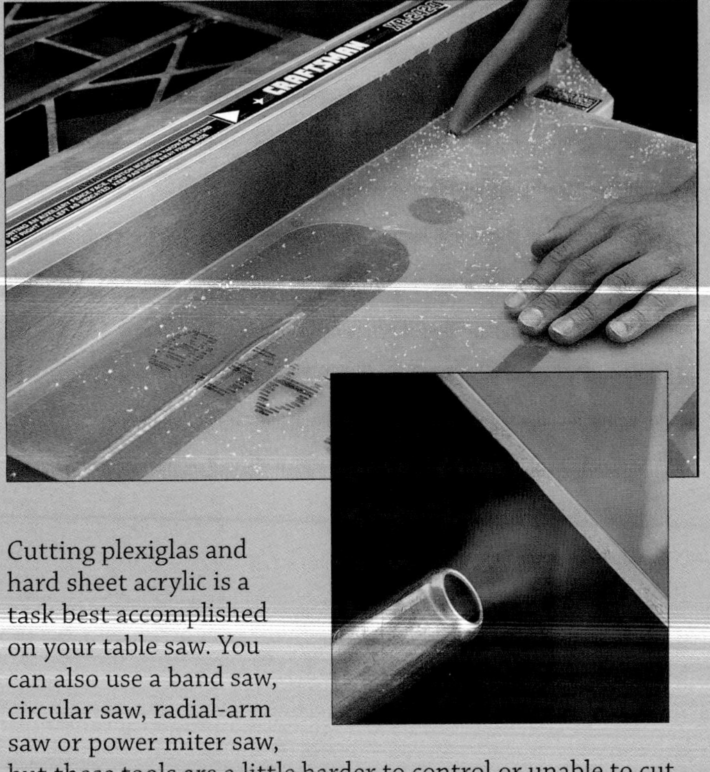

Cutting plexiglas and hard sheet acrylic is a task best accomplished on your table saw. You can also use a band saw, circular saw, radial-arm saw or power miter saw, but these tools are a little harder to control or unable to cut larger sheet goods, and they are more prone to overheating and causing the material to melt at the edges of the cut. Whichever saw you use, use a blade with a high number of teeth per inch (tpi). The table saw above is equipped with a plywood cutting blade. If the material has a paper or poly facing, leave it on until the cut is finished. The edges of the cut can be sanded or rounded over with very fine sandpaper or emery cloth. For a clear edge, run the flame from a propane torch carefully along the edge (inset photo).

Drilling

Drilling precise and uniform holes is an overlooked art form in most workshops. But the fact is, it doesn't take much longer to set up drilling guides that will help make your drilling projects virtually foolproof. Choosing the right tool and the right style of bit is also very important to drilling success. The basic selection of drill types includes:

Hand drills (brace-and-bit, egg-beater style and others). These tools are becoming less common with the advent of the cordless power drill, but they're still nice to have around for drilling a few quick holes onsite (and the battery never runs down).

Corded portable drills. These too have lost prominence to the cordless, but every shop should still be equipped with one of these workhorses. With few exceptions, they can still create more torque than cordless drills, and they're very reliable for large projects, like screwing down decking.

Cordless drills. How did we ever get along without these tools? Technology continues to evolve, but generally a 12-volt model with an exchangeable battery pack will perform just about any workshop drilling task.

Drill press. For power and precision, a drill press is unbeatable. For most tasks, a benchtop model will do the job. But if you do a lot of woodworking or metalworking, look for a floor-standing model with easily adjustable speed and a larger throat capacity.

A BACKER BOARD PREVENTS TEAROUT

Regardless of the type of drill and bit you're using, bits will cause splintering and tearout when they exit a board. To prevent this from happening, simply slip a backer board beneath the workpiece before drilling. Any piece of wood scrap can be used as a backer board. For a more permanent backer board, many woodworkers attach pieces of scrap wood to their drill press table with screws driven up through the guide holes in the table. In addition to preventing tearout, a wood auxiliary table on your drill press helps prevent damage that can occur to drill bits if they're inadvertently driven into the metal table.

DRILL PRESS SPEEDS

MATERIAL	HOLE DIA.	SPEED (RPM)
Plastic	1/16 in.	6000-6500
	1/4 in.	3000-3500
	1/2 in.	500-1000
Soft metal	1/16 in.	6000-6500
	1/4 in.	4500-5000
	1/2 in.	1500-2500
Steel	1/16 in.	5000-6500
	1/4 in.	1500-2000
	1/2 in.	500-1000
Wood	0-1/2 in.	3000-4000
	1/2-1 in.	2000-3000
	1+ in.	700-2000

Note: Multispur bits should be used at very low speed (250 to 700 rpm)

Portable drill types

Hand-held power drills are made in two basic handle styles: the *T-handle* and the *pistol grip*.

If you use your drill for extended periods of time, the T-handle is probably a better choice because it's more balanced and won't cause fatigue as soon. The T-handle also is easier to control for precision drilling. Pistol-grip drills are preferred by people who work with harder materials because the design allows you to apply more downward pressure directly over the bit—but never press too hard.

T-handle

Pistol grip

Secure a sphere

Drilling holes into a wood sphere is easy with this homemade holder. Drill holes slightly smaller than the diameter of the sphere into the centers of two small pieces of scrap wood. Sandwich the sphere between the holes and secure with a wood-screw clamp.

Steady a cylinder

A block of wood with a V-groove will hold dowels and other cylinders steady during drilling. Simply set the blade on your table saw to 45° and cut 1-in.-deep grooves from opposite ends, forming a "V" in the center of the board. Adjust the width and depth of the "V" according to the diameter of the cylinder.

DRILL BIT DIAMETERS

BIT TYPE	RANGE OF DIA.
Twist	1/64 to 1 in.
Spade	1/4 to 1 1/2 in.
Brad-point	1/64 to 5/8 in.
Masonry (3/8-in. drill)	1/8 to 1 in.
Masonry (1/2-in. drill)	1/8 to 1 1/2 in.
Forstner	1/4 to 2 1/8 in.

Drill perfect pilots on the fly

Take the guesswork out of drilling pilot holes for finish nails by chucking one of the nails into your drill and using it as a drill bit.

SPECIAL-PURPOSE DRILLS & ACCESSORIES OFFER SOLUTIONS

Hammer drill for concrete

The hammer drill (available in ⅜- and ½-in. models) uses percussion to help drill bits cut into stubborn concrete. Be sure to use a masonry bit (see page 48) and wear hand, ear and eye protection.

Fly cutter for circular cutouts

The fly cutter is an adjustable drill press accessory that will make smooth circular cutouts up to 6-in. dia. Use the lowest drill press speed setting and be sure to clamp your workpiece to the drill press table.

Bit extension for deep holes

Ever wondered how to drill a cord hole in a lamp base, or how to drill through an 8-in. timber with a 6-in.-long bit? By chucking a bit extension into your drill you can add 12 to 24 in. of drilling capacity.

HOW TO DRILL CLEAN HOLES IN CERAMIC TILE

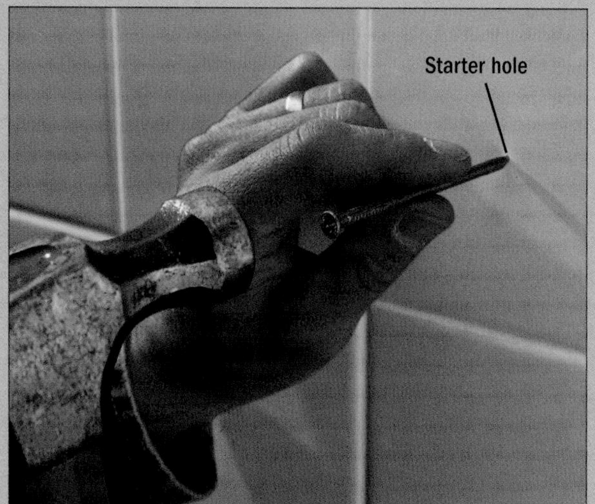

1 Before drilling into glazed tile, break the slick surface by lightly tapping the tile with a center punch or nail at the centerpoint of your drilling mark. This will create a starting point for the drill bit (without a starter hole, the bit will wander across the surface of the tile, scratching and gouging as it travels).

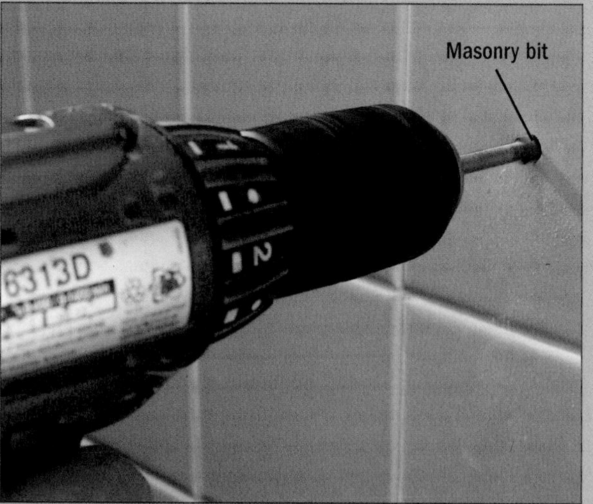

2 Use a masonry bit to drill through the tile. If you have a variable speed drill, set the tool on its slowest setting. Don't force the bit or you risk cracking the tile.

HOW TO CUT WOOD PLUGS WITH A PLUG CUTTER

1 Select a plug cutter that matches the diameter of the holes you will be filling. Install the cutter in the drill press. Or use a plug cutter designed to use in a cordless drill. Next, cut the plugs in a piece of scrap wood that features similar grain orientation to the wood with the holes that will be filled.

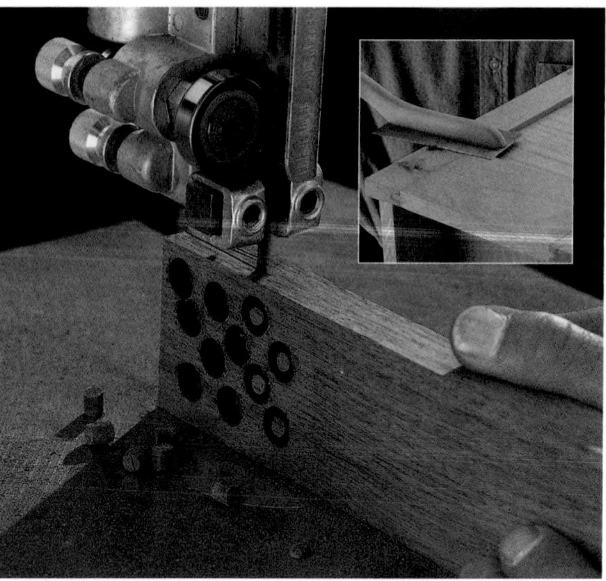

2 If you are making plugs from dense hardwood, then use a band saw to cut them out. In softwood you can simply break each plug loose using a flat blade screwdriver. Apply glue to each plug and then tap them into the holes. Trim and sand them flush after the glue has cured.

USING A HOLESAW

A hole saw is a popular hole-cutting device that can be fitted onto your portable power drill or your drill press. Frequently used to drill holes in doors for locksets, hole saws are sold in standard sizes on fixed mandrels, or as adjustable tools where hole saws of differing diameter can be fitted and secured onto a single mandrel. The free end of the mandrel is chucked into the drill and the pilot bit on the other end is used to start the hole and keep the hole saw cutting on-center.

1 When cutting with a hole saw, position the tip of the pilot bit over the drilling point and begin drilling at slow speed until the teeth of the hole saw engage the workpiece. Adjust the drill speed so the saw is cutting productively, but without bogging down or burnishing the edges of the hole. Hold the drill perpendicular to the workpiece

2 Cut as deeply into the work area as you can, without cutting all the way through. Make sure the pilot bit has cut through, however. Withdraw the hole saw and finish the cut from the other face of the workpiece (this prevents tearout from the hole saw).

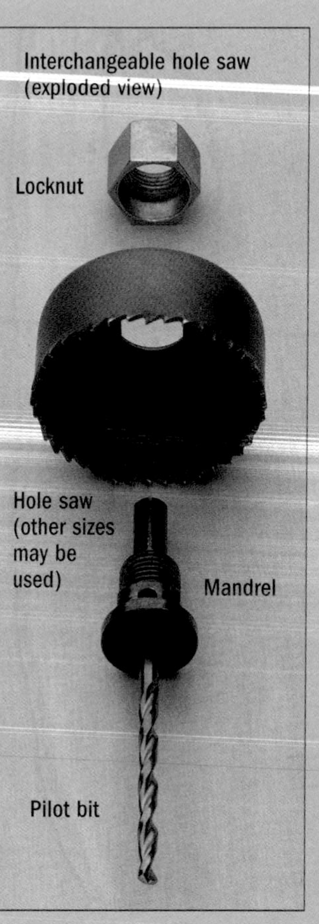

GUIDE TO COMMON DRILL BITS

1. Twist bit will bore through angle iron, flat iron or sheet metal and can be used for rough drilling in wood and other materials. Twist bits are available in a wider range of diameters than any other bit type.

2. Brad-point bit looks like a twist bit, but has a center spur and side spurs to keep it from wandering. These bits can make clean cuts in wood and softer materials (but not metal).

3. Auger bit will bore deep, straight holes into timber or thick softwood. The threaded bit point helps keep the bit cutting true while the spiral cutting head carries wood shavings to the surface. Best used with hand-powered brace-and-bit or a power right-angle drill.

4. Counterboring bit creates a pilot hole and countersink hole to accommodate a screwhead and wood plug. Some bits are fully adjustable as to their depth. Common sizes are for #5, 6, 8, 10, 12, or 14 wood screws and 1/4-, 3/8- (most common) or 1/2-in. wood plugs.

5. Forstner bit will cut very clean holes with flat bottoms. It is especially useful in fine woodworking or when drilling into hardwoods. The bit will produce holes in any grain direction. Sold individually, or in sets. Use with a drill press only.

6. Masonry bit has hard cutting flanges, designed to penetrate concrete and other masonry, including ceramic tile. Best used with a hammer drill.

7. Countersink bit will ream out an existing hole so a screw can be driven flush, or slightly recessed, into the wood surface.

8. Spade bit is useful for boring through wood where precision is not critical. It is the bit of choice when boring wiring holes through studs or removing wood before chiseling (as when cutting a mortise).

9. Vix bit is designed to drill perfectly centered screw pilot holes through guide holes in hardware plates.

Portable drill guide

This drilling accessory gives a portable power drill the precision of a drill press. You can use it to drill perfectly straight holes on the job site, and many models are scaled to drill at precise angles.

Guide for shelf pin holes

A strip of perforated hardboard (pegboard) makes a handy guide for drilling evenly spaced shelf pin holes in shelf standards. Typically, holes are spaced about 1 in. apart and are drilled with a ¼-in. bit.

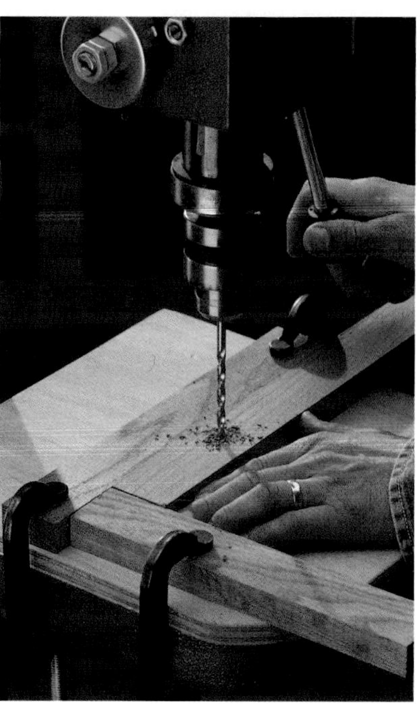

Drill press table stopblocks

Straight lengths of scrap wood can be clamped to your drill press table to make stopblocks for drilling uniform holes in multiple workpieces.

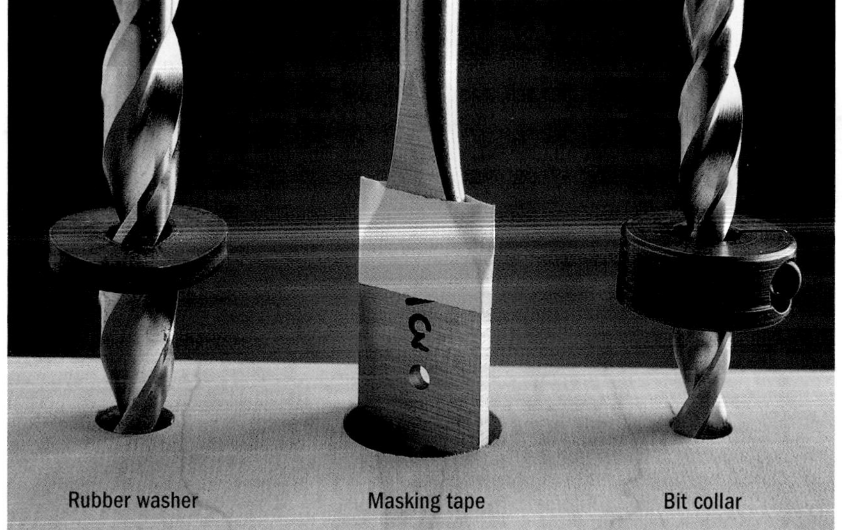

Do-it-yourself depth stops for portable drills

Drilling depth can be set with a gauge on your drill press, but what about with a portable drill? To take the guesswork out of drilling holes to an exact depth, mark the drill bit at the appropriate depth with a rubber washer or masking tape. You can also use special drill bit collars that are sold at most building centers and hardware stores.

Drilling template

Plot out hole spacing on a paper or hardboard template for woodworking projects. The template will help you drill identical hole patterns on matching workpieces.

Shaping

Shaping is a fairly broad category when it comes to workshop skills. In one sense or another, just about anything you do to a workpiece with a tool alters its shape. But this chapter concerns shaping exercises that don't necessarily change the size of the workpiece, but rather alter its appearance or, in some cases, prepare it to be joined with another workpiece. Routing, planing, filing and shaving or paring are the activities normally done for this purpose.

Shaping is the area of woodworking where hand tools are still used most prevalently. Hand planes, files, drawknives, spokeshaves and other hand-powered tools offer a level of precision and control that's hard to find with power tools. But for their part, power tools (particularly the router) are much faster and, for some types of shaping tasks, more accurate. Making grooves, rabbets, dovetails and other joinery cuts is a perfect chore for the router, provided you use the correct router bit. Shaping complex edge profiles, like ogees and coves, is much easier to do with a router bit than with any hand tool.

Whether you're using hand or power tools, the key to good results when shaping wood is not to try to remove too much material at one time. Make a habit of making several precise, controlled passes with the tool whenever possible. This will yield cleaner, more accurate results, and you're less likely to ruin your workpiece: it's tough to put wood back on once you cut it off.

INVEST IN A ROUTER TABLE

A router is one of the most versatile power tools ever created, but mounted in a router table its usefulness and accuracy become even greater. Commercial models are available, but many DIYers prefer to build their own. You can purchase kits for making the mounting plate, fence and even the table surface. The router table shown to the right is made using an inexpensive bathroom vanity as a cabinet, with a piece of post-form countertop for the tabletop. If you plan to use your router table frequently, it's a good idea to buy a dedicated router for it. Look for a fixed-base model with a ½-in. collet. A soft start feature will make the router table safer and easier to manage.

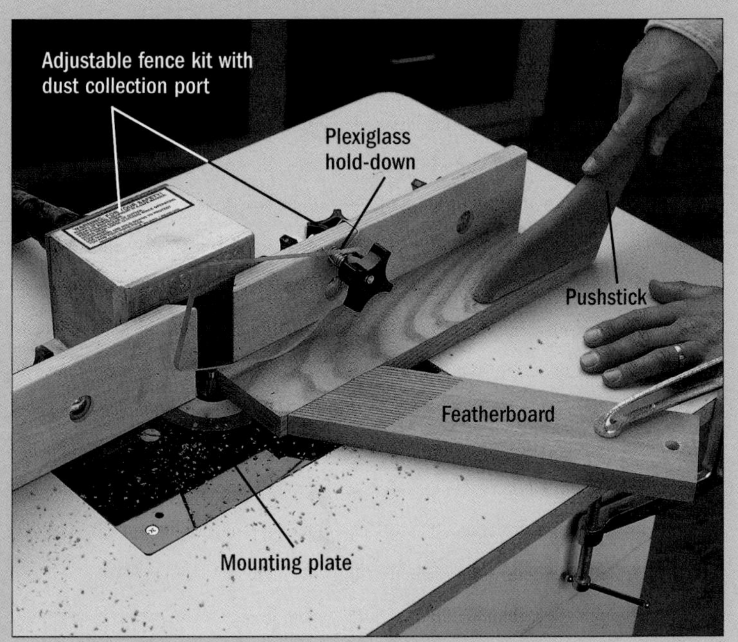

Three common hand planes for workshop use are the block plane, jack plane and jointer plane. **Block planes** are very handy general purpose tools. They can be used to plane with the grain, but they have shallow blade angles and flat soles so they can also plane end grain effectively. Their small size makes them easy to manage and convenient to store in your tool box. **Jack planes** are medium-sized planes with a slight curve in the sole. Their main purpose is to reduce board thickness by surface planing (see photo above). **Jointer planes** (also called *try planes*) have long soles that can ride a board edge smoothly. Their main use is to smooth board edges, especially in preparation for edge gluing.

SHAPING

THICKNESS PLANING WITH A HAND PLANE

If you don't own a power planer and need to reduce the thickness of a board slightly, a jack plane is the tool you'll want to use. The fastest way to remove stock is by *roughing* with the plane: scraping the plane diagonally to the direction of the grain. To remove smaller amounts of material, and to smooth out after roughing, use a smoothing motion: orient the blade so the blade is diagonal to the wood grain, but follow the grain direction as you push the tool across your workpiece.

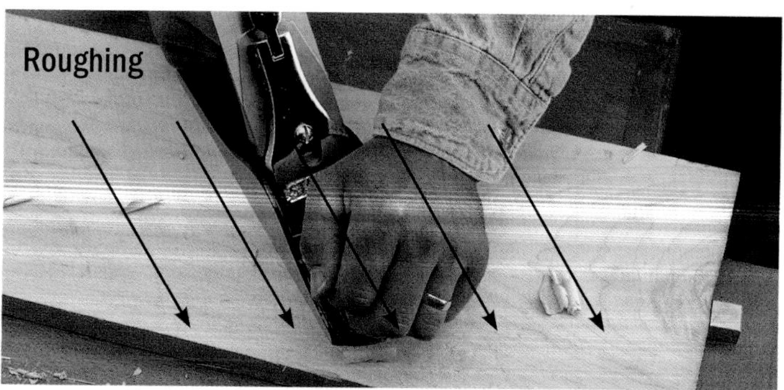

SHARPENING PLANE IRONS

Plane blades (called *irons*) are sharpened in much the same way as wood chisels, typically at an angle of 25° (see page 40). To maintain a steady angle on the irons, you can purchase a *honing guide* through most woodworking catalogs.

FOLLOW THE GRAIN AS YOU PLANE

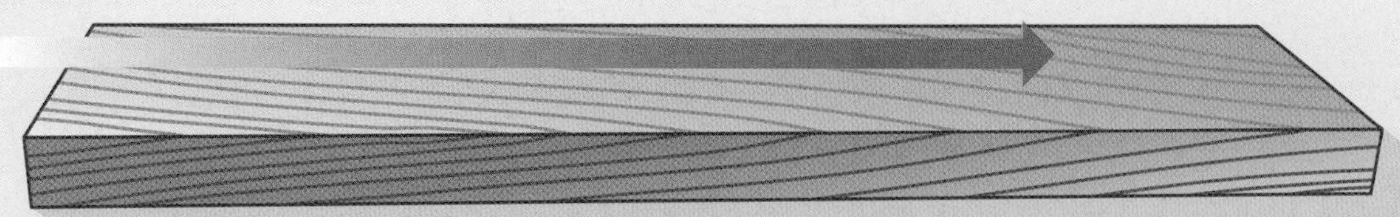

Straight grain: Plane following the upward grain slope

For best results when planing, pay attention to the direction of the wood grain, keeping in mind that the grain is a three-dimensional feature of the wood. In addition to running longitudinally along a board, it also has a general up or down slope on most boards. Inspect the edge of the board to see which direction the grain is running (illustration above) and plane the board to follow the wood grain upward. On some face-sawn boards, the wood grain is wavy or cupped from the side view. On such boards, you'll need to switch planing direction as you work along the board, always planing toward a crest in the wood grain.

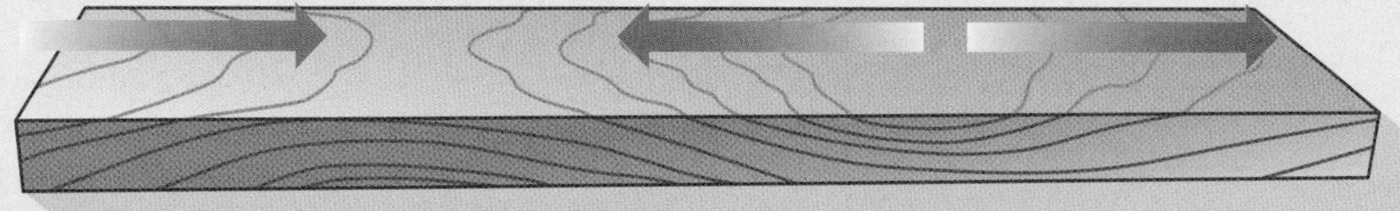

Wavy grain: Switch directions to plane toward crests

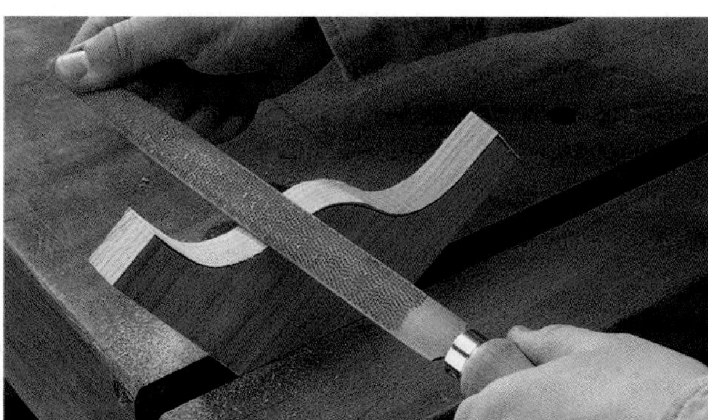

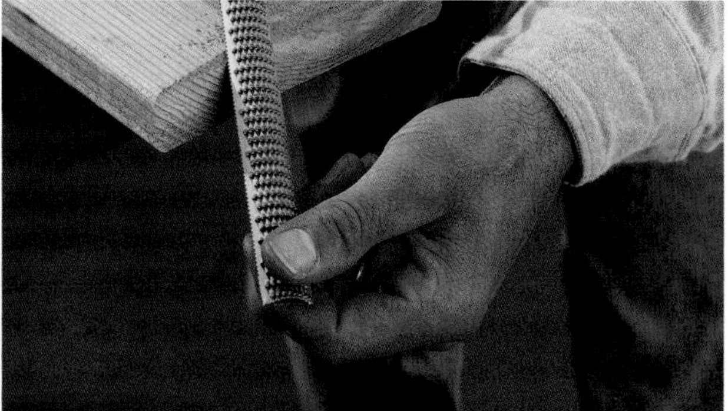

Hand tools excel at delicate work

When performing intricate woodworking tasks, reach for your hand tools.

Overlooked shop tool has multitude of uses

Remove bulges, dips and bumps from contoured cuts by filing them away with a flat or half-round, single cut file. A file or rasp also makes quick work of cutting a roundover or easing a sharp edge.

TRADITIONAL SHAPING TOOLS HAVE A PLACE IN ANY SHOP

Drawknife works quickly and cleanly

Once used primarily to strip bark from felled trees, the drawknife can resurface a piece of rough or damaged wood stock as fast as any belt sander, but without the dust and noise. They're also a good choice for chamfering sharp edges on woodworking projects. When left unsanded, the surface marks created by the drawknife can add rough-hewn charm to your project.

Spokeshave makes easy roundovers

You don't need to be a wheelwright to make good use of this time-honored tool. The spokeshave can round over just about any furniture leg or table edge. And many woodworkers enjoy using the spokeshave to make chair spindles and other round parts. Spokeshaves are made in several different sizes with concave blades of varying radii.

SHAPING

YET ANOTHER USE FOR THE VERSATILE DRILL/DRIVER

For enlarging holes or reshaping internal cutouts, try installing a rasp bit into your drill/driver. Most tool catalogs and hardware stores carry a nice selection of rasp bits that vary by size and shape. You can also use the rasp bits to strike off bumps and imperfections from contoured cuts.

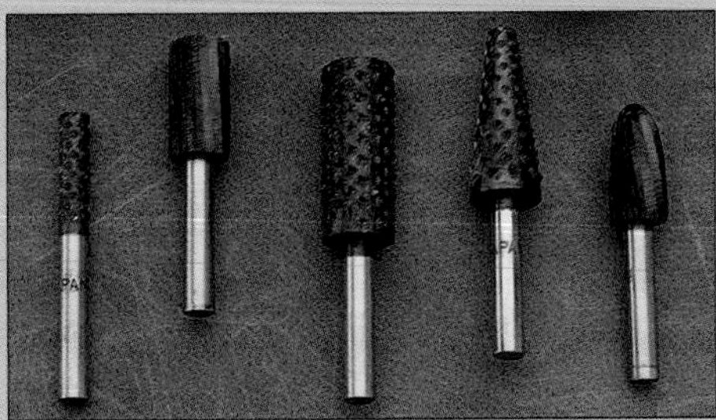

Here's a sampling of the dozens of rasp bits you can purchase for your drill/driver.

A primer on router usage

It's not unusual for beginning do-it-yourselfers and woodworkers to be a little intimidated by routers. They're loud, aggressive shaping tools and they sometimes seem to have a mind of their own when it comes to following a guide or the edge of a board. But by keeping a few basic points in mind, and with some practice, these extremely versatile tools will amaze you with the variety and quality of work they can produce.

Setup is a very important aspect of correct router usage. Make sure the bit is well secured in the collet and set to an appropriate cutting height. The workpiece must be secured, either with clamps or bench dogs or with a non-slip router pad like the one shown at right. If using a piloted edge-forming bit, you won't need a straightedge or guide for the router base to follow, although you should secure scrap pieces the same thickness as the workpiece at each if you're routing one side (this prevents the router from following the corner and cutting into the adjacent sides). With non-piloted groove-forming bits, you'll need to use a straightedge or router guide to keep the tool cutting on line (see photo, right).

Whether you're using a fixed-base router or a plunge router, the bit should be spinning at full speed before you apply it to the workpiece. Wearing hearing and eye protection, engage the bit into the workpiece and draw it toward yourself, keeping your body out of the line of the tool as best you can. To be effective, the bit should cut against the rotation of the bit. In most cases, this means you should feed the router counterclockwise. Maintain an even cutting pace, and don't set the router down until the bit has stopped spinning. Always practice your cut on scrap wood before cutting the workpiece.

Use a guide when grooving

Guides for making groove cuts can be as simple as a straight piece of scrap wood clamped to the workpiece. You can also use an extruded steel straightedge (see photo, above), or an edge guide that connects to the base.

Find router base setback

To figure out how far from the cutting line to secure your guide, measure the router "setback." Secure a straightedge to scrap and make a practice cut, following the guide. Measure from the closer shoulder of the cut to the guide.

ROUTER BITS

Router bits fit into two general categories: *edge-forming bits* and *groove-forming bits*. Edge-forming bits are used to cut decorative profiles on the edges of boards; they are equipped with integral pilots that guide the bit along the edge of the material being cut. Some more inexpensive bits have fixed pilots that are an extension of the bit shank, but most today have ball-bearing pilots that allow the cutter to spin but won't burn the edge of the board as fixed pilots can. Groove-forming bits cut channels of various profiles into the material. Except when carving freehand, they require a cutting guide. Most basic bits are made with either a ¼-in. or ½-in.-dia. shank. Bits with a larger cutting radius can only be used with a router that accepts a ½-in. shank. Unless otherwise noted, the sizes listed below refer to cutting radius.

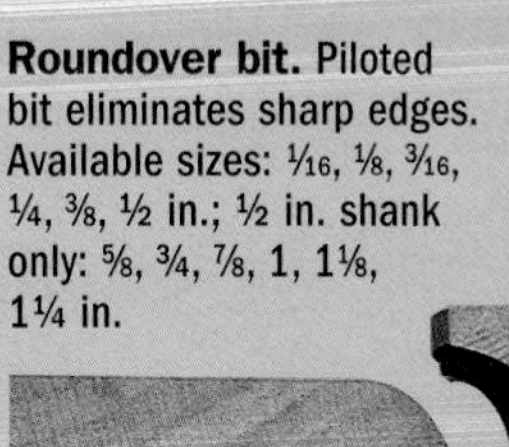

Roundover bit. Piloted bit eliminates sharp edges. Available sizes: 1/16, ⅛, 3/16, ¼, ⅜, ½ in.; ½ in. shank only: ⅝, ¾, ⅞, 1, 1⅛, 1¼ in.

Core box bit. Grooving bit for fluting, veining and carving. Available sizes: ¼, ⅜, ½, ⅝, ¾ in.; ½ in. shank only: ⅞, 15/16, 1 in.

Flush-trimming bits. Piloted edge-trimming bits for trimming laminates and pattern routing; 2 or 3 flutes. Available sizes: ¼, ⅜, ½ in.; ½ in. shank only: ¾, 1*, 1⅛* in.

*top-mounted bearing typical

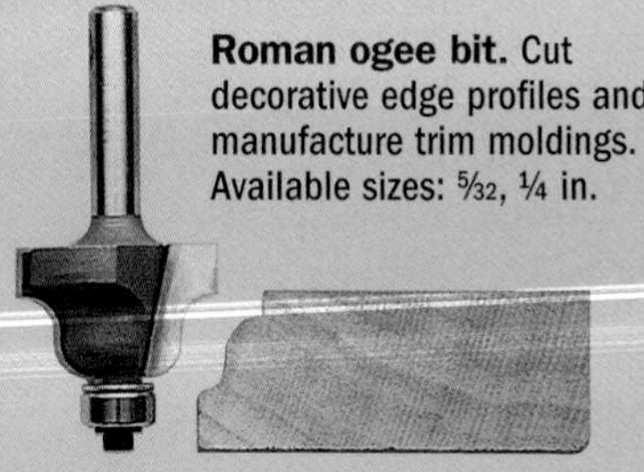

Roman ogee bit. Cut decorative edge profiles and manufacture trim moldings. Available sizes: 5/32, ¼ in.

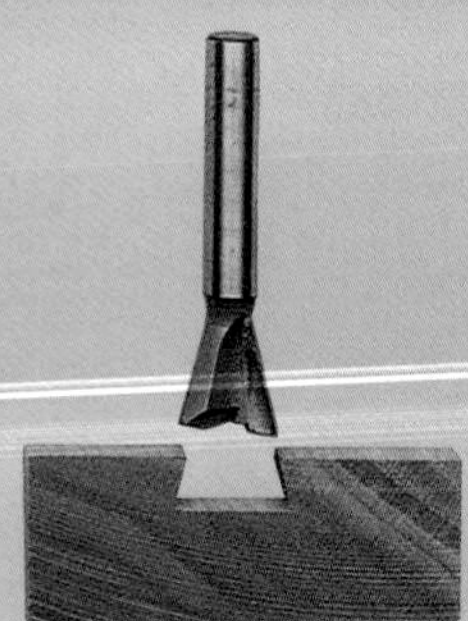

Dovetail bit. Used to cut dovetail joints, generally with a dovetail jig. Angles of flutes vary between 7 and 14°. Available sizes: ¼, 5/16, ⅜, ½, ⅝, 1 1/16, ¾ in.; ½ in. shank only: 13/16, 1 in.

Chamfer bits. Piloted bit eliminates sharp edges, making smooth, clean angle cut. Vast majority are 45° angle (both ¼ in. and ½ in. shank). Can find bits with 15, 22½ and 30° cutting angles as well.

Piloted rabbeting bit. Cut rabbets, tongue-and-grooves and shiplap joints without need for straightedge or other guide. Available sizes (by depth of cut): ¼, ⅜, ½ in.; ½ in. shank only: ¾ in. Can also purchase rabbeting bit with interchangeable bearings varying rabbet depth.

Veining (V-groove) bit. Used for carving, lettering and cutting decorative V-shaped veins. Most are 90° cutting angle, but 45° and 60° bits can be found. Available sizes: ¼, ⅜, ½, ⅝, ¾ in.; ½ in. shank only: 15/16, 1, 1¼, 1½, 2 in.

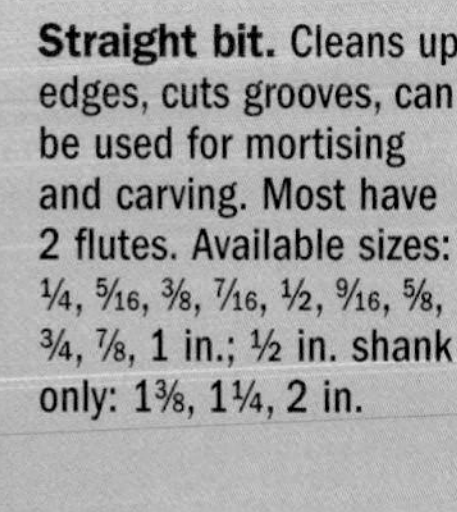

Straight bit. Cleans up edges, cuts grooves, can be used for mortising and carving. Most have 2 flutes. Available sizes: ¼, 5/16, ⅜, 7/16, ½, 9/16, ⅝, ¾, ⅞, 1 in.; ½ in. shank only: 1⅜, 1¼, 2 in.

Rabbeting with a straight bit

Many woodworkers prefer to make rabbet cuts with a straight bit rather than a piloted router bit for a couple of reasons: piloted bits have a tendency to jump and will follow any imperfections in the edge of the board; they also will cut rabbets of only a set depth (even piloted rabbet bits with interchangeable bearings are limited to four set depths). By using a jig like the one shown to the left, you increase the bearing surface, preventing jump-outs, and you can adjust the relationship of the jig to the bit to cut rabbets of any depth up to the maximum cutting capacity of the bit. To make the jig, simply choose a straight piece of scrap about 1 ft. long, make a notch slightly deeper than the bit diameter, and clamp the jig to the router base so the bit protrudes to the depth of the cut.

Double Roman ogee bit

Save money and increase trim options by cutting your own trim molding with a router

Anyone who's done much trim carpentry knows that milled trim moldings can be very expensive, especially if they're made of hardwood. It can also be very difficult to find the size, profile and wood species you're looking for from stock millwork. One good solution to this dilemma is to cut your own trim moldings. Simply choose an edge-forming bit with the profile you like and rout the shape into a piece of stock. You can rout the shape freehand, using a piloted bit, but make sure the stock is wide enough to provide a stable bearing surface for the router base. If you own a router table, use it to make the profile cuts. After the profile is cut, rip-cut the profiled board to the desired trim width on your table saw. If you need more molding, rout the profile into the cut edge of the stock then rip-cut again.

Any edge-forming bit (and some groove-forming bits) will cut a suitable edge. But as you experiment with cutting your own moldings, look into new bit options with more sophisticated profiles, like the double Roman ogee bit shown here. If you're using a router that can accept a ½-in. shank, you'll find a wide selection of interesting bits in just about any woodworking catalog. You can also use two or more bits in combination to form complex and interesting edge treatments.

Use a roundover bit to remove sharp edges or renew a beat-up edge

The piloted roundover bit is a quick and reliable tool for easing sharp edges on just about any piece of furniture or trim. In most cases, the best time to roundover the edge is after the furniture is assembled, as with the picnic table that's receiving the roundover treatment in the photo to the right. A roundover bit doesn't have to be used on new furniture projects only. It's also a great device for giving a shot of new life to an older piece of furniture that has damaged, dented or even rotted edges. A bit with a ⅜- or ¼-in. cutting radius is a good general purpose choice.

For information on making circular cutouts with a router, see page 34.

SHAPING

HOW TO TRIM & SHAPE COUNTERTOP LAMINATE

One of the most common uses for routers is to trim and profile laminate surfaces on countertops (if you do a lot of this work, look into buying a laminate trimmer, which is essentially a scaled-down router). When you bond the laminate to the countertop surface, make sure to leave ⅛ to ¼ in. overhanging the edge (don't try to align the laminate with the countertop edge—your chances of success are quite low).

1 Install a piloted, flush-trimming bit (the cutting radius doesn't matter) into your router and trim the laminate so the edge is flush with the outside edge of the countertop or countertop trim.

2 Use a piloted edge-forming bit to create a decorative profile on the top edge of the countertop. A chamfer bit, shown above, makes a clean profile that's free from sharp edges.

Clamping, Gluing & Fastening

No matter how carefully you cut project parts and no matter how painstakingly you form the joints, without good clamping, gluing and fastening techniques your project likely will fail.

Clamping serves two fundamental purposes in woodworking: first, it draws parts together tightly and ensures that joints that should be square are square; and second, it holds parts together until the glue that will hold them together permanently sets. For non-woodworking shop projects, clamping is also very important. Among its more common jobs are holding workpieces together while fasteners are driven; securing jigs for cutting and drilling; and holding small workpieces so they stay steady while you work on them.

Successful gluing is a matter of choosing the best adhesive for the job, making sure the mating surfaces are properly prepared, and applying the correct amount of glue. From bonding retaining wall blocks together with construction adhesive to applying cabinet veneer, gluing is a skill every handyman should possess.

Fastening is an easy project step to rush through. By the time you're ready to fasten, the last thing you want to do is spend additional time fussing with pilot holes, counterbores and screw patterns. But take the time—there's no more discouraging shop experience than to see a project fail because you neglected to drill a pilot hole and the wood split.

THE VISE SQUAD

Choosing the best vise for your needs is an important decision. The two types used most frequently in the workshop are the *bench vise* (sometimes called a *machinist's vise*) and the *woodworker's vise*. Lighter-duty *clamp-on vises* can be set up on a sawhorse at your job site, or stored out of the way in your shop and set up on an as-needed basis. If your main interest is woodworking, you should definitely look into a woodworker's vise for your shop. Normally attached to the end of a workbench, the woodworker's vise has smooth jaws designed to be fitted with wood inserts that won't damage wood as a the jaws on a bench vise can. Because woodworker's vises are mounted so the tops of the jaws are flush with the worksurface, make sure the jaw width will fit your bench and that the benchscrew will have enough clearance when the jaws are in a closed position.

Woodworker's vise

LOCKING PLIERS

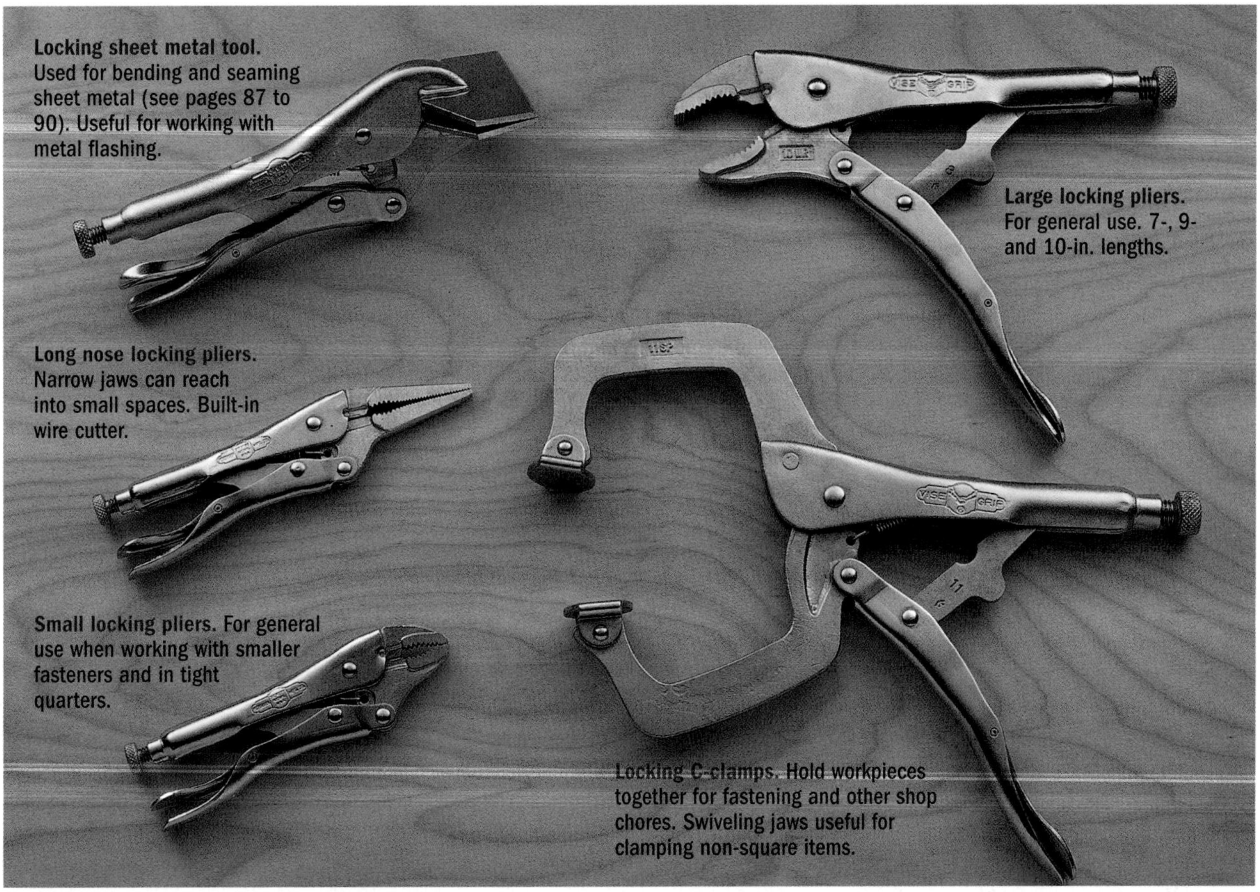

Locking sheet metal tool. Used for bending and seaming sheet metal (see pages 87 to 90). Useful for working with metal flashing.

Large locking pliers. For general use. 7-, 9- and 10-in. lengths.

Long nose locking pliers. Narrow jaws can reach into small spaces. Built-in wire cutter.

Small locking pliers. For general use when working with smaller fasteners and in tight quarters.

Locking C-clamps. Hold workpieces together for fastening and other shop chores. Swiveling jaws useful for clamping non-square items.

Locking pliers can do more than just grip nuts and bolts, especially with the assortment of special-purpose tools that are made by most locking pliers manufacturers. The locking technology has been adapted to C-clamps and sheet metal seamers, as well as downsized versions of the standard locking pliers and pliers with specially shaped jaws for tough-to-reach spots.

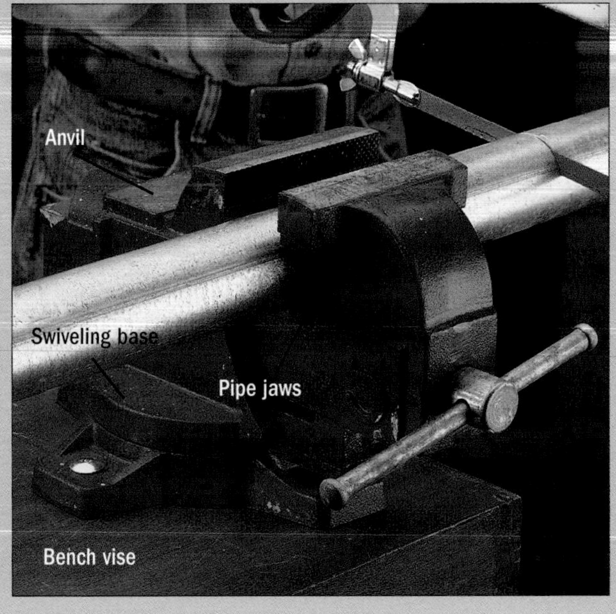

Bench vise

Clamp-on vise

Trouble gripping small finish nails & brads?

Make handling small fasteners a snap by drilling a small guide hole in a piece of thin wood (like a popsicle stick) to create a nail holder.

TIP: WAX YOUR SCREW THREADS

Keep a block of beeswax in your shop to lubricate the threads of screws. The wax greatly reduces friction, which makes for less work and fewer stripped screw heads. You can use hand soap for a similar purpose, but it's more likely to discolor the wood.

FOLDING WORKTABLES

Portable, folding worktables like the Black & Decker Workmate add versatility and efficiency to the workshop—especially the smaller workshop. They're also valuable tools when working on the job site. In addition to their most basic function as a sturdy set-up table that stores out of the way easily, you can use the bench dogs to secure workpieces for machining. The two opposable sections of the worksurface can be clamped together to secure round items like conduit, or one section can be positioned perpendicular to the other and clamped down like a wood caul.

Bench dogs can secure workpieces

Gap between table sections form vise

Narrow table section forms wood caul

ATTACHING OBJECTS TO CONCRETE SURFACES

Attaching sole plates for stud walls in the basement or garage and tacking furring strips to your foundation wall when insulating are just two of many do-it-yourself projects that require the use of masonry anchors. Here are a few of the most commonly used systems for screwing or bolting to concrete.

Lead sleeve. Driven into large guide hole before sole plates or furring strips are positioned. Threads of lag screws dig into soft lead as screws are driven. Sleeve expands to create pressure fit in guide hole. Excellent holding power.

Bolt sleeve. Requires same size guide hole for board and for concrete, so can be driven through board and into concrete at same time. Bolt causes sleeve to flare and grip guide hole as nut is tightened. Excellent holding power.

Self-tapping masonry screws. Driven into pilot holes in board and concrete. Hex-head and slotted, countersink versions. Good holding power, fast to install.

Powder-actuated stud driver. Gun powder charge drives masonry nail through sole plate and into concrete floor. Driver can be rented. Good holding power, fast to use, but loud and can split plates.

Concrete nails. Driven with hammer into pilot holes. Poor to good holding power, nails bend easily.

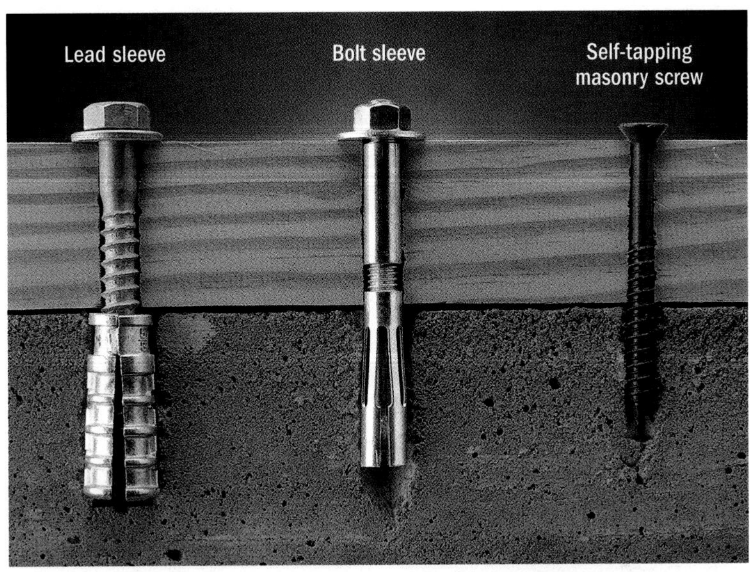

WALLBOARD ANCHORS

Light duty: Plastic sleeve tapped into pilot hole

Medium duty: Self-tapping plastic anchor threaded into pilot hole

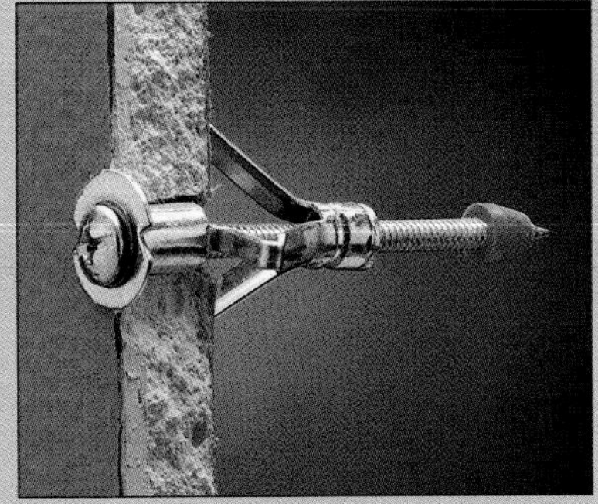

Heavy duty: Toggle screw driven through pilot hole

SELECTING THE RIGHT ADHESIVE FOR YOUR BONDING TASK

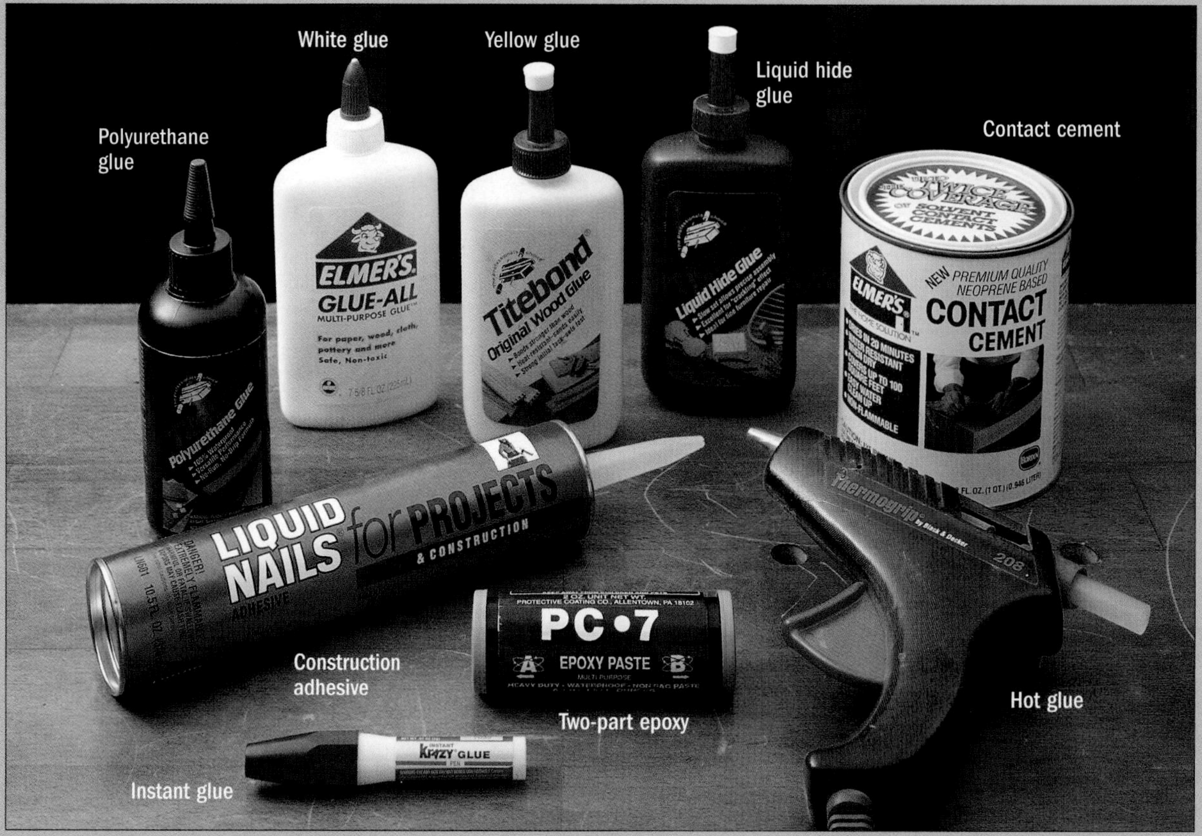

White glue: Used on wood, paper or cloth. Interior use only. Dries in several hours and has a moderately strong bond. Poor resistance to water and heat. Emits no harmful odors. Cleans up with soap and water.

Yellow glue: Used on wood, paper or cloth. Interior use only. Dries faster than white glue and has a slightly stronger bond. Moderate resistance to water and heat. Emits no harmful odors. Cleans up with soap and water.

Liquid hide glue: Ideal for fine wood furniture or musical instruments. Interior use only. Sets slowly. Has good bond and is resistant to solvents and wood finishes. An eye irritant. Will clean up with soap and water.

Polyurethane glue: Used to bond a variety of materials including wood, metal and ceramics. Sets quickly and produces a strong bond. Waterproof. *Warning:* this glue can cause immediate and residual lung damage. This product should only be used with excellent ventilation. Asthmatics and people with chronic lung conditions should not use this product. Cleans up with acetone or mineral spirits.

Construction adhesive: Used on framing lumber, flooring and roof sheathing, plywood and paneling, wallboard, masonry. Dries within 24 hours and has a very good bond. Cleans up with mineral spirits.

Contact cement: Joins laminates, veneers, cloth, paper, leather, and other materials. Sets instantly and dries in under an hour. Produces a bond that is not suitable for structural applications. Very flammable and an irritant to eyes, skin and lungs (non-flammable contact cement is also available). Cleans up with soap and water.

Hot glue: Joins wood, plastics, glass and other materials. Sets within 60 seconds. Strength is generally low, but depends on type of glue stick. Good resistance to moisture, fair to heat. Heat will loosen bond.

Two-part epoxy: Joins wood, metal, masonry, glass, fiberglass and other materials. Provides the strongest bond of any adhesive. Bond has excellent resistance to moisture and heat. Drying time varies. *Warning:* fumes are very toxic and flammable. Cleanup sometimes possible with acetone.

Instant (cyanoacrylate) glue: Bonds smooth surfaces such as glass, ceramics, plastics and metal. Has excellent strength, but little flexibility. Dries in just a few seconds. Has excellent resistance to moisture and heat. Warning: toxic and flammable, and the glue can bond skin instantly.

Options for cleaning up glue squeeze-out

A damp rag will remove glue squeeze-out before it gets a chance to penetrate into the wood pores, which reduces the wood's ability to absorb stain or topcoat products. The only downside is that it will raise the wood grain and require light sanding when dry.

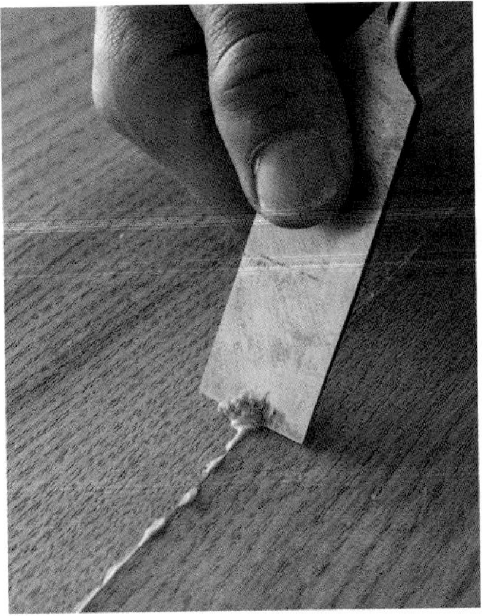

An old wood chisel can be used to scrape congealed glue squeeze-out from edge-glued joints, or from any flat surface. Keep the beveled edge of the chisel down to avoid marring the wood. Make certain the chisel edge is free of nicks.

A sharp floor scraper will make quick, neat work of removing dried glue from joints. Don't get too aggressive, though. You'll likely need to sand the area before finishing to get even finish results.

CLAMPING TIPS

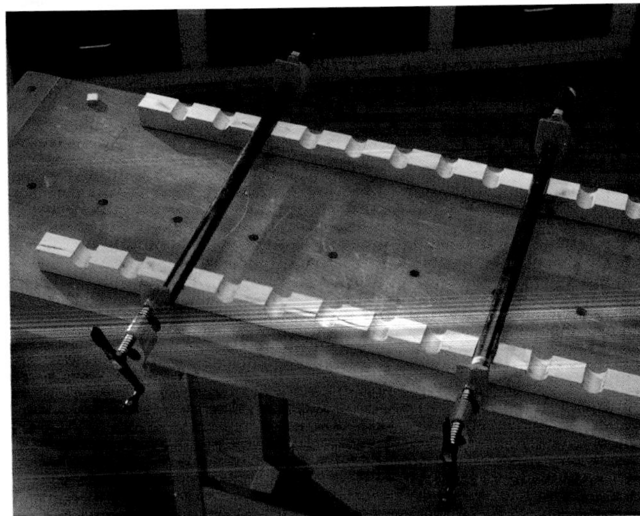

Quick & easy pipe clamp supports

Pipe clamps can be awkward to use when laid flat on a workbench. To remedy the problem, drill a series of 1½-in.-diameter holes down the center of a 4-ft.-long 2 × 4, then rip-cut the board in half. The resulting semicircular cutouts will cradle the pipes, increasing their stability and improving access to the cranks.

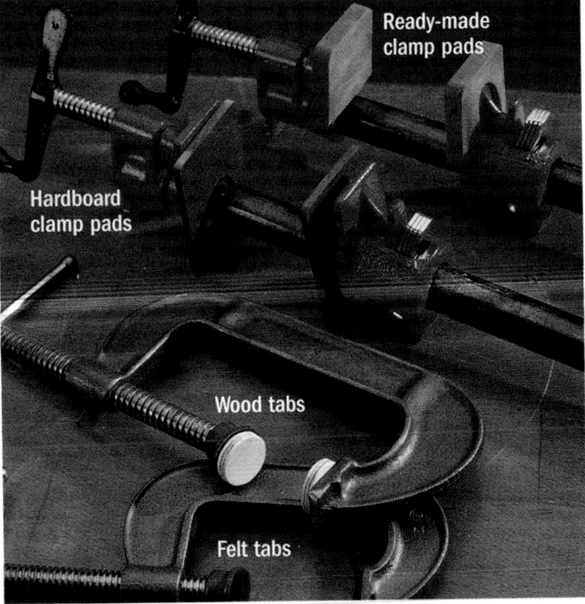

Attach pads for hands-free clamping

Eliminate the hassle of trying to slip loose clamping pads between the jaws of your clamps and your work-piece by attaching pads directly to your clamps or clamp jaws. Hot-glue tabs of wood or felt to C-clamp jaws. Slip ready-made clamp pads on the heads of your bar clamps, or make your own bar-clamp pads by drilling 1-in.-dia. holes in pieces of scrap hardboard.

"Wedge-gluing" panels

Applying clamp pressure to the edges of a glue-up panel ensures strong, tight joints, but it does little to prevent the panel from buckling. In fact, the side pressure from the clamps can even contribute to buckling problems. To help keep your glue-up panel from looking like corrugated metal, try this simple technique. Alternate the bar clamps on opposite faces of the panel (this is easier to do if you use clamp supports, like those shown on the previous page). Then, cut several hardwood wedges. Drive the wedges between the clamping bars and the panel (don't get too aggressive here). Visually inspect the panel to make sure the pressure is even and it's not buckling. If necessary, adjust the pressure of the wedges.

Clamping aids come through when duty cauls

Because most clamp jaws are less than 2 in. wide, tightening the clamps directs the clamping pressure to only a small section of the workpiece. As a result, joints (and entire woodworking projects) can be pulled out of square. A good solution to this effect is to use wood cauls when gluing up your projects.

Wood cauls are simply strips of wood that are slipped between clamps and the workpiece to distribute the clamping pressure evenly. Woodworkers have been using them for centuries to help create strong, square joints. You can use any hardwood, or even strips of plywood, to make your own wood cauls. Be sure to have plenty on hand before beginning the glue-up.

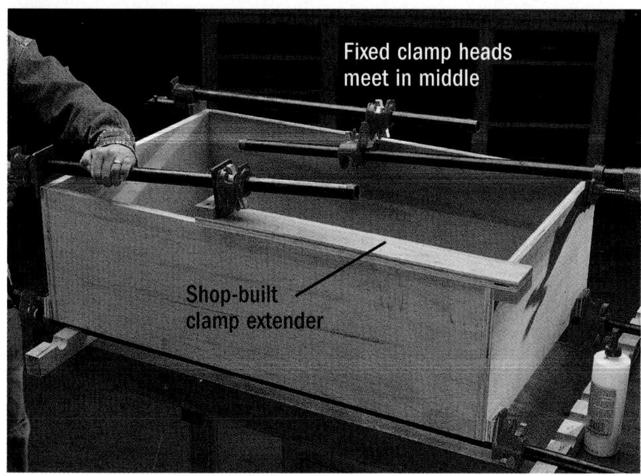

Two simple tricks for stretching pipe clamps

For those occasions when you get caught short during glue-up, here are two clever ways to get more reach out of your pipe clamps. If you have two clamps that are both too short, arrange the fixed heads so they meet in the middle: the clamping pressure will hold them together. Or, you can build a clamp extender like the one above from scrap wood.

One way to get around this clamping problem

Clamps aren't designed to work well with round workpieces, such as the tabletop shown above. One way to get even clamping pressure on round workpieces is shown above. Trace the arc of the workpiece onto the edges of two sturdy boards, then cut out the arc with a jig saw to make your clamping aids.

A foolproof system for clamping frames

Build this frame clamp with a few pieces of scrap wood and a woodscrew clamp. It will apply equal pressure on all four corners of a frame. Cut four equal-length wood strips and drill center holes at 1- to 2-in. increments. Cut two shorter strips and drill a hole near each end. Fabricate four L-shaped corner braces out of scrap wood (or an old frame) and drill a hole in the corner of each. Form the strips into two V-shaped assemblies with wing nuts, as shown above. Attach the corner braces, set the frame inside the corners, then use a woodscrew to draw the "V" together.

Wooden bridge extends C-clamp capacity

C-clamps are useful for many tasks, but their relatively shallow throats limit their range. Extend the reach of the clamp by fashioning a clamping bridge with two pieces of scrap wood. One piece (the *spacer*) should be the same thickness as the workpiece being pressed down. The second scrap (the *bridge*) needs to be long enough to span over the spacer and the workpiece. Set the spacer between the workpiece and the edge of the support surface, then lay the bridge across the spacer and over the workpiece. Clamping down on the bridge creates clamping pressure on the workpiece.

Gallery of Clamps

The corner clamp

A corner clamp holds mitered corners firmly in alignment. When fastening frames, glue and clamp opposite corners and let them dry before gluing the remaining two corners.

The strap clamp

Reinforced webbing is wrapped around irregular shapes and tightened with a ratcheting cinch. Perfect for gluing up round tabletops and casework, as well as repairing table legs, lamp bases, and other hard-to-clamp objects. Also called *band clamps* or *web clamps*.

The C-clamp

This classic clamp has nearly unlimited applications in the workshop. Keep a wide assortment of sizes on hand, including a few deep throat C-clamps. No clamp type works better for laminating, as above.

The pipe clamp

Another indispensable weapon in the clamp arsenal, the pipe clamp is the workhorse of wood glue-ups. The clamp heads are purchased separately from the pipes. Typically, ¾- or ½-in. black pipe is used (diameter depends on hole size in clamp heads). One clamp head is fixed in rough position, then the adjustable head is tightened with a hand screw.

The woodscrew

Also called *handscrew clamps* or *Jorgenson's* (after their primary manufacturer), these all-wood clamps have excellent gripping power, wide throat capacity and the wood jaws won't dent or mar most types of wood. Jaw lengths range in size from 4 to 16 in.

The quick clamp

This trigger-activated bar clamp head lets you tighten the clamp with only one hand. They're great for holding workpieces in rough position for fastening. The bars are sold with the clamps. They range from 6 to 50 in. in length.

The 3-way clamp

The right angle screw in the spine of the clamp is used to apply downward pressure on the edge of a workpiece after the jaws at the top and bottom of the throat are tightened. Perfect for attaching edge trim to sheet goods or for repairing moldings.

IMPACT DRIVERS

The cordless impact driver may look like a small drill/driver, and both tools can drive threaded fasteners, but the similarities end there. Impact drivers are smaller, lighter and more powerful at driving fasteners than cordless drill/drivers, advantages that have made them very popular in the construction trades.

A drill/driver has one mechanical action—rotation. If the tool meets resistance, the motor must work harder to overcome it. An impact driver also rotates, but when it meets resistance, it adds an impact action that increases the bit's torque. The action of an impact driver is triggered by rotational resistance and is perpendicular to the bit. The effect is similar to hitting a wrench with a hammer to free a stuck bolt, except the hammering action happens very quickly, as many as 3,000 times a minute. The rapid-fire impact is noisy. Ear protection is highly recommended.

An impact driver doesn't require the same amount of downward force to be applied to the fastener as a typical drill/driver. This makes the tool great for overhead and reaching applications when it is difficult to get adequate leverage behind the tool.

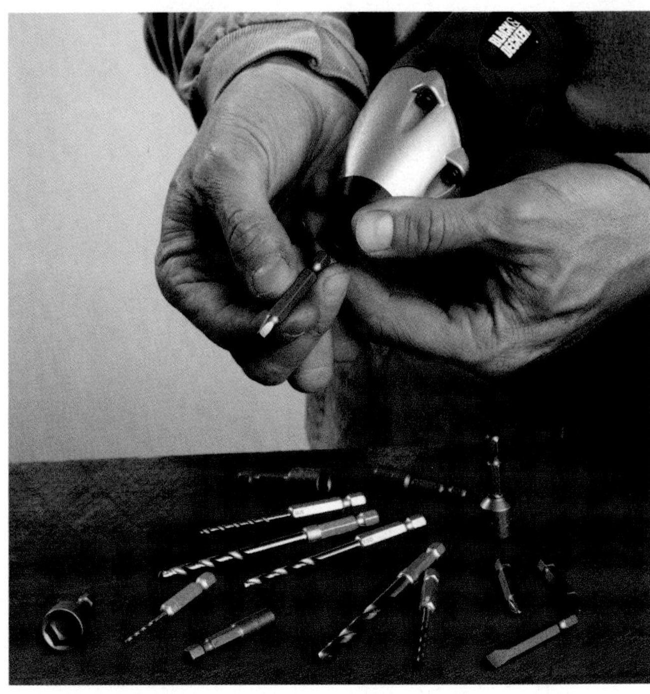

The hex chuck on an impact driver isn't limited to screw driving bits. You can attach any bit that features a hex shank, including sockets, hex bolt drivers and twist drill bits.

An impact driver has no problem driving a lag screw into pressure treated lumber – even without a pilot hole. It's important to use only adapters, sockets and bolt drivers made from hardened steel that is intended for use with impact drivers.

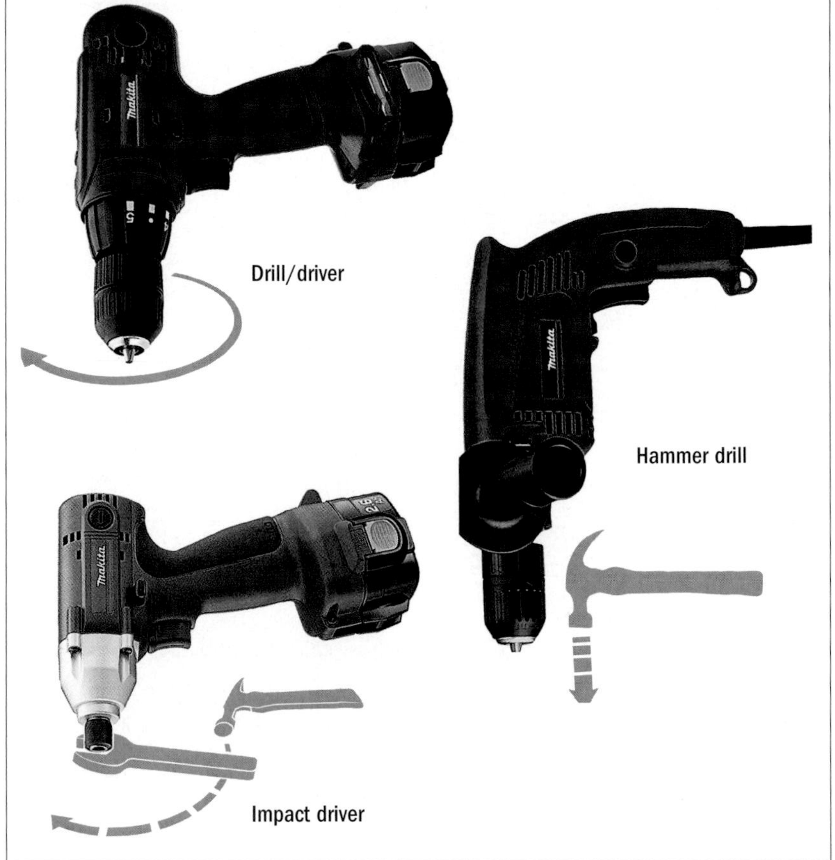

Adding air tools can take your workshop to a new level

Compressed-air-powered fasteners can dramatically decrease the amount of time you spend on a project. Many tools will fire fasteners as fast as you can pull the trigger. Most air nailers require a ½ to 1 hp compressor with tank capacity of at least 3 gallons of air. Smaller air nailers and staplers usually run on 2 to 5 cubic feet per minute (cfm) or air volume at a pressure of 70 to 90 pounds per square inch (psi). Larger framing nailers can require as much as 9 cfm and 100 to 120 psi. If you already own a compressor, check to make sure it's able to drive new air tools before purchasing them. When working with air-powered fasteners, it is essential to wear approved safety goggles and ear protection. Familiarize yourself with the operation of the tool before beginning work. A device that can send a nail deep into a 2 × 4 can do a great deal of harm to the human body. Note: Recently, a similar tool to air nailers, the cordless power nailer, has become available for home use or for rental (see description below).

Pneumatic staplers: Air-powered staplers can drive crown-style staples from ¼ to ½ in. wide, and up to 2 in. long. Smaller staplers are useful for installing carpeting, roofing felt, floor underlayment and insulation. Larger capacity staplers can attach fence boards, strip flooring and even roof decking (check with your local building codes first).

Framing nailers: The "big boy" of air-powered fasteners, these powerful, high-capacity tools will drive nails up to 3½ in. long for all types of frame construction. The magazine can hold upwards of 100 nails.

Brad nailers: Drive brads up to 2⅛ in. long. Used to attach trim, carpet strips and moldings. This lightweight tool allows you to nail one-handed, a real help when aligning trim molding pieces.

Finish nailer: Drives finish nails from ¾ to 2⅛ in. long. Useful for installing siding, flooring, door and window casing and most types of finish carpentry.

Cordless power nailer: Relies on battery power and disposable fuel cells to power-drive nails. Also called impulse nailers. Require special fasteners, generally 16 gauge, from 1½ to 3¼ in. long, depending on the model. Each fuel cell will drive from 1200 to 2500 nails, depending on length, and a single battery charge will drive up to 4000 nails.

HOW TO USE A POCKET HOLE JIG

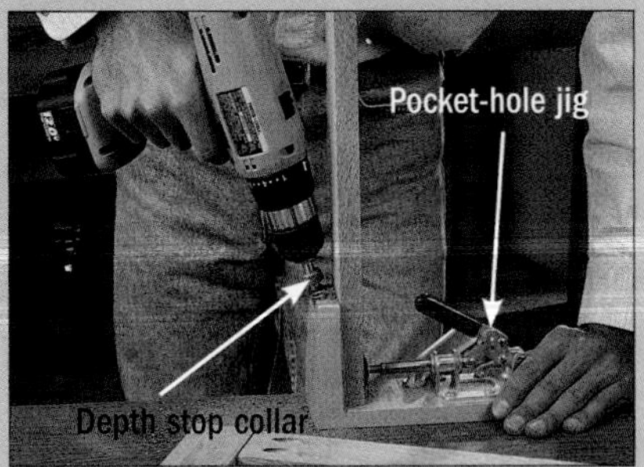

1 Clamp the workpiece that will contain the screw starter holes (usually the rails on a face frame, as shown above) into the pocket screw jig. The center of the jig should align with the centerline of the workpiece. Mount the step drill bit that came with the jig into a portable drill, then drill through the guide bushings and into the workpiece until the depth stop makes contact with the mouth of the guide.

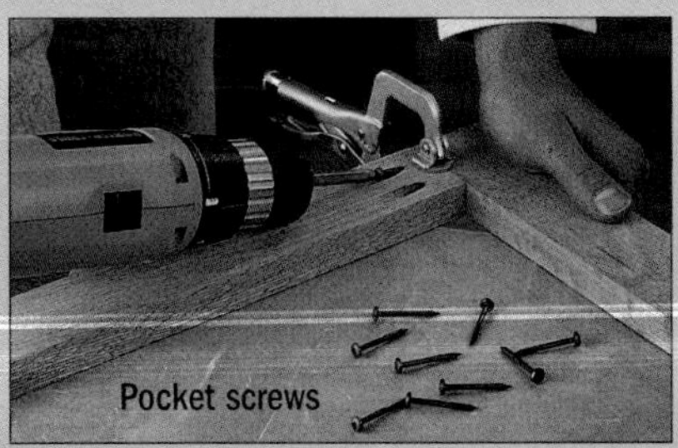

2 Clamp the workpiece containing the starter holes to the mating workpiece, then drive pocket screws through the starter holes and into the mating workpiece. Pocket screws are sold in packets at woodworking stores. They're thinner than regular wood screws to prevent the workpieces from splitting when they're driven. Most have square-drive heads. Take care not to overdrive the screws.

INSTALLING POCKET SCREWS

Driving pocket screws into a butt joint is a little like toenailing with a screw. Pocket-hole jigs allow you to drill pocket holes quickly and accurately for reinforcing butt joints with pocket screws. For best results, use the special drill bit, driver and screws that are usually sold along with the pocket hole jig. Pocket joints are especially handy when making face frames for cabinetry and furniture.

NAIL TYPES

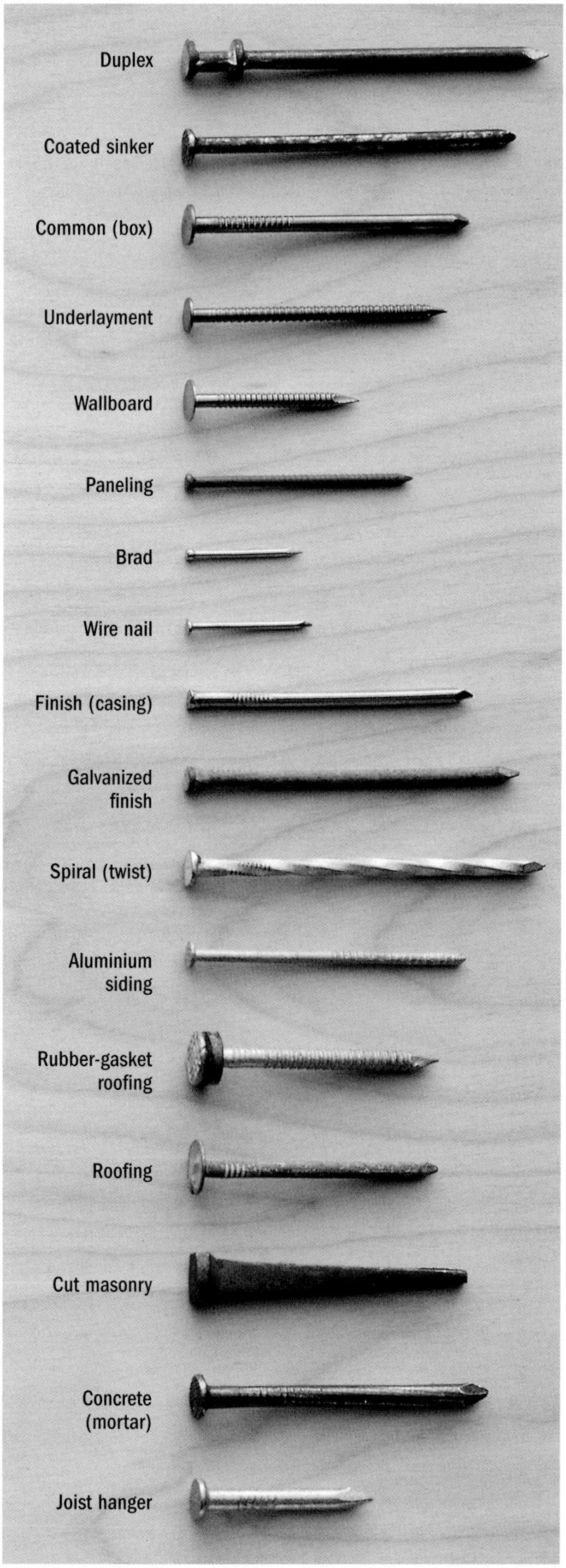

Duplex
Coated sinker
Common (box)
Underlayment
Wallboard
Paneling
Brad
Wire nail
Finish (casing)
Galvanized finish
Spiral (twist)
Aluminium siding
Rubber-gasket roofing
Roofing
Cut masonry
Concrete (mortar)
Joist hanger

SCREW TYPES

A
B
C
D
E
F
G
H
I
J

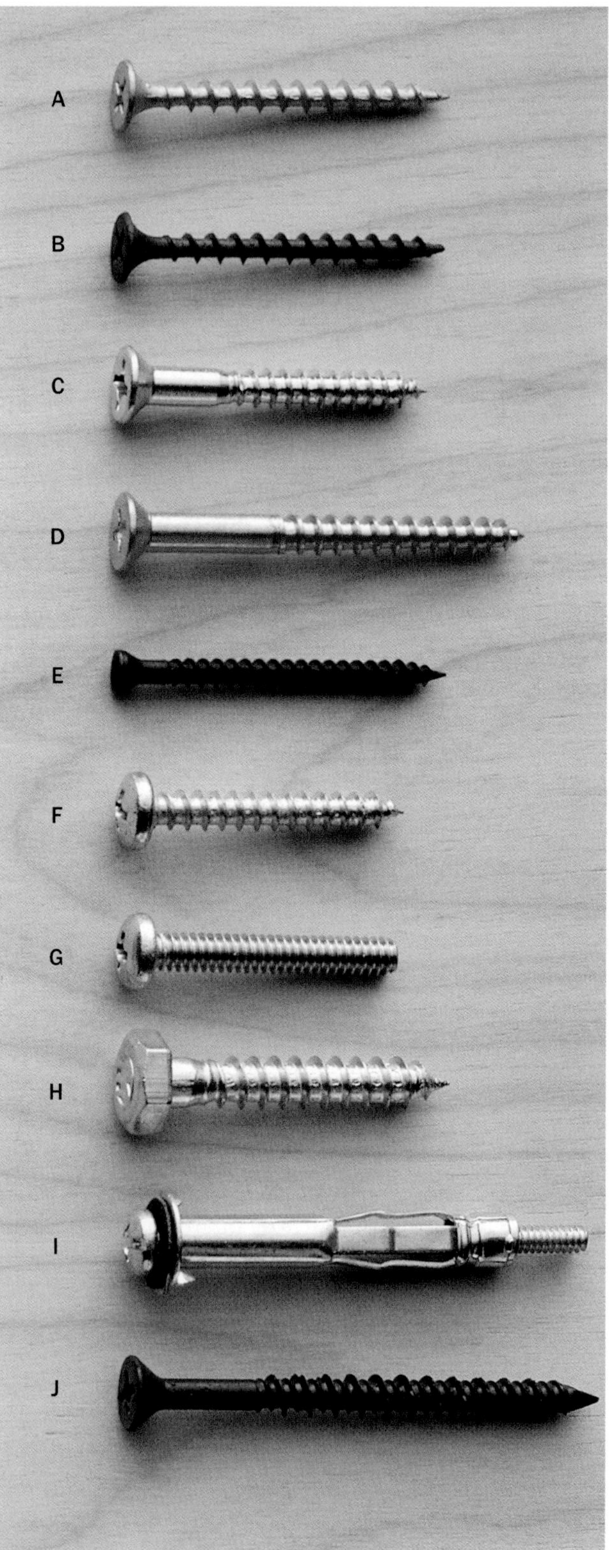

Useful types of screws for the workshop include: (A) deck screws; (B) wallboard screws; (C) wood screws; (D) brass-plated wood screws; (E) trim head screws; (F) sheet metal screws; (G) machine screws; (H) lag screws; (I) wall anchor screws; (J) high-low thread screws.

WOOD SCREW SIZES

GAUGE NO.	NOMINAL DIA. (IN.)	NOMINAL DIA. (MM)	LENGTH (IN.)	LENGTH (MM)
0	0.060	1.52	3/16	4.8
1	0.070	1.78	1/4	6.4
2	0.082	2.08	5/16	7.9
3	0.094	2.39	3/8	9.5
4	0.108	2.74	7/16	11.1
5	0.122	3.10	1/2	12.7
6	0.136	3.45	5/8	15.9
7	0.150	3.81	3/4	19.1
8	0.164	4.17	7/8	22.2
9	0.178	4.52	1	25.4
10	0.192	4.88	1 1/4	31.8
12	0.220	5.59	1 1/2	38.1

NAIL SIZES

PENNYWEIGHT (IN.)	LENGTH (CM)	LENGTH (IN.)	DIAMETER (CM)	
2d	1	2.5	.068	.17
3d	1 1/4	3.2	.102	.26
4d	1 1/2	3.8	.102	.26
5d	1 3/4	4.4	.102	.26
6d	2	5.1	.115	.29
7d	2 1/4	5.7	.115	.29
8d	2 1/2	6.4	.131	.33
9d	2 3/4	7.0	.131	.33
10d	3	7.6	.148	.38
12d	3 1/4	8.3	.148	.38
16d	3 1/2	8.9	.148	.38
20d	4	10.2	.203	.51

SCREW HEAD STYLES

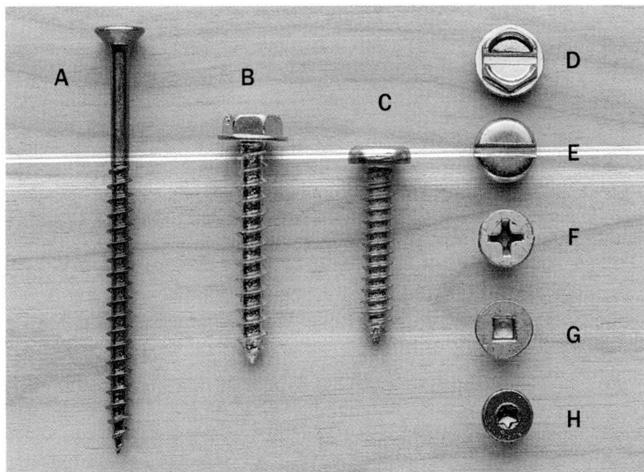

Common types of screw heads include: (A) flathead wood screw; (B) hex head; (C) panhead. Slot styles include: (D) hex/slot; (E) straight; (F) phillips head; (G) square drive; (H) torx.

NUTS, BOLTS & WASHERS

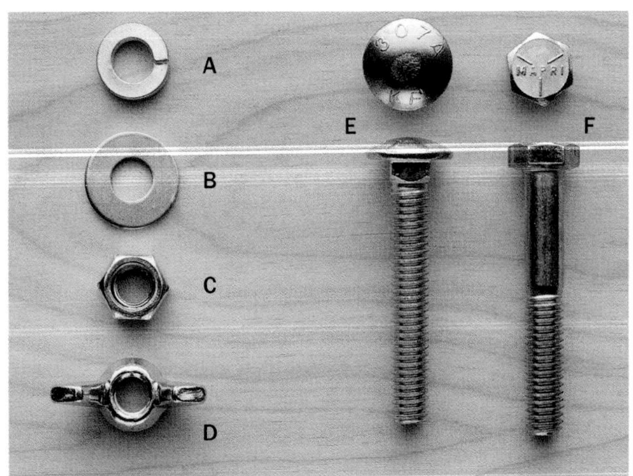

Nuts, bolts and washer types include: (A) lock washer; (B) flat washer; (C) hex nut; (D) wing nut; (E) carriage bolt; (F) hex-head bolt.

STANDARD STAPLE SIZES

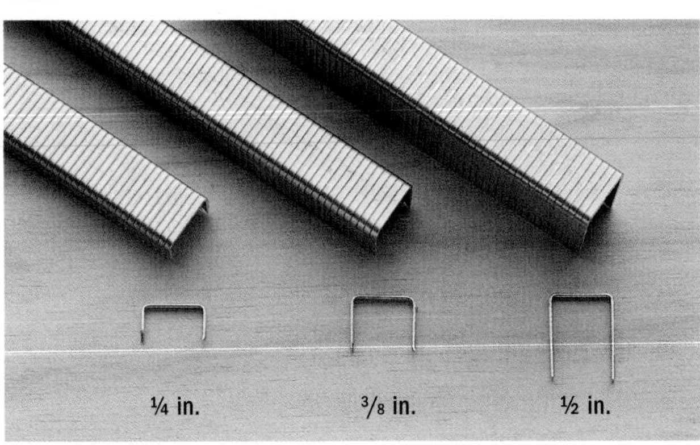

CHOOSING CAULK

TYPE	EASE OF USE	DURABILITY
Acrylic latex	Easy	Very Good
Butyl	Difficult	Good
Latex	Easy	Poor
Oil	Easy	Poor
Paintable silicone	Moderate	Very Good
Polyurethane	Moderate	Excellent
Silicone	Moderate	Excellent
Synthetic rubber	Difficult	Good

Sanding & Finishing

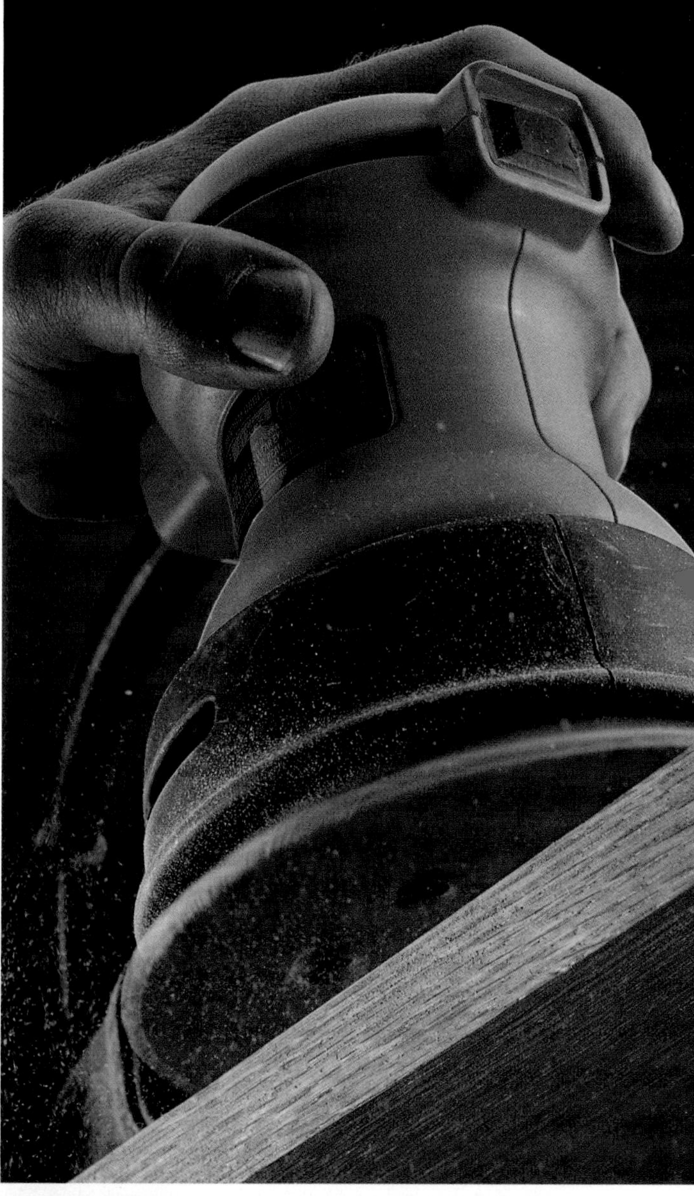

After spending hours, days or even months of labor on a workshop project, don't let an incorrectly or hastily applied finish spoil all your hard work. Take the time to prepare the wood for the finish by sanding thoroughly with a sequence of finer-grit sandpapers. Make sure all screw plugs are securely in their counterbores and flush with the wood surface. Don't let the project sit for more than 48 hours between final sanding and finish application so that it has time to attract dust. Then, choose the finishing products that best meet your needs: both in terms of protection and appearance. And once the finish is applied, patch up any dents, nail holes or small cracks with tinted wood putty.

Choosing the best finishing products can be very daunting. There are dozens upon dozens of paints, stains, dyes, varnishes, penetrating oils, lacquers and countless other finishing products on the shelves of most building centers. Deciding which to use is a matter of learning a little bit about the products. Don't rely too much on the claims you'll see on the labels—look for basic information on the composition of the product and see how it fits into finish selection charts, like the ones on pages 80 and 81. But with today's labeling practices it's sometimes difficult to determine exactly what kind of product you're examining even after reading the label top to bottom. In such cases, don't be shy about asking the store clerk for information. And whenever you decide to try a product you've never used before, always test it out first on some scrap.

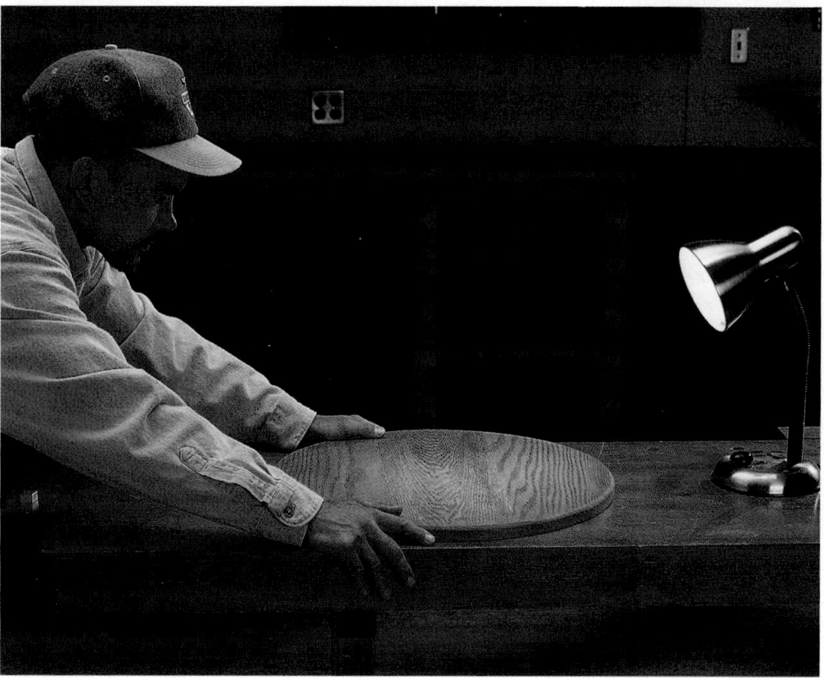

Highlight surface flaws

Sanding marks, small scratches and dents and other minor surface flaws can be very difficult to detect—until you apply your wood finish, when they show up with glaring clarity. To spot these surface imperfections before applying your finish, use a desk lamp or other low lamp source (a 60-watt bulb is about right). Set the lamp next to the surface so the light hits it at a low angle. From the opposite side of the workpiece, view the surface. Even slight scratches and flaws will be highlighted by the shadows created by the light. Mark flawed areas with a light pencil mark, sand them away, then check again.

Prolong life of sandpaper and sanding belts

Sandpaper, sanding pads and sanding belts will gum up quickly when sanding, losing most of their tooth. But don't throw them away. Belts, pads and papers can be cleaned with a sanding stick (shown above) or just about any clean, uncolored rubber (an old tennis shoe sole, for example). With power sanders, simply turn on the tool and apply the sanding stick to the paper until the residue disappears.

Turn a band saw into a band sander

Stationary belt and disc sanders are powerful tools that remove a lot of material quickly. This characteristic is great for many sanding tasks, but if you're doing more delicate work more power isn't what you're looking for. The band saw can provide a solution for delicate sanding projects. Simply replace the band saw blade with an abrasive band to create a sanding tool that lets you remove very small amounts of wood.

Keep belt sanders on track

To impart a smooth, crisp edge on a board, use a belt sander. To prevent the sander from rocking and causing roundovers along the edge, sandwich the workpiece between two pieces of scrap wood, making sure all three edges are flush. Clamp the "sandwich" into the vise in your workbench.

Smooth rough cuts with a cabinet scraper

A lot of experienced woodworkers view sanding as a last resort. It's messy, noisy, time-consuming and it creates sanding marks. A cabinet scraper is a better tool for smoothing out rough cuts. It works equally well on curved surfaces, as above, or on broad, flat surfaces. See page 77 for more information on using cabinet scrapers.

SANDPAPER TYPES

Emergy cloth for metal and plastics

40-grit aluminum oxide

100-grit aluminum oxide

220-grit aluminum oxide

400-grit wet/dry

SANDPAPER GRIT CHART

GRIT NUMBER	DESCRIPTION	USE
12	Very Coarse	Very rough work requiring high speed, heavy machinery. Used for unplaned woods, uneven wood floors and rough-cut lumber.
16		
20		
24		
30	Coarse	Rough carpentry.
36		
40		
50		
60	Medium	General carpentry.
80		
100		
120	Fine	Preparation of hardwoods and final smoothing of softwoods.
150		
180		
220	Very Fine	Final and between-coat sanding. Used to remove sanding marks left by coarser grits.
240		
280		
320	Extra Fine	Sanding between finish coats and wet sanding paints and varnishes.
360		
400		
500	Super Fine	Sanding metal, plastics, ceramics and wet sanding.
600		

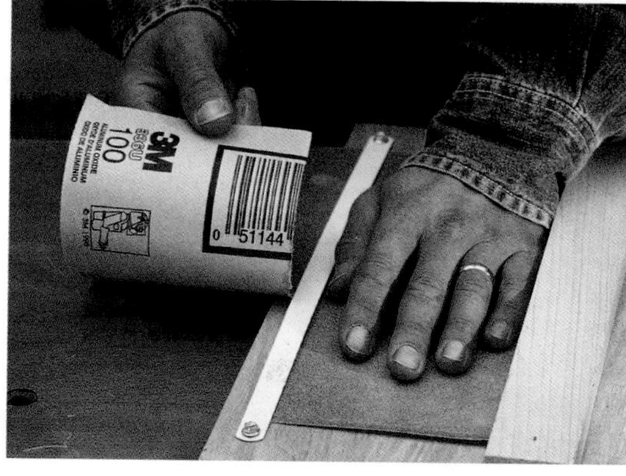

Slick trick for a rough customer

Sandpaper is difficult to tear in a straight line, and cutting it with scissors or a utility knife will dull blades very quickly. Build yourself a sandpaper cutter by attaching a hacksaw blade to a piece of scrap wood, with the sharp edge of the blade facing toward the edge of the board. Attach a strip of wood parallel to the blade. Position the strip so it's the same distance from the cutting edge of the blade as the most common dimension you'll need to fit your pad sander. Slip a piece of sandpaper underneath the blade and up against the strip. Pull upward against the blade for a neat cut.

Keep sandpaper scraps on file

An expanding, accordion-style file holder makes a great storage center for sandpaper scraps. Assign a grit number to each storage compartment and file your sandpaper sheets in the appropriate compartment so they'll be easy to find when needed.

A sander for any sanding task

Assemble a team of sanders for your woodworking and carpentry projects. The most versatile sander is the *random-orbit sander.* The irregular sanding action of this tool keeps sanding marks to a minimum, and is suitable for both rough sanding and fine finish sanding. *Belt sanders* can remove a lot of material in a hurry, making them useful for resurfacing as well as smoothing very rough stock. A *detail sander* has a small, triangular pad that can get into those hard-to-reach spots. A *¼ or ⅓ sheet finishing sander* does a fine job preparing surfaces for a finish, and is cheaper than a random-orbit sander.

A sampling of sanders and sanding blocks

Fabricated sanding blocks have soft pads and are designed to be easy and comfortable to grip. *"Tear-drop" sanding blocks* are made to fit the most common molding profiles. *Sanding sponges* can remove surprising amounts of material quickly and will conform to irregular surfaces.

HOW TO MAKE CUSTOM SANDING BLOCKS FOR MOLDING & TRIM

1 Cut a 4- to 6-in. strip of the molding or trim you need to sand. Tack a small piece of scrap wood to each end of the molding strip to create "forms." Fill or cover the molding with auto body filler, smoothing the filler so it's level with the tops of the forms. Let the filler dry according to the manufacturer's recommendations.

2 Remove the molded auto body filler and hot-glue a block of wood to the flat face to give the sanding block greater rigidity and durability. Wrap a piece of sandpaper around the shaped face and start sanding. Note: This technique also works with convex sanding profiles.

SANDING TIPS

Sanding wallboard

Use a wallboard sanding block fitted with metal sanding mesh to smooth out dried wallboard compound on taped wallboard seams. The sanding mesh removes compound smoothly, without creating fine dust.

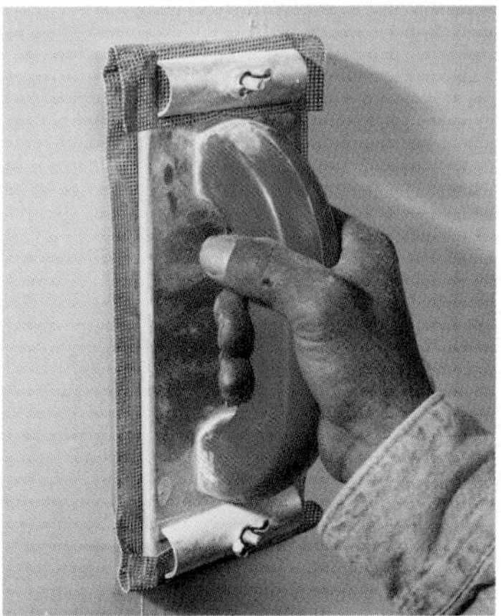

Try detail sanders

New power sanders are hitting the market all the time. Many of the more recent innovations are in the detail sander area. These compact tools have triangular sanding pads that let them fit into areas that otherwise could only be hand-sanded.

Build a drum sander dust-collection box

Drum sander attachments for the drill press are terrific for smoothing curves and sanding interior cutouts, but they can make quite a mess. Keep sanding dust in check by building a dust collection box that's clamped to your drill press table. Make a cutout in the side of the box for a vacuum hose port, and another cutout on the top for the sanding drums to fit into. The top of the box also comes in handy as a sanding table.

CABINET SCRAPERS

The cabinet scraper isn't just a tool for cabinetmakers. This simple metal blade can do away with almost all of the need for sanding in woodworking shops. As long as the cutting burr is sharp, the cabinet scraper will shave off paper-thin wisps of wood, leaving behind a glass-smooth surface that has no sanding marks. If you've never used a cabinet scraper, it's well worth investing a few dollars to try out this valuable tool. You may never go back to sanding again.

To use a cabinet scraper, hold the ends and press in with your thumbs to cause a slight flex. Hold the scraper at a fairly steep angle and push it away from yourself, applying downward pressure as you push (you can also flex the scraper inward and draw it toward yourself).

HOW TO MAKE SHARP BURRS ON CABINET SCRAPER EDGES

1 File down any traces of the old burrs on all edges of the cabinet scraper, using a fine single-cut metal file. Don't get too aggressive with the file—it doesn't take much power to remove a fine burr.

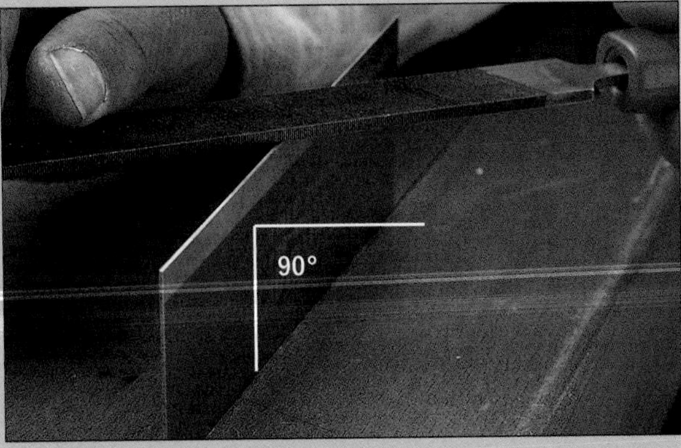

2 With the cabinet scraper held firmly in a vertical position, file the edges flat at an exact 90° angle, using the metal file. Take care not to overwork the edge.

3 With the scraper lying flat on a worksurface, rub across the edges of the scraper with a burnishing tool held at a very slight angle. If you don't have a burnishing tool, any piece of round hardened steel (like the top of a chisel shank) will do. The edge of the scraper should be set back just slightly from the edge of the worksurface to prevent you from burnishing at an angle that's too steep.

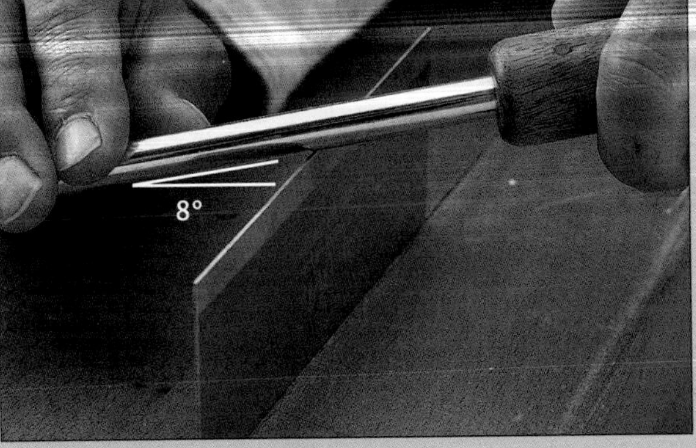

4 With the scraper lying flat on a worksurface, rub across the edges of the scraper with a burnishing tool held at a very slight angle. If you don't have a burnishing tool, any piece of round hardened steel (like the top of a chisel shank) will do. The edge of the scraper should be set back just slightly from the edge of the worksurface to prevent you from burnishing at an angle that's too steep.

PLUGGING SCREW COUNTERBORES

Screw hole counterbores can be plugged with matching wood plugs or with contrasting plugs that give the project decorative flair, as above.

SCREW COUNTERBORE SIZES

GAUGE	HEAD BORE	SHANK BORE	PILOT HOLE
2	11/64	3/32	1/16
3	13/64	7/64	1/16
4	15/64	7/64	5/64
5	1/4	1/8	5/64
6	9/32	9/64	3/32
7	5/16	5/32	7/64
8	11/32	5/32	7/64
9	23/64	11/64	1/8
10	25/64	3/16	1/8
12	7/16	7/32	9/64
14	1/2	1/4	5/32

HOW TO COUNTERBORE AND PLUG FOR WOOD SCREWS

1 Drill a counterbored pilot hole using a counterboring bit (see page 48) or by drilling a pilot hole, then counterboring for the screw shank and the screw head, according to the dimensions in the chart above.

2 After the screw is driven, apply wood glue to the end of a screw plug. Set the plug into the counterbore hole with a wood mallet. For contrast, the grain in the plug should be perpendicular to the workpiece grain. For concealment, align the patterns.

3 After the glue has dried, trim the plug flush with the wood surface using a flush-cutting saw (see photo, above left). Take care not to mar the surrounding wood surface. Sand the plug smooth.

TINTED OR UNTINTED WOOD PUTTY?

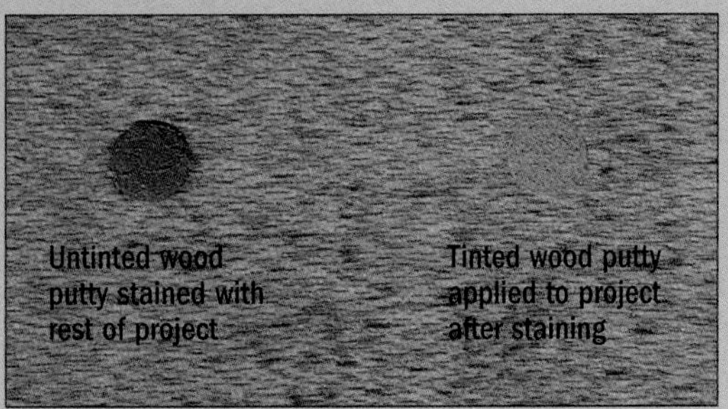

Debate over the best method to conceal nail and screw heads with wood putty has raged for generations. We've had the best success filling holes with putty tinted to match the finished color of the surrounding wood, rather than applying untinted putty and staining it at the same time as the rest of the project.

For information on how to cut your own screw counterbore plugs, see page 47.

STEEL WOOL TYPES AND USES

TYPE	DESCRIPTION	SUGGESTED USES
#3	Coarse	Remove old paint and varnish
#2	Med. coarse	Clean rough metal, concrete or brick. Clean garden tools, remove paint from molding
#1	Medium	Clean resilient floors, copper pipe and fittings
#0	Med. fine	Clean grills, pots, pans. Remove rust from metal tools (use oil)
#00	Fine	Buff painted finish. Clean screens and frames. Remove old finish from antiques
#000	Very fine	Polish aluminum, copper, brass and zinc. Remove minor burns from wood and leather
#0000	Super fine	Buff woodwork, shellac and varnish. Smooth clear finishes. Clean delicate tools

Steel wool and abrasive pads (synthetic steel wool) have many uses in the shop, from general cleanup to buffing to stripping old finishes.

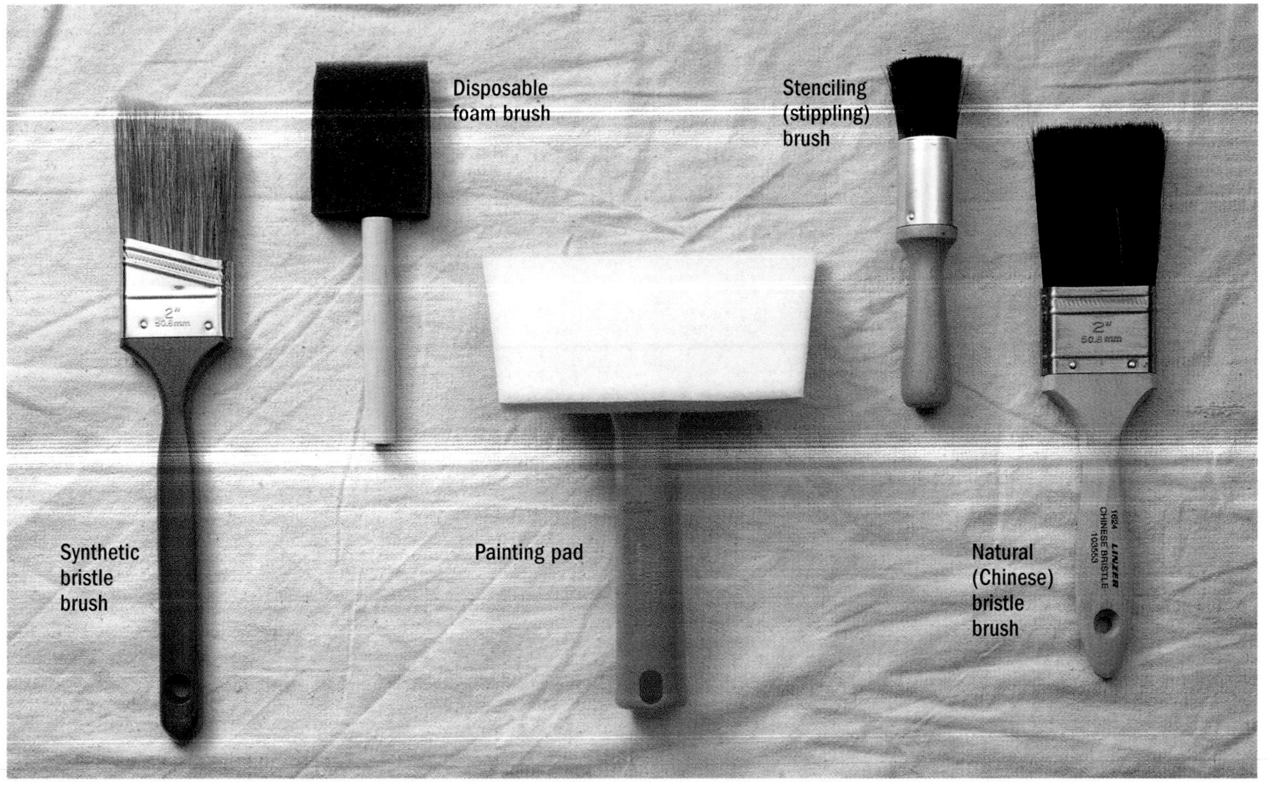

SANDING & FINISHING

Paintbrushes & pads

Choosing the best paintbrush or pad for your application has a great effect on the speed and quality of the job. As a general rule, use the widest paintbrush that will fit the principal surfaces being painted (for example, the lap siding boards on your house). If using a water-based (latex) paint, you can use a brush with either natural or synthetic bristles. If using oil-based products, a natural bristle brush is a better choice—the oils will break down the synthetic bristles. Use a painting pad for broad flat surfaces or for heavily textured surfaces. Because brush cleanup is messy, you may prefer to use disposable foam brushes.

WOOD COLORING AGENTS

TYPE	STRENGTHS	WEAKNESSES	RECOMMENDED FOR:
Liquid stain	Can be built up to control color. Both conditions and seals the wood. Spray-on application can speed up and simplify application process.	Difficult cleanup. Application can be messy Slow curing time allows dust to settle in the finish. May show brush marks	Previously stained wood. Touching up wood finish.
Gel stain	Neat and easy to apply, with no running. Even drying. Color can be deepened with layering. Buffing will result in a hard surface.	High cost, difficult clean-up and limited color selection. Requires buffing between coats. Does not penetrate wood. Vulnerable to streaking.	Woodwork with vertical surfaces. Furniture with spindles and other rounded parts.
Aniline dyes	Color can be lightened or changed with a solvent long after initial application. Wide range of colors available. Greater control of tone.	Granular dyes must first be mixed with a solvent. Do not penetrate or bond well with pores of open-grain woods like oak or ash, requiring application of wood filler in spots.	Touch-up and repairs. Coloring or tinting a topcoat made of a similar solvent.

Do-it-yourself tack cloths

Make your own tack cloths for wood finishing by dampening cheesecloth with equal amounts of boiled linseed oil and varnish. Store them in a covered jar.

Sand lightly between coats of finish

After each coat of finish dries, sand it lightly with 400- to 600-grit sandpaper to knock down bubbles and surface defects. Wipe with a tack cloth when done.

Store finishing materials in a metal cabinet

Finishing materials and other potentially flammable or dangerous chemicals should be stored in a sturdy, lockable metal cabinet. Used office furnishing stores are an excellent source for this kind of cabinet.

WATER-BASED VS. OIL-BASED FINISHING PRODUCTS

Wood coloring agents and topcoating products are available in both water-based and oil-based varieties. Each has its own advantages and drawbacks.

1960s' clean-air legislation prompted manufacturers to produce water-based finishes, and recent health concerns have bolstered their popularity. They are nontoxic and nonflammable. They also have weaker odors than oil-based varieties and can be cleaned up with soap and water. However, the transparent nature of water-based products produces a flatter finish than the oil-based versions, which tend to carry a more vivid sheen. It is easier to achieve an even application when finishing with oil-based products than with water-based.

Another characteristic of oil-based products is their enhanced workability, due to their slower drying times and weaker penetration of the wood. Water-based versions are absorbed deeper into the wood, drying quickly and producing an extremely hard finish. They also have a tendency to raise the wood grain.

Although technology for creating non-petroleum-based finishing materials is advancing quickly, the majority of tradespeople still prefer the oil-based products. But when deciding between the two finish types, be sure to consider the available ventilation and whether or not there are youngsters present. If ventilation is poor or kids may be in the area, water-based products may be a better idea.

TOPCOAT TYPES AND CHARACTERISTICS

TYPE	USES	CHARACTERISTICS
Oil-based polyurethane	High-use furniture and outdoor projects.	A durable, hard finish that resists water and alcohol.
Water-based polyurethane	Floors, interior woodwork (especially eating surfaces and toys).	Dries fast and cleans up easily while resisting water and alcohol. Nontoxic and nonflammable.
Lacquer	Low-use furniture.	Medium durability in a rich-looking finish that is easily buffed to a luster.
Paste wax	Floors, antiques and fine furniture.	Provides a natural appearance that is easily renewed, but wears away quickly and must be reapplied with some regularity.
Shellac	Initial sealer coat and repairing blemishes in other finishes.	Highly resistant to humidity. Nontoxic and long lasting.
Tung oil	Uneven surfaces (e.g. chairs with spindles) and wood with highly figured grain.	A durable, moisture-resistant and nondarkening finish. It gives a low-luster, natural appearance while being easily applied or renewed.
Danish oil	Low-use furniture and antique restoration.	A durable, easily repaired finish that gives a warm, natural-looking tone with higher sheen than tung oil.
Linseed oil	Antique restoration.	Provides a low-luster, hand-rubbed look, but lacks durability and longevity.

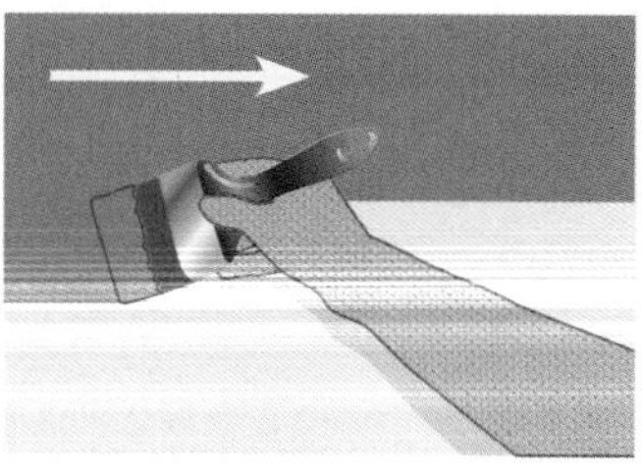

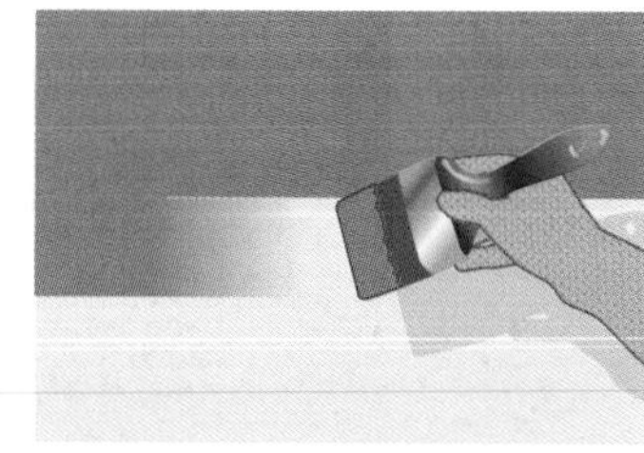

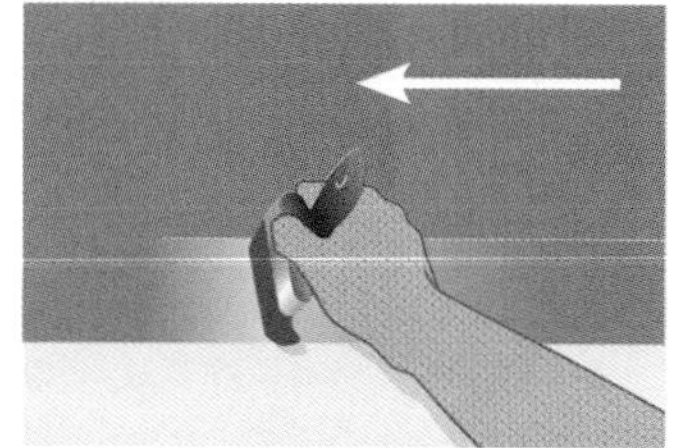

Feather paint for a smooth finish

Painting large, broad surfaces with a brush can produce streaking and brush strokes that remain visible after the paint has dried. Using the proper feathering technique is the best way to ensure that painted surfaces are smooth and even. Start by applying a fully loaded brush (paint should be ⅓ to ½ way up the bristles) across the surface from left to right—always begin at the top of the project area. As soon as the paint coverage begins to thin out, lift the brush slowly. Then, reload the brush and apply paint from right to left, in line with the previous stroke. Slowly lift the brush as you approach the endpoint of the previous stroke. Partially load the brush with paint and sweep it back and forth in the area between the two strokes to blend them together.

HOW TO REVITALIZE HARDENED PAINTBRUSHES

Most of us have a few old crusty paintbrushes that have been lying around the basement for months or even years. Whether they were cleaned improperly or not cleaned at all, we can't bring ourselves to admit that they're ruined. Well, they may not be. Try one of these tricks for softening bristles and giving new life to old hardened brushes. If the brush was used to apply shellac, simply soak it in alcohol overnight, then rinse and wash in a trisodium phosphate (tsp) solution. Use a brush comb to help clean and condition the bristles. For brushes that are crusted with other materials, try soaking them in paint and varnish stripper to dissolve the gunk, then rinse with tsp and comb. If you know the exact type of solvent used for the product that has dried, try soaking the brush in that product (for example, lacquer thinner) before opting to use stripper.

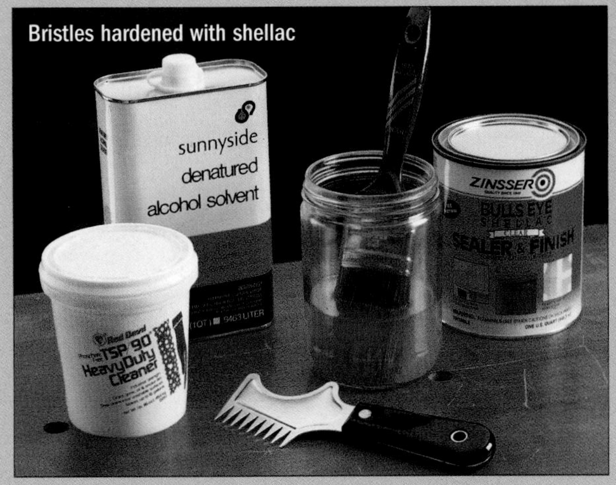

Bristles hardened with shellac

Bristles hardened with other finishing products

A one-two punch for cleaning oily hands

You should always wear rubber gloves when working with finishing materials, but just in case some product does get on your hands, here's an effective trick for cleaning it off. Wash your hands in ordinary vegetable oil to dissolve the oily mess. Then, rinse your hands with grease-dissolving dish detergent and warm water. You'll be amazed at the effectiveness of this one-two punch.

Suspend discarded oily rags in water

There is perhaps no greater fire hazard in the workshop than oily rags. Left crumpled in a corner or, worse yet, in a pile, rags containing petroleum distillate are highly flammable, and have been known to spontaneously combust. Don't take any chances. When you're through with an oily rag, drop it into a bucket of water until it can be properly disposed of at a hazardous waste collection site.

STORING HAZARDOUS FINISHING MATERIALS

All oil-based products, most solvents and paint removers, and even some water-based products fall into the hazardous waste classification. Leftovers should be handled and stored with care until they can be disposed of properly at a hazardous waste disposal site. Here are a few tips to note:

- Store in a cool, dark location, away from direct sunlight and heat sources.
- Do not set metal cans on damp concrete floors.
- Leave the product in the original container so you know exactly what it is and how to handle it.
- Do not store products in old food or beverage containers.
- Dispose of all products in a timely fashion. Most local waste management centers operate hazardous waste collection programs.

Evaporate unused paint before disposing of cans

Containers for water-based paints and finishes that are not considered hazardous wastes (see tip, left) can be disposed of in your normal trash collection if they are completely empty and dry. Before disposal, set open cans in a well-ventilated area and allow the old product to evaporate until only a dry residue remains.

USING CHEMICAL STRIPPERS

Get the facts on chemical strippers before making your choice

Chemical strippers are very controversial these days. Most of the traditional strippers contain dangerous solvents that can cause health issues if proper protection isn't taken. Methylene chloride, acetone, tuolene and xylene are some of the active ingredients in chemical strippers that are considered dangerous. Because of these hazards, "safer" paint and varnish strippers have been introduced. Some have organic active ingredients that are less caustic, others simply evaporate more slowly, reducing the exposure. Many people who have tried these newer strippers have found them to be less effective than the older types (although frequently the problem is a failure to follow the directions properly). The best advice is to try a few different products, taking care to follow the manufacturer's directions, and decide which one you prefer. Perhaps even better advice is to avoid using chemical strippers altogether. A good sharp scraper will remove most finishes quickly and safely.

Save those planer shavings

The messiest part of using chemical strippers is scraping off and disposing of the goo and residue that's created by the stripping process. To make this step a little neater, scatter shavings from your power planer (sawdust is ineffective) onto the stripper after it has done its job, and allow the chemicals to soak into the shavings. Then, simply wipe up the shavings and dispose of them properly.

Metalworking

Many DIYers who are right at home working with wood and other common building materials balk at the thought of working with metal. But in many regards, metal is actually easier to work and more forgiving than wood. All it takes is the right tools, a little know-how and some practice. Light-gauge sheet metal is a very versatile, easy-to-handle workshop material. It is worked mostly by cutting, bending and joining with mechanical fasteners. Light-gauge metals, such as aluminum, copper and brass, are also easy to cut and shape. Heavier-gauge steel requires more patience and, eventually, will require you to develop welding skills.

COMMON METAL PROPERTIES AND USES

METAL OR ALLOY	PROPERTIES	USES
Stainless steel	Tough but difficult to work. Will not rust or corrode.	Kitchenware, furniture, picture frames and sinks.
Aluminum	Light, soft and malleable. Easy to work or cast.	Siding, roofing, gutters, flashing and auto parts.
Copper	Soft and easily worked. A good electrical conductor.	Plumbing and wiring. Also a major component of brass and bronze.
Brass	Soft. Can be worked either hot or cold. Casts and polishes well.	Marine fittings, architectural trim and bearings.
Tin	Soft, malleable, resists corrosion.	Galvanizing and alloys.
Cast iron	Hard and brittle. Slow rusting.	Engine blocks, machine bases, fireplace equipment and bathtubs.
Medium-carbon steel	Hard and strong. Fast rusting.	Nuts, bolts, axles and pins.

FABRICATED METAL TYPES & DATA

Sheet steel is manufactured in a variety of thicknesses or gauges. Lower gauge numbers indicate thicker metal (see chart, right). Thin galvanized sheet metal (#28 and #30), used commonly for bending projects, flashing and ductwork, is sold at most building centers, usually in the ductwork section. Thicker rolled steel sheets are usually sold only through metal distributors.

SHEET STEEL GAUGES

GAUGE	LBS./SQ. FT.	THICKNESS (IN.)
#6	8.12	0.2031
#7	7.50	0.1875
#8	6.87	0.1719
#10	5.62	0.1406
#12	4.37	0.1094
#14	3.12	0.0781
#16	2.50	0.0625
#18	2.00	0.0500
#20	1.50	0.0375
#22	1.25	0.0312
#24	1.00	0.0250
#26	0.750	0.0187
#28	0.625	0.0156
#30	0.500	0.0125

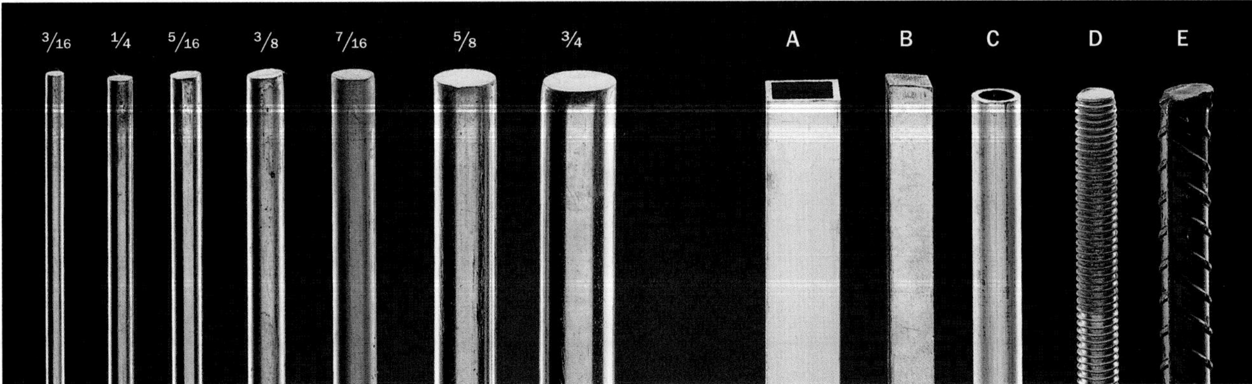

Metal rods. Steel, brass and aluminum rods are sold in many building centers in the stock diameters above, usually in 24-in. and 36-in. lengths. You can also purchase square metal tubes (A), square rods (B), round tubes (C), threaded rods (D) and rebar (E) to use as raw materials for your metalworking projects.

Corrugated sheet metal. Used mainly as cladding or roofing material for outbuildings, corrugated sheet metal is typically sold in 2- or 3-ft.wide sheets sheets with a variety of profiles and finishes. Overlapping seams are sealed with foam tape and secured with self-tapping screws fitted with rubber washers.

Flashing. Even if you haven't attempted much metalworking in the past, you've probably worked with metal flashing. The most common types are step flashing (left) and roll flashing (right). Both can be purchased in aluminum or galvanized steel.

Gallery of Metalworking Tools

Metal snips: Pay attention to handle color

Aviator snips for cutting metal are coded by handle color. Green-handled snips are used to cut curves to the right, yellow-handled snips are best used to make straight cuts, and red-handled snips cut left curves.

Hacksaw

This everyday workshop tool can be used to cut metal up to ⅓ as wide as length of the hacksaw blade (10 or 12 in. for most saws). Hacksaw blades are made of hardened, tempered steel, featuring 14, 18 or 24 teeth per inch (tpi)—use higher tpi blades for denser metal. Carbide chip blades are available for cutting milder metal.

Cold chisel

The wedge-shaped cold chisel is used to shape edges, score metal and shear off bolt heads.

Center punch

Used primarily to punch starter indentations for drilling metal.

Reciprocating saw

Fitted with a metal-cutting blade, this versatile saw will cut through rebar, metal posts and just about any other tough-to-cut metal.

Hook-nose aviator snips

The broad, flat jaw rides on the metal surface for greater stability when cutting delicate curves.

Metal files

A collection of metal-working files will allow you to apply a finished edge to just about any metal type. The rat-tail file has a round, tapered shape for deburring or reaming out holes (shown with interchange-able wood file handle); the double-cut flat file has an aggressive bite for rough shaping of metal edges; the single-cut flat file is designed for finer edge finishing.

Ball peen hammer

Used to strike metal chisels and punches, it is well balanced and weighted to concentrate the force of the blow.

3-lb. maul

Used mostly to flatten metal on an anvil surface, or to drive heavy-duty punches and shapers.

Hand seamer

Bends and flatten sheet metal edges for hemming, seaming and crimping.

Locking sheet metal tool

This variation of the popular locking pliers design is used to bend or seam sheet metal and flashing.

Anvil

Use an anvil as a surface for hammering, punching and bending metal. Anvils are made in a wide range of sizes, with larger ones weighing in at 400 pounds or more. The old anvil shown here is actually fashioned from a section of railroad track.

Use two hands for better hacksaw control

For best results when cutting with a hacksaw, first clamp the workpiece securely in a vise, with the cutting line close to the jaws of the vise (if cutting metal strips, scribe the cutting line with a punch or diamond-point chisel). Make a light forward stroke to score the cutting line, then steady the front of the blade with your free hand and proceed with the cut. Cut with light pressure when moving the blade forward, and do not apply any pressure on the return stroke.

Angle grinder and cutting wheel

An angle grinder equipped with a metal cutting wheel is an excellent way to cut metal. Make sure the cutting wheel is the appropriate size for the grinder that you are using. Secure the piece that you are cutting with clamps and wear safety gear, including gloves, eye protection and hearing protection.

Make a metal sandwich when cutting soft, thin sheet metal

Many mild metals used for decorative purposes can be cut easily with power saws and a metal cutting or jeweler's blade. But there's just one problem: these delicate materials rip easily from the force of the saw blade. An effective solution to the dilemma is to sandwich the material (light-gauge copper sheeting is shown here) between two pieces of thin plywood or hardboard. Secure the "metal sandwich" with masking tape, then draw your cutting lines and make your cuts through the wood and the metal at once (you can also gang-cut several sheets of metal at one time using this method).

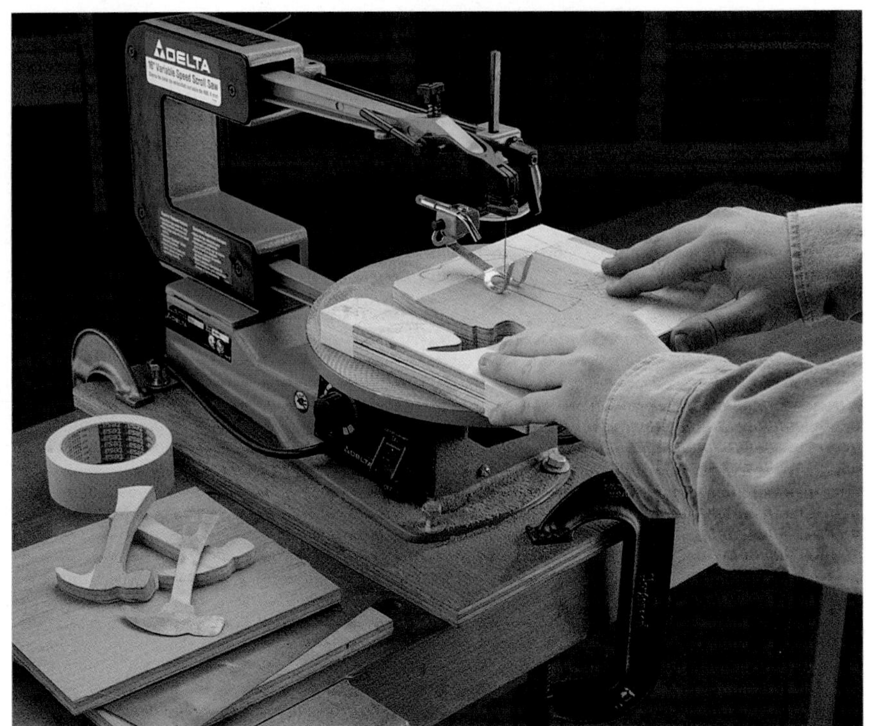

Use a tough saw to cut tough metal

A reciprocating saw with a metal cutting blade is one of the few tools that can cut rebar and other stubborn steel materials. Be sure to secure the metal object in a vise or with clamps as close to the cutting line as possible (this will help dampen vibrations). Cut with the foot of the saw up against the rebar, and do not force the cut—the weight of the saw provides more than enough downward pressure.

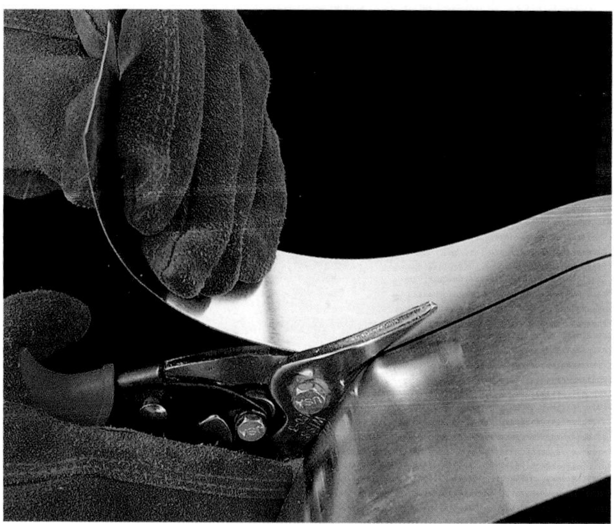

Keep waste out of the way with aviator snips

Practically everyone has cut flashing or other light-gauge metal with aviator snips or tin snips, but few people have done it correctly. If you're making a straight cut, be sure to use the yellow-handled snips designed for straight cutting (see page 86). Start your cut, holding the waste section with your free hand. Peel the waste away as you cut, preventing it from causing the snips to bind in the saw kerf. To keep the cut from kinking, never close the jaws of the snips all the way.

Keep cool when drilling metal

Use light machine oil for lubrication when drilling holes in metal. Create a depression for the bit to follow with a metal punch first. Select hardened metal twist bits to drill holes in metal, and set your drill press or portable drill at its slowest drilling speed (see page 45).

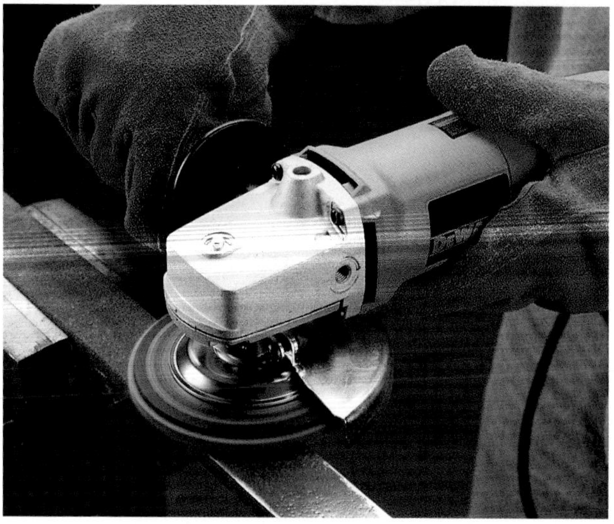

Grind away rust with an angle grinder

For fast removal of rust from heavy metal items, use an angle grinder fitted with a flap-style abrasive grinding disc. Always wear eye protection and gloves when operating this or any other metalworking tool to protect your eyes from flying sparks or bits of metal.

Rounding corners with a bench grinder

Create a roundover on strap steel and other metal types with your bench grinder. Use the tool rest as a guide to keep the edge of the roundover perpendicular. Cool the metal by dabbing it with a damp sponge.

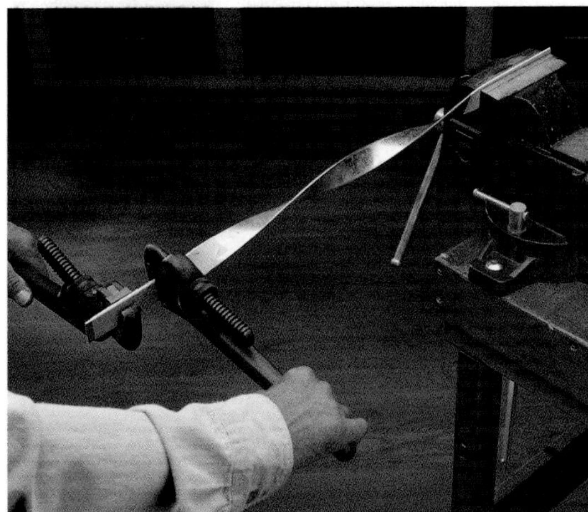

How to twist metal straps

Metal strap steel can be twisted into a regular spiral shape with this simple trick. Clamp one end of the strap in your machinist's vise and grasp the free end with a pipe wrench. Tighten another pipe wrench an inch or two in from the end of the strap, then slowly spin the wrenches as if you were turning the steering wheel of a car. The metal will develop even twists for a spiral effect. Protect the end of the strap with masking tape before attaching the pipe wrenches. You can use the twisted strap or straps for many metal-working projects, including plant hangers and stair rail balusters.

HOW TO BEND METAL STRAP

1 Measure and lay out the desired location of the bend. Lay the strap on an anvil or on the anvil portion of a bench vise and score along the bending line by rapping a cold chisel with a hammer.

2 Secure the strap in the jaws of your vise so the scored bending line projects above the jaws of the vise slightly. Slip a piece of metal conduit over the free end of the strap. Gently pull down on the conduit so the direction of the force is in line with the flat face of the strap. This will cause the strap to bend at its weakest point: the scored line. Pull down until the desired angle is achieved.

3 If making a 90° bend, use a hammer or maul to flatten the corner of strap at the bending line. For a very crisp, 90° bend, remove the strap and hammer both legs of the corner on an anvil until they're as smooth and crisp as possible.

Fasteners for metal

Joining metal with mechanical fasteners is much the same as joining wood. The trick lies in doing careful layout and preparation work, drilling pilot and guide holes accurately, and selecting the right fastener for the job. Whenever possible, select hardware made from the same type of metal as the parts being joined.

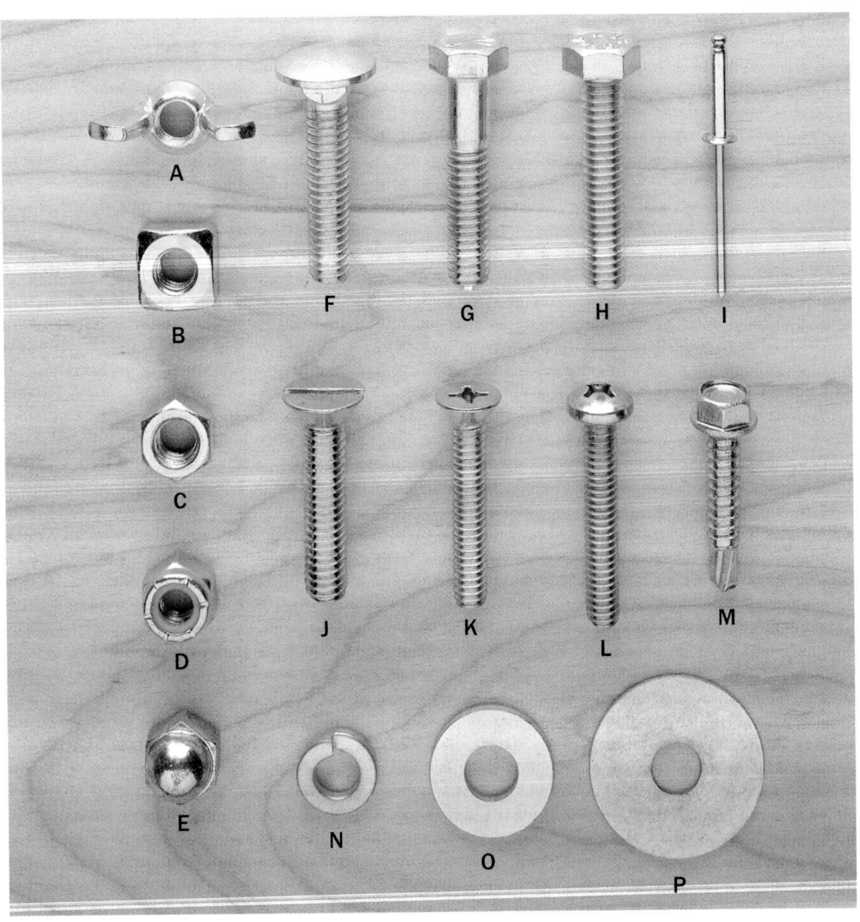

Common nuts used in metalworking include: (A) wing nut; (B) square nut; (C) hex nut; (D) stop nut (locks down when tightened); (E) cap nut (conceals bolt heads).

Common fasteners used in metalworking include: (F) carriage bolt; (G) machine bolt; (H) tap bolt; (I) pop rivet; (J) stove bolt; (K) flathead machine screw; (L) roundhead machine screw; (M) self-tapping metal screw.

Common washers used in metalworking include: (N) lock washer; (O) flat washer; (P) fender washer.

TWO WAYS TO BEND FLASHING & LIGHT SHEET METAL

Use a hand seamer or locking sheet metal tool (see page 87) to crease and bend seams in small pieces of roll flashing or step flashing. The hand seamer is also an effective tool for hemming and seaming sheet metal (see next page). Start bending or creasing in the middle of the workpiece, and work your way toward the ends, alternating from side to side.

Use a straightedge, like the top of a sawhorse, as a guide for hand-bending roll flashing (for example, to make hip or valley flashing when roofing). Clamp or attach a stopblock to set the distance of the crease from the edge of the flashing. Wearing gloves, simply press down on the flashing along the bending line until a neat crease is formed in the metal.

THREE WAYS TO DEBURR CUT METAL

Use a rotary grinding tool with a grinding wheel to smooth away burrs from the inside edges of metal tubing or conduit.

Use a metalworking file (see page 87) to smooth out rough edges from rolled steel and plate steel. Use a double-cut file for roughing and a single-cut file for final smoothing.

Use a bench grinder to smooth out burrs on metal used for rough construction, like the conduit shown above. The grinding wheel does fast, neat work but has a limited range of angles from which to apply the workpiece.

FOLDED SEAMS & HEMS FOR SHEET METAL

Seams and hems are keys to strength in fabricated sheet metal projects

Many useful and decorative items can be built by fabricating sheet metal: tool boxes, drawers, roofing fixtures, workshop jigs, and birdhouses, just to name a few. When building with sheet metal, draw patterns for the project parts directly onto the metal with a wax crayon. At joints between parts, use folded seams for strong construction that's free of sharp edges. The folded seams and hems illustrated here are bent using a hand seamer (see page 87). Be sure to allow for the width of seams and hems when laying out your patterns.

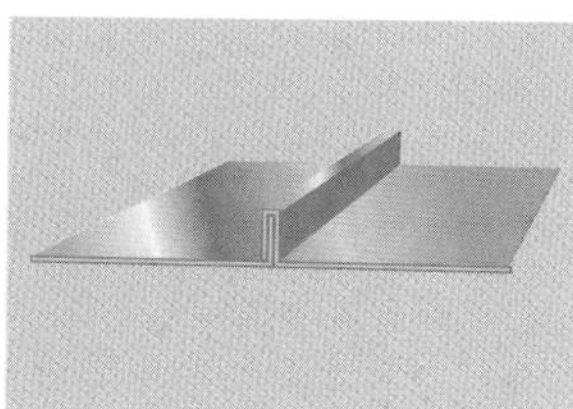

Standing seam: used for rectangular or square ductwork. Mating parts are folded, then hooked together. Seams can be up to 1 in. high.

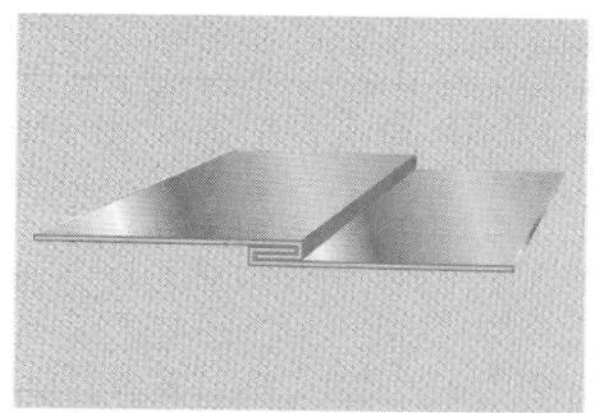

Folded seam: used mostly for installing metal roofing and siding. Mating parts are folded, then hooked together. Typically 1/4 in. wide.

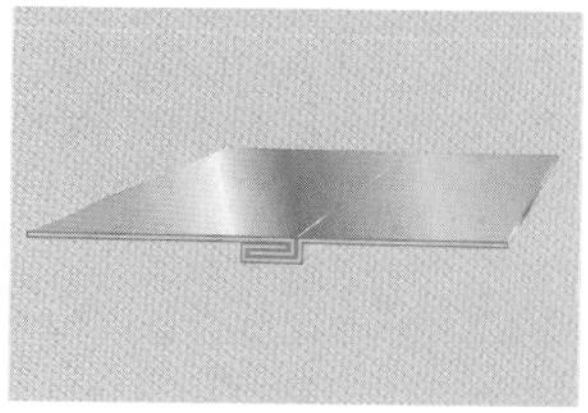

Grooved seam: used mostly for long joints and cylinders. Prefolded and hooked, then final side is hammered flush. Typically 1/4 in. wide.

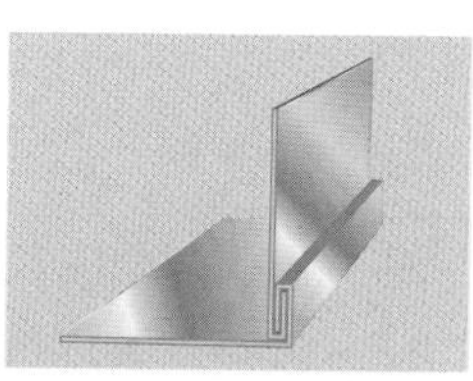

Double seam: used to join vertical and horizontal planes. Prefolded, then folded again after sheets are hooked together. Typically 1/4 in. wide.

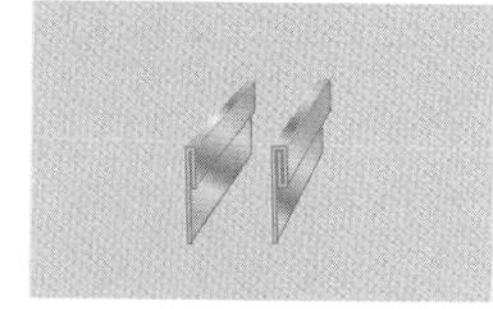

Single fold hem (left) and **double fold hem** (right).

HOW TO USE A POP RIVET GUN

Pop rivets are easy-to-use fasteners that join two or more pieces of light-gauge metal. They're especially useful for repairing sheet metal objects, like file cabinets, that have come apart at the seams.

1 Start by positioning the parts to be joined and drill a guide hole through the seam for each pop rivet. The guide hole should be the same diameter as the pop rivet mandrel (shaft).

2 Insert the mandrel of a pop rivet into the hole in the nosepiece of the pop rivet gun. Squeeze the gun handles together to hold the rivet and insert the end of the rivet into the guide hole. The head of the rivet should be flush on the surface of the metal. Avoid rocking the gun.

3 Squeeze the gun handles together repeatedly until they resist squeezing. Check to make sure the head of the rivet is still flush on the metal surface. Squeeze the handles together again (this can take some effort) until the pressure from the gun causes the mandrel to snap off from the head of the pop rivet. Check the fit of the rivet: you may need to drive the top of the mandrel stump down into the rivet head with a punch.

Coatings & treatments used with metal

Most metals are well suited for painting, but you should use special paints and coatings designed for use with metal.

Among the more common of these are: (A) enamel spray paint; (B) high-temperature spray paint for grills, stoves, etc.; (C) spray version anti-rust primer; (D) rust-inhibiting metal paint; (E) chain link fence paint; (F) rust-inhibiting metal primer; (G) naval jelly for dissolving rust; (H) rust stop solution for preparing rusted metal surfaces for paint.

LUBRICANTS FOR GENERAL WORKSHOP & METALWORKING USE

Penetrating machine oil: A general lubricant used for drilling, cleaning and removing rust from metal.

Spray silicon: A multi-use lubricant that won't attract dirt. Non-corrosive, lubricates, waterproofs and insulates metals and other materials.

Spray graphite: An exceptionally slick lubricant used for locks, bearings and other precise mechanical parts.

Penetrating lubricants: Lubricate and condition metal, dissolve rust and loosen rusted hardware. Protects metal from corrosion. Brand names include WD40 and others.

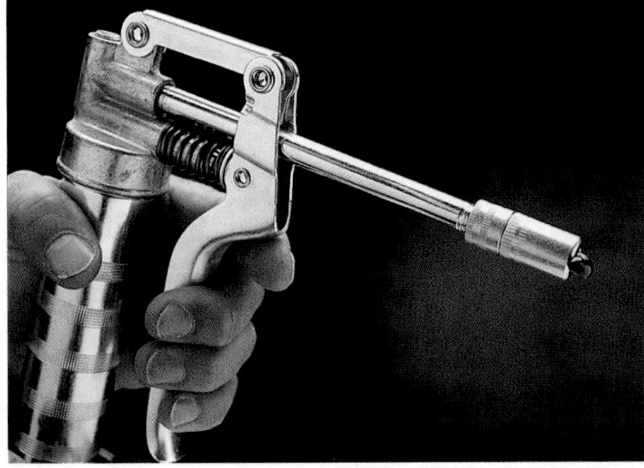

Lithium grease: Mechanical joint lubricant that's cleaner, longer lasting and more heat resistant than standard petroleum-based grease lubricants.

Paste wax: When buffed onto metal surfaces creates a smooth, resistance-free finish and protective barrier. Used on stationary tool tables.

Plumbing

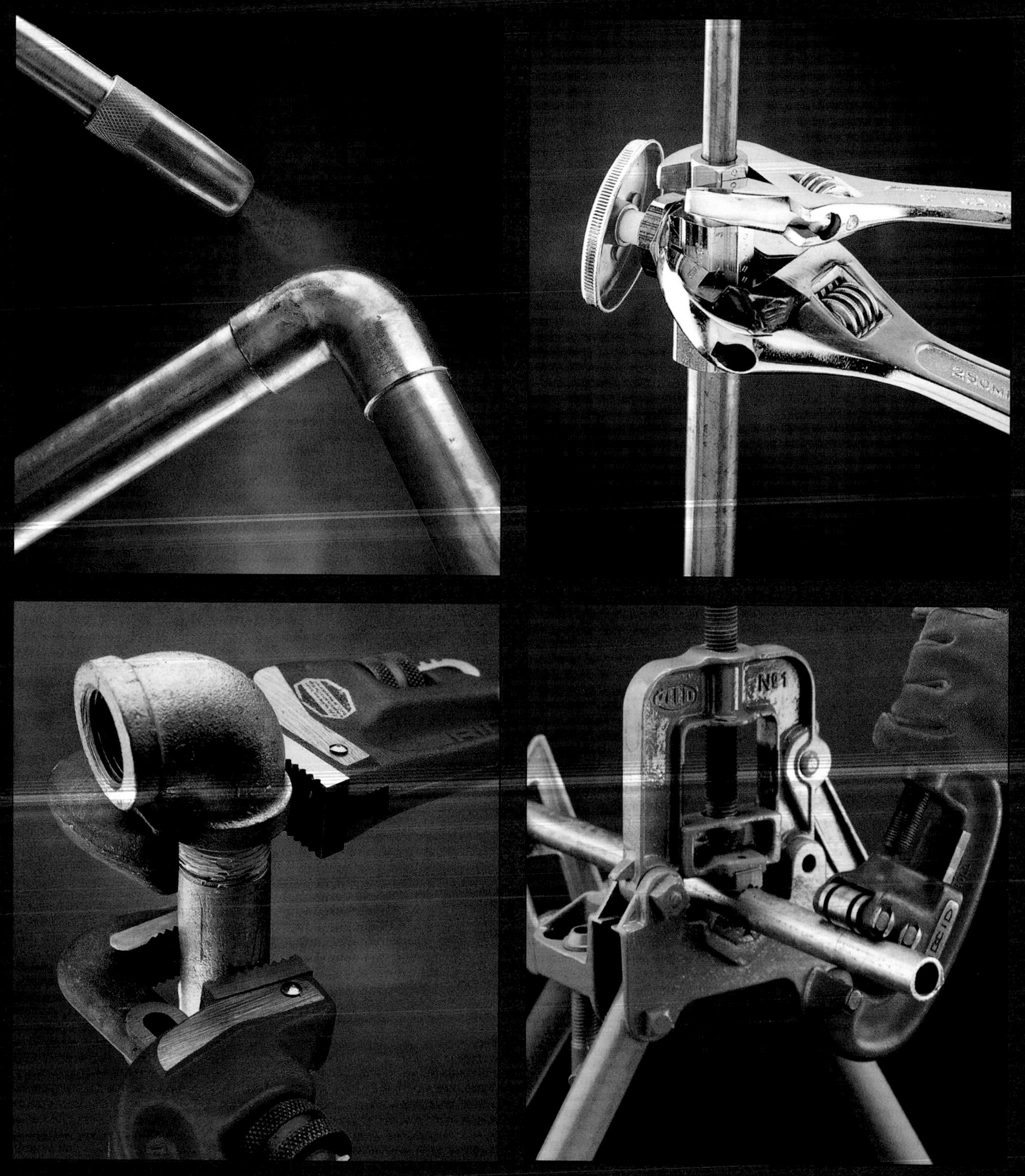

Plumbing Systems

Once you understand the basic theories behind moving water through a home and get to know the basic materials and materials handling techniques, you'll be able to tackle just about any plumbing repair or project with confidence.

In a nutshell, here's how plumbing works: Water is brought into the home under pressure through a metered water main. The main is connected to supply pipes, usually ¾-in.-dia. copper. The supply pipes run in parallel pairs throughout your home. One takes a detour at the water heater, then rejoins the cold water supply pipe to carry hot water to sinks, bathtubs and showers. The supply pipes typically run through joist and wall cavities, passing through floors or walls near plumbing fixtures, where they're connected to the fixtures with water supply lines, usually ½-in. copper or plastic. Usually, several plumbing fixtures are serviced by one loop of the supply pipes. Throughout the network of pipes, and at each plumbing fixture, shutoff valves are inserted into the supply lines so the water flow can be stopped if needed.

The water leaves your home through a network of drains that form the drain/waste/vent (DWV) system. Individual fixtures are connected to a vertical main drain stack via branch drains that run at a slight downward slope through floor and wall cavities. The main stack connects directly to the sewer or septic line outside the home. To prevent pressure and gas buildup, the entire DWV system is connected to a network of vent pipes that also work their way back to the main stack, which rises all the way through your home and exits through the roof in the form of a roof vent.

PLUMBING CODES

Because of the potential for disastrous water damage and the high cost of repairing a plumbing system once its up and running, plumbing is a closely regulated practice. The Uniform Plumbing Code (UPC) is a national set of codes that's updated every three years. It forms the foundation of most local plumbing codes. But for a number of reasons, including climate, local codes often vary from the UPC standards—usually on the more restrictive side. Use the UPC as a general guide when planning a plumbing project or repair, but make sure to consult with your local building inspection department before beginning any work. For new installations, a permit is normally required.

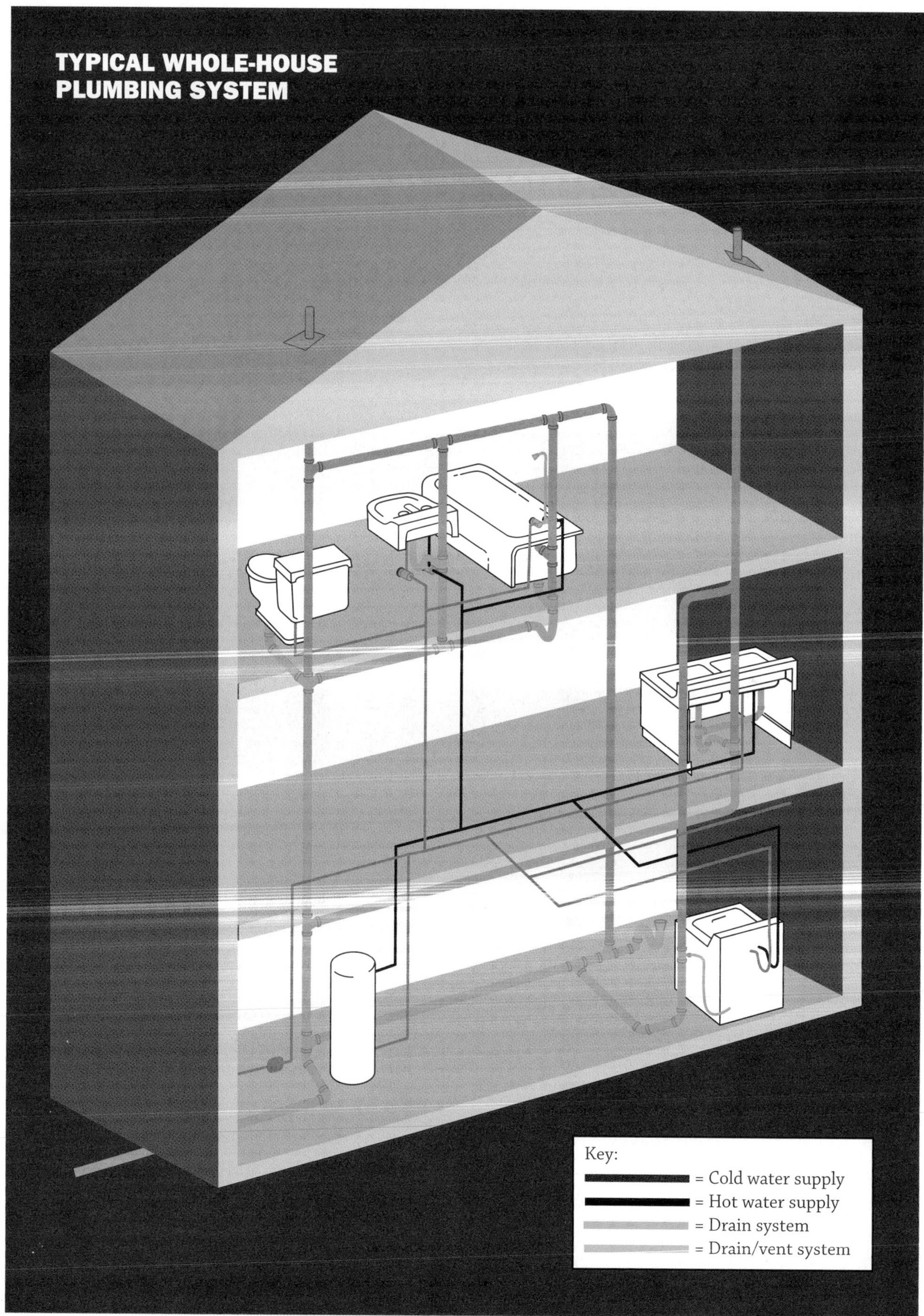
TYPICAL WHOLE-HOUSE PLUMBING SYSTEM
Key:
= Cold water supply
= Hot water supply
= Drain system
= Drain/vent system

THE DRAIN/WASTE/VENT SYSTEM

TYPICAL DWV SYSTEM

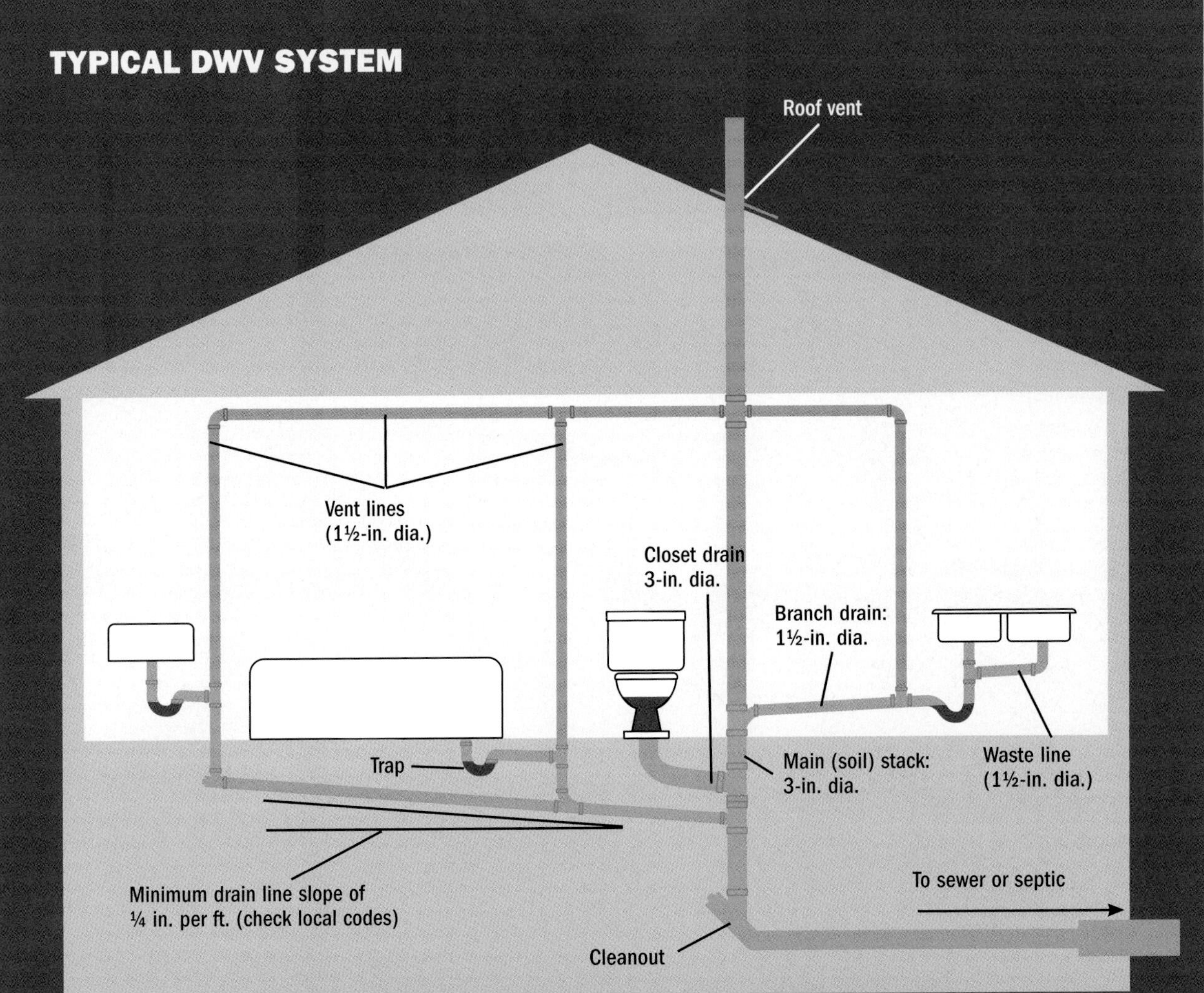

DWV SYSTEM BASICS

Waste and sewage are removed from the home through a system of drains and branch drains that are vented through the roof via a network of vent pipes. A large-diameter drain pipe, called the soil stack or main stack, runs vertically through the house. All other branch drains tie into this stack, the bottom of which terminates at a large drain pipe leading directly to the sewer or septic system. The vent system also ties into the main stack, although it's not uncommon to have a secondary vent stack that also exits through the roof. The branch drains that tie into the main stack are connected to individual plumbing fixtures with waste lines. Each waste line contains a trap that is always filled with water to prevent sewer gases from escaping through the drain system and into the house.

Both the branch drain and the waste pipes must slope toward the main stack at a rate of at least ¼ in. per ft. to ensure steady flow. Vent lines should slope upward slightly to keep water and condensation from accumulating and weakening the pipes.

Today, drain and vent systems almost always are constructed with PVC pipe. But many houses still contain DWV systems with a cast iron main stack and galvanized steel branch and waste lines. Consult your local building inspection office for specific information on drain and vent pipe size, slope and spacing requirements in your area.

HOW TO CUT COPPER PIPE WITH A TUBING CUTTER

While copper tubing can be cut with a hacksaw, a tubing cutter produces a much smoother, more even cut, which helps ensure a tight solder joint. Because it doesn't stress the pipes as a saw does, it can be used on pipes that have been soldered. And its small profile allows it to fit into tight areas where other tools can't be used.

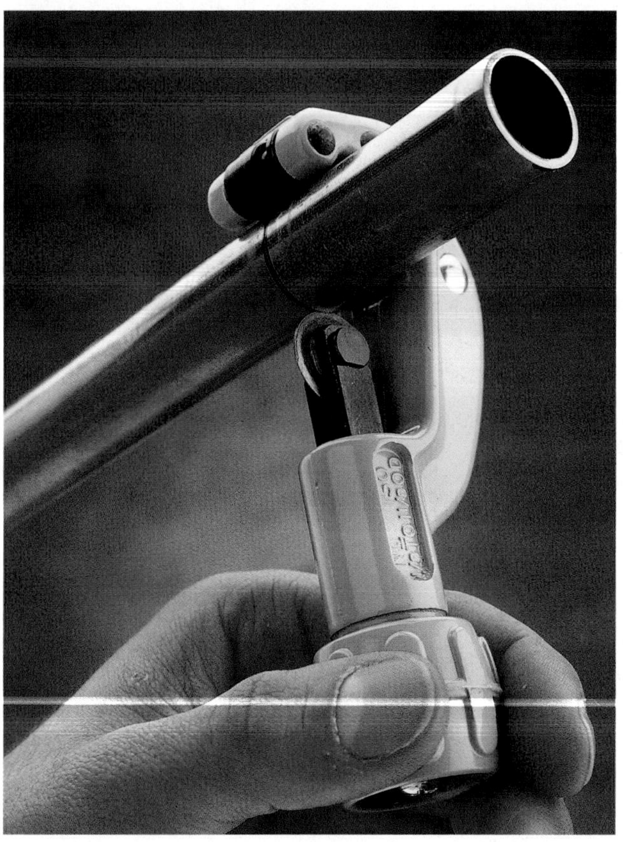

1 Mark the length you want to cut with a black magic marker. Then place the tubing cutter over the pipe and tighten the handle. The cutting wheel should be aligned with the cutting line and both rollers on the tubing cutter should be making contact with the pipe. Turn the tubing cutter one complete rotation, scoring a continuous straight line around the pipe.

2 Rotate the cutter in opposite directions, tightening the handle slightly after every two rotations until the cut is complete and the waste piece of pipe drops free.

3 Remove burrs from the inside lip of the pipe with the reaming blade found on the back of the tubing cutter, or use a rat-tail file. Removing all the burrs and creating a perfectly smooth edge is critical to successful soldering. It also ensures good water flow and fewer deposits over time.

HOW TO SOLDER COPPER PIPE

Making a sweated joint

A well-soldered copper joint will be watertight and durable. When soldering, enough heat must be applied to the pipe to draw the solder into the gap between the pipe and the fitting. Too much heat, or uneven heating, can result in a faulty joint. In addition, pipes and fittings must be clean and dry before and during soldering. If you're sweating a brass or bronze fitting, such as a shutoff valve, be aware that it takes these metals a little longer to reach the melting point of the solder. Be patient, and resist the temptation to force the solder into the joint before the metal is sufficiently heated. Also, first remove any rubber or plastic parts from the fittings like valve stems or washers to keep them from melting or distorting as you solder. Reinstall these parts after the solder joints have completely cooled.

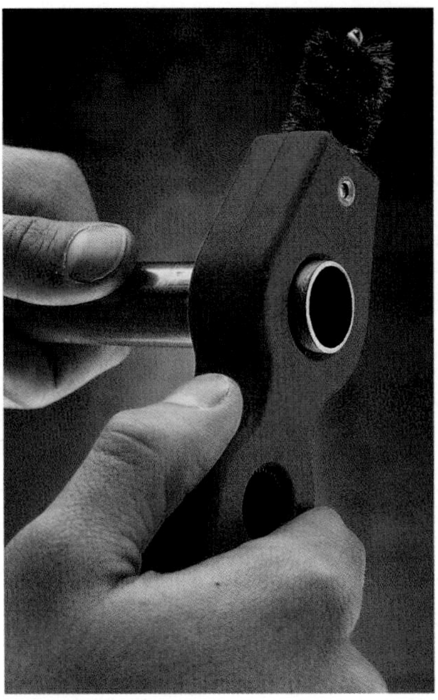

1 Clean the pipe. Copper pipes must be clean and burr-free before soldering. A brush tool allows you to clean both the inside and outside of pipes, and to scuff the copper slightly, creating a bonding surface for the solder.

2 Clean the fitting. Here, a brush tool is used to clean the inside of an elbow fitting. Avoid touching the mating areas of the pipes and fittings—the oil residue from your skin can interfere with the bond. For best protection, wear rubber gloves.

3 After a pipe is clean and dry, apply a thin layer of soldering flux (sometimes called soldering paste) to the ends of the pipe. The flux cleans and prepares the copper surface for the solder. It should cover about 1 in. of the pipe end.

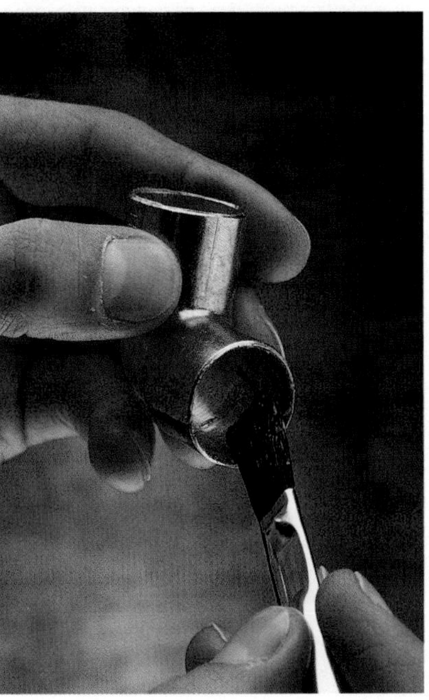

4 Apply flux to the inside, mating surface of the fitting, using the flux brush.

5 After assembling the joint so it fits together snugly, heat the fitting—not the pipe—with a propane torch for several seconds. The flux should begin to sizzle. Heat all sides of the fitting.

HOW TO SOLDER COPPER PIPE (CONT.)

6 Before heating the joint, prepare the wire solder by unwinding about 1 ft. of wire and bending the first two in. into a right angle. Then, when the joint is hot, touch the solder to the pipe. If the solder melts, the pipe is ready. Remove the torch and quickly push ½ to ¾ in. of solder wire into the joint. You don't need to move the solder around the pipe, capillary action will draw melted solder into the joint. A thin bead of solder should form all the way around the lip.

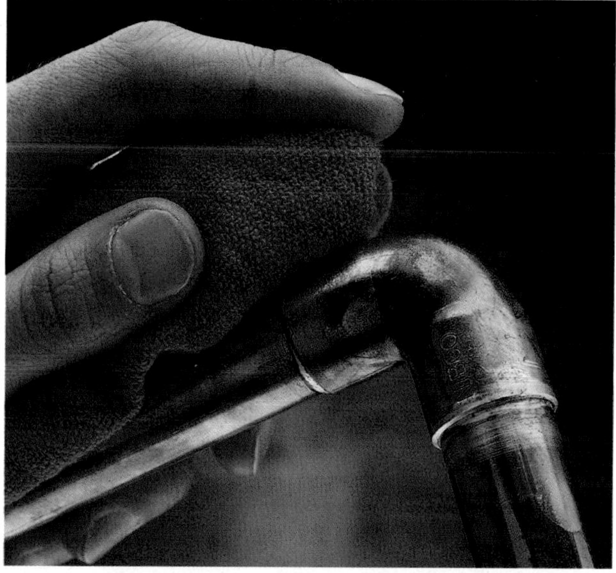

7 With a dry rag, wipe away any excess solder from the joint. Take care: the pipes will be extremely hot. When the pipe has cooled, turn on the water and check for leaks. If water does seep from a joint, drain the pipes, resist the urge to reapply additional soldering paste to the rim of the joint and reapply solder. This fix usually fails.

HOW TO BREAK A SOLDERED JOINT

1 If a soldered joint fails, the best solution is to break the joint, clean up the pipes, and try again with a new fitting. First, turn off the water supply in the house and drain the pipes by opening the highest and lowest faucets. Then, heat the fitting using a propane torch. Hold the flame to the fitting until the solder begins to melt.

2 Using channel-lock style pliers, grip the pipe and pull it free from the fitting before the solder re-sets. Be careful to avoid any steam trapped inside the pipe.

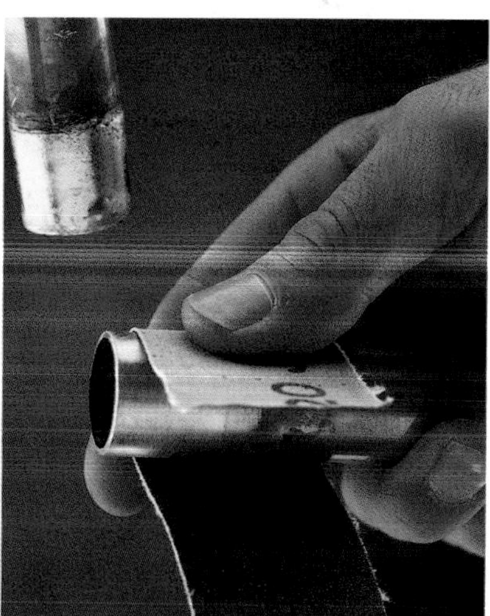

3 Allow the pipe to cool (you can speed cooling by wrapping the pipe in a damp rag). Clean the old solder residue from the pipes using emery paper and a pipe brush.

HOW TO CONNECT COPPER TUBING USING A FLARE FITTING

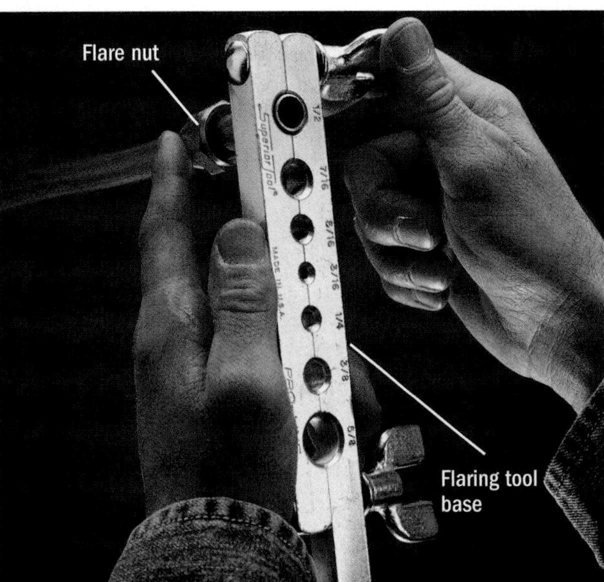

1 Flare fittings are used in situations where the pipe may need to be disconnected (such as at a shutoff valve before a fixture), or where soldering is unsafe or difficult. Flare fittings are also often used for flexible copper gas lines. When flare fittings are used on water supply lines, the connections must not be concealed by walls. To flare copper, you'll need a two-piece flaring kit and brass flare fittings. Slide the flare nut over the tubing, then clamp the tubing into the flaring tool. The tubing end must be flush with the face of the flaring tool base. Note: Do not attempt to use a flare fitting with rigid copper; flare fittings should be used with flexible copper only.

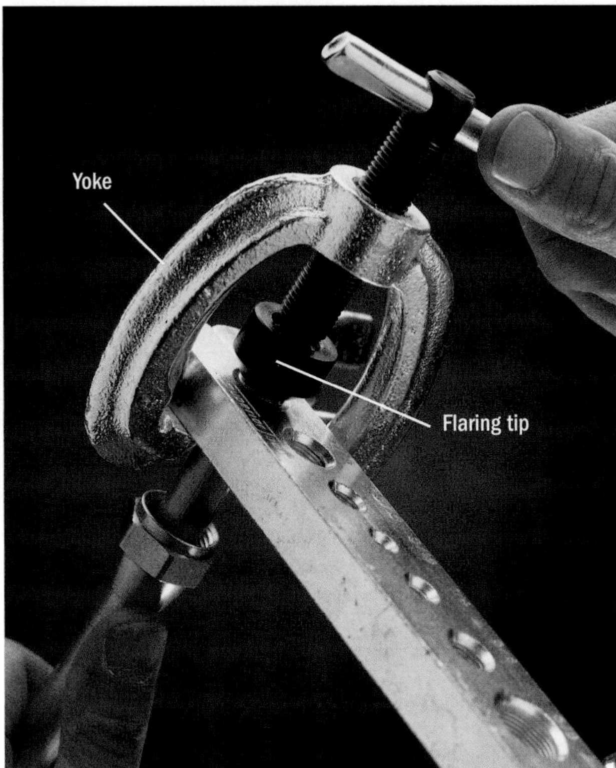

2 Slip the yoke part of the flaring tool around the base. Center the flaring tip of the yoke over the pipe. Turn the handle until it stops against the face of the flaring tool base, resulting in a flared end on the tubing. Tip: Oiling the flaring tip will produce a smoother flare.

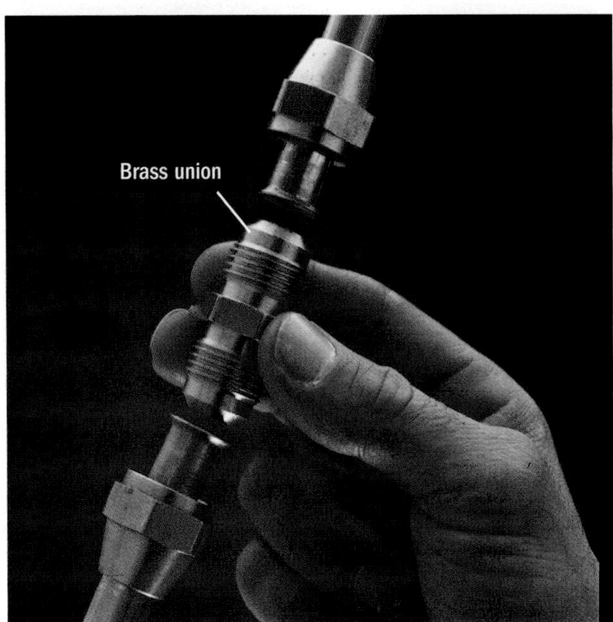

3 Flare the end of the other tube, then place the brass union between the flared ends.

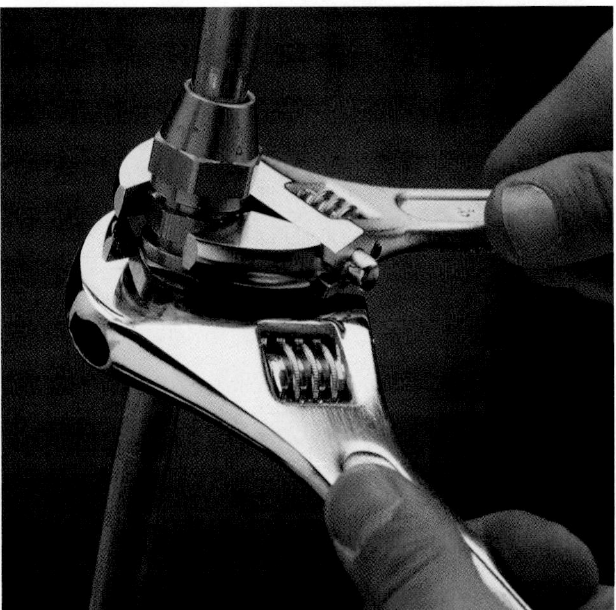

4 Tighten the flare nuts onto the union using two pliers or wrenches and turning in opposite directions. Joint compound is not necessary. Check for leaks. If the fitting leaks, tighten the nuts slightly.

Shutoff Valves

According to the Uniform Plumbing Code, every water supply line leading into a plumbing fixture should have a working shutoff valve. If you're repairing a toilet, you need to turn off the water supply without affecting the rest of the house. And if a fixture should somehow spring a leak, you'll need to turn off the water immediately before your house suffers from water damage. Here you'll see how to attach a shutoff valve featuring a compression fitting to a fixture supply tube.

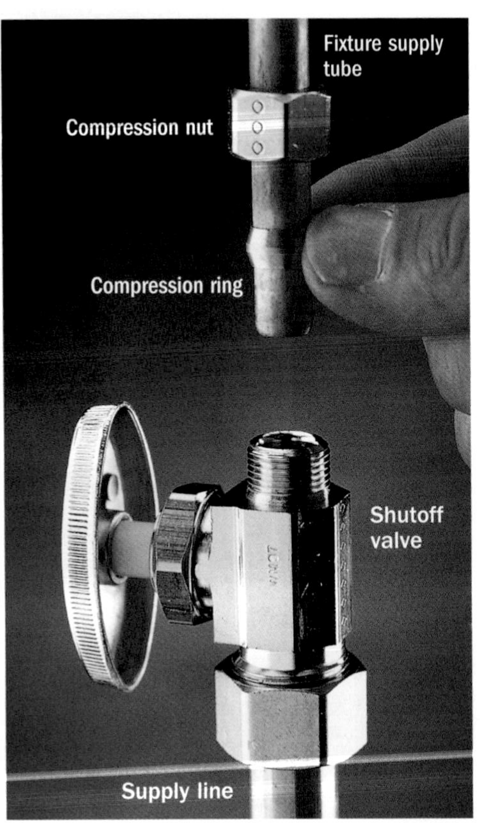

1 Solder the shutoff valve to the incoming supply line, then cut the fixture supply tube to length, allowing ½ in. for the portion that will fit inside the shutoff valve. Slip a compression ring and compression nut (usually included with valve) onto the end of the fixture supply pipe.

2 Apply pipe joint compound to the threads of the valve opening. The compound will serve as a lubricant during compression.

3 Insert the fixture supply tube into the valve and hand-tighten the compression nut over the compression ring.

4 Tighten the compression nut with two wrenches. Turn on the water supply. If the fitting leaks, try gently tightening the nuts.

Transitions & Unions

When connecting copper pipe to galvanized iron pipe, you need to install a *dielectric union* between the two materials. That's because if copper and iron come in contact with each other, a chemical reaction between the metals will create increased corrosion. The dielectric union will prevent this corrosion from occurring.

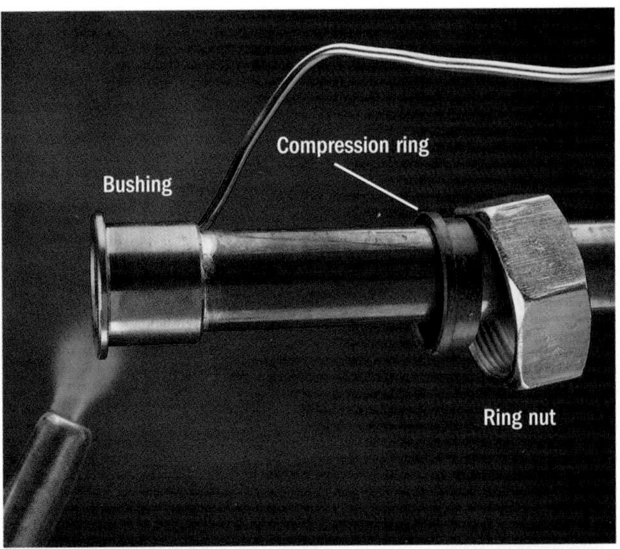

1 Solder the copper or brass bushing from the dielectric union onto the copper pipe using normal soldering techniques: apply flux, insert the fitting, heat the pipe for several seconds until the flux begins to sizzle, then quickly push the solder wire into each joint. The soldered joint should have a thin bead of solder around the lip of the fitting. Make certain not to damage the plastic spacer with the heat from the torch.

2 Screw the galvanized portion of the union onto the galvanized pipe. First apply a bead of pipe joint compound on the threaded end of the pipe. Use two wrenches to apply the fitting: one to hold the galvanized iron pipe steady and the other to turn the union fitting.

3 Connect the parts of the dielectric union. Make certain the spacer is properly aligned, and then tighten the ring nut that draws the dielectric union together, using two wrenches.

Galvanized Pipe & Fittings

Galvanized pipe is rarely installed in new construction today for one main reason: it's time-consuming to install. Compared to soldering copper tubing, or solvent-welding plastic pipe, putting together galvanized pipe is slow work. However, replacing a section of old galvanized pipe with new galvanized pipe is a reasonable project for the do-it-yourselfer.

Galvanized pipe is connected with threaded joints. You'll need to rent a pipe vise, a reamer and a threader to thread your own galvanized pipes at home. Get a threader with a head that is the same nominal diameter as the pipe you are planning to thread. You'll also need a bottle of cutting oil.

Like all metal pipe, galvanized iron will eventually corrode and need replacing. But replacing an entire system of galvanized pipe is a big, time-consuming job. Remember that with galvanized iron, you cannot simply unscrew a middle section of piping without first disassembling the entire run.

Occasionally, however, galvanized pipe will corrode in just a small area. How do you replace the damaged section without removing a whole run of piping? Simple. Use a three-piece union. The union will allow you to sidestep the laborious job of disassembling an entire run of pipe.

When shopping for replacement pipe, specify the interior diameter (ID) of the pipe you need. Prethreaded pipes, called nipples, are available in lengths up to 1 ft. or longer. For longer runs, have the store cut and thread the pipe to your dimensions. You can also thread your own by following the steps outlined on the next page.

One warning: Galvanized iron pipe, which has a silver color, is sometimes confused with "black iron" pipe. Black iron pipe is used only for gas lines and will corrode shut very quickly if used to carry water.

GALVANIZED PIPE FITTINGS

(A) union; (B) reducing coupling; (C) reducing tee; (D) 45° elbow; (E) hex bushing; (F) square head plug; (G) coupling; (H) tee; (I) 90° elbow; (J) 90° reducing elbow; (K) 90° street elbow; (L) cross connector; (M) cap.

Lubing & sealing mechanical joints

Pipe joint compound and Teflon tape are each used to lubricate, seal and protect the joints on pipe threads. Pipe joint compound comes in tubes, cans or sticks. Some pipe joint compound contains Teflon, which can be used on PVC and other plastic pipe. Often, the choice comes down to convenience. Tape is considered easier for a do-it-yourselfer, while pipe joint compound usually costs less.

HOW TO REPLACE A SECTION OF GALVANIZED PIPE

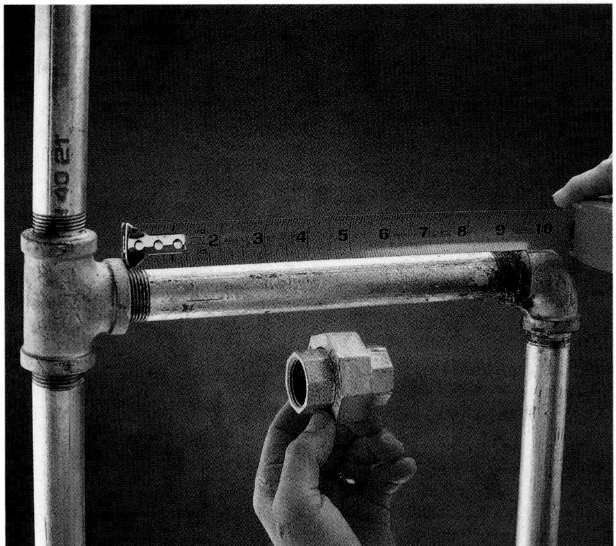

1 Measure the length of replacement pipe you will need. Make certain to include ½ in. for each threaded end that inserts into a fitting. However, subtract the width of the union from the measurements. When assembled, the union and replacement pipe must equal the length of the section being removed.

2 Cut through the old galvanized pipe with a hacksaw or reciprocating saw fitted with a metal-cutting blade.

3 Remove the corroded pipe with a pipe wrench. If the fitting is stubborn, grasp the fitting with a second pipe wrench. If the joint still won't loosen, heat it with a propane torch for five to 10 seconds, making certain not to ignite any nearby materials. Once the fitting is removed, clean the pipe threads with a wire brush.

4 To remove corroded fittings, use two wrenches. Face the jaws in opposite directions and use one wrench to remove the fitting while the other wrench holds the pipe in place.

5 To attach a new fitting, apply pipe joint compound on the threaded ends of all pipes and nipples. Screw the new fitting onto the pipe and tighten with two pipe wrenches. Leave the fitting about ⅛-turn out of alignment to permit installation of the union.

HOW TO REPLACE A SECTION OF GALVANIZED PIPE (CONT.)

6 Attach a new pipe, or nipple, to the fitting. Apply pipe joint compound or strips of Teflon tape to all threads. Tighten with a pipe wrench. Wrap the tape counterclockwise to keep it from unwinding as you thread the pipe into the fitting.

7 Slide a ring nut onto the installed nipple. Then screw a hubbed union nut onto the nipple. Tighten with a pipe wrench.

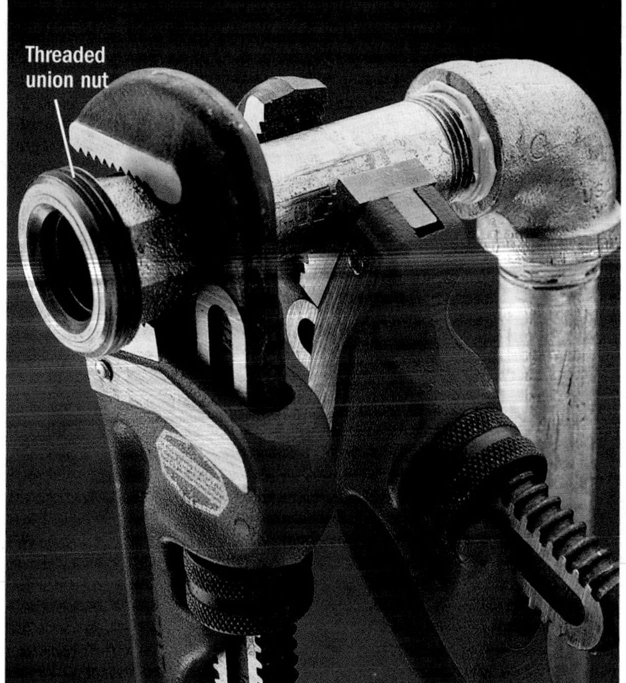

8 Attach the second nipple to the opposite fitting. Tighten with a pipe wrench. Then screw the threaded union nut onto this nipple. Hold the nipple with a second wrench while attaching the union nut.

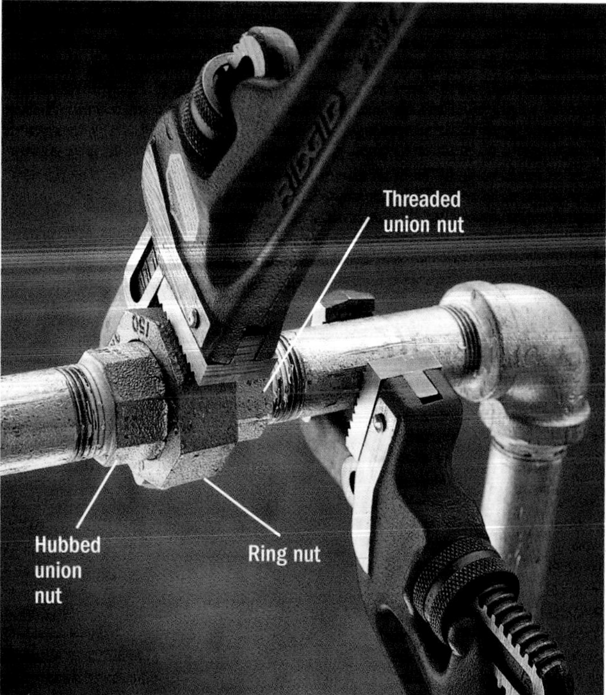

9 Align the pipes so the lip of the hubbed union nut fits inside the threaded union nut. Tighten the connection by screwing the ring nut onto the threaded union nut.

HOW TO THREAD GALVANIZED PIPE

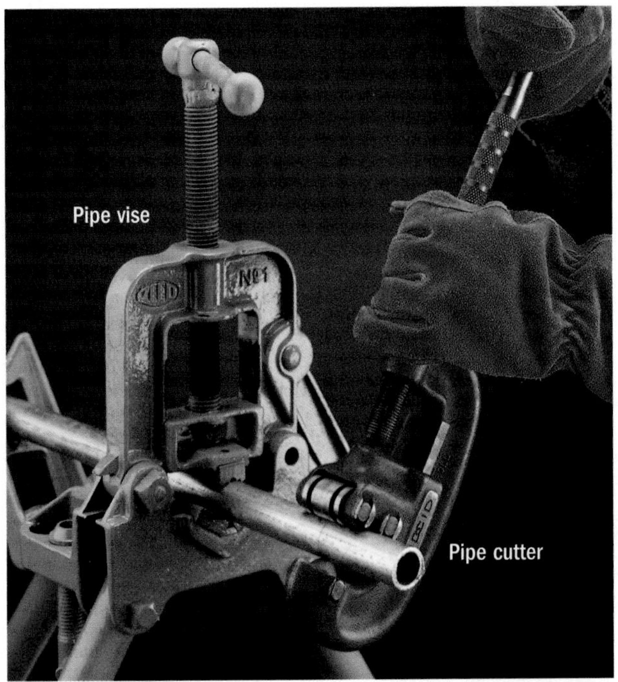

1 Before cutting, mark the length you want. Then, secure the pipe in the pipe vise (pipe fitting tools can be rented at most rental centers). Tighten a pipe cutter on the mark and rotate the cutter first one direction, then the other. Tighten the cutter every two rotations until the pipe is cut all the way through.

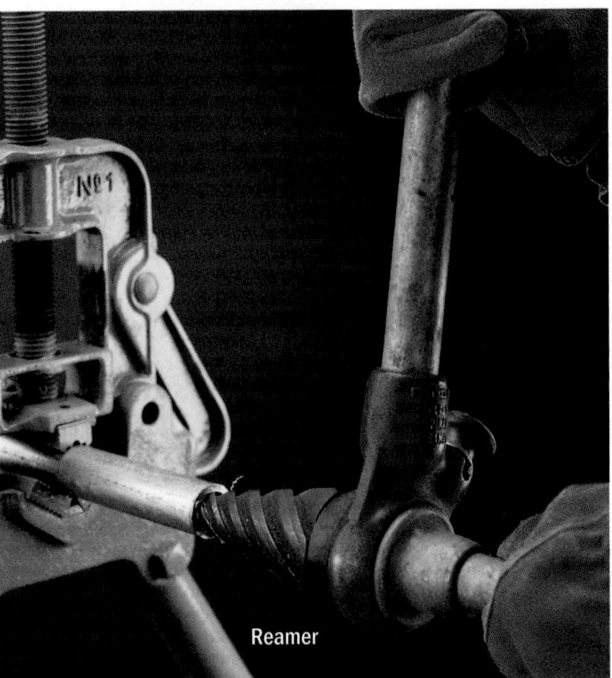

2 A reamer will remove burrs and jagged edges inside the pipe. Simply insert the nose of the reamer into the pipe, push and turn clockwise. Put a catch basin under the work area to collect pipe shavings and oil as you work.

3 To thread the pipe, slip the head of the threader over the end of the pipe. Push down on the threader and tighten it until the threader's head, also called the die, bites into the pipe. At that point stop tightening the tool and turn it clockwise around the pipe. Apply lots of cutting oil while turning. Keep turning the threader until the cutting head has cleared the pipe by at least one full turn. If the threader sticks, metal chips are probably blocking progress. In that case, rotate the tool backwards slightly and blow the chips away.

4 When done threading, remove the threader and clean the newly cut threads with a stiff wire brush.

Specialty Pipe & Fittings

PEX TUBING AND FITTINGS

Cross-linked polyethylene or PEX is fast becoming the tubing of choice for hot and cold plumbing supply lines. This flexible tubing is popular for several reasons. First, it is fast and easy to connect. PEX lines are connected with clamp, crimp or push-on fittings. Second, because PEX does not require any heat or an open flame to connect, there are no fire hazards in the installation. Third, PEX is flexible, making it easier to route through a house and requiring far fewer fittings. Finally, whole-house PEX systems utilize a central manifold which diverts the water to designated water lines, much like the breaker box in an electrical system.

A crimping tool is used to squeeze the crimp ring that secures the line to the fitting.

PEX fittings are available in several styles, similar to the fittings used with other types of supply line tubing.

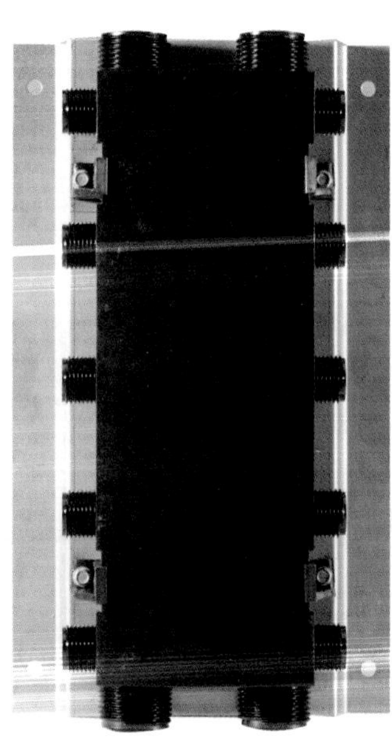

A manifold in a PEX whole-house system acts much like a breaker box in a home electrical system. It diverts the main water supply to the various branch lines throughout the house. Some manifolds feature shutoff valves that allow you to turn off the water to individual lines.

POLYETHYLENE CONNECTIONS

Polyethylene (PE) is soft, synthetic rubber tubing that's used primarily for light-duty outdoor plumbing projects, such as installing an underground sprinkler system. The sections of PE tubing are joined using rigid plastic connectors with flared grip rings at the ends. The connectors are simply slipped into the ends of the PE tubes **(see photo 1)**, then secured with a small hose clamp **(see photo 2)**.

PVC Pipe & Fittings

As a building material, PVC pipe is inexpensive, easy to work, lightweight and relatively forgiving. PVC and ABS are rigid forms of plastic pipe that are used almost exclusively for drain and vent systems.

PVC DRAIN & VENT FITTINGS

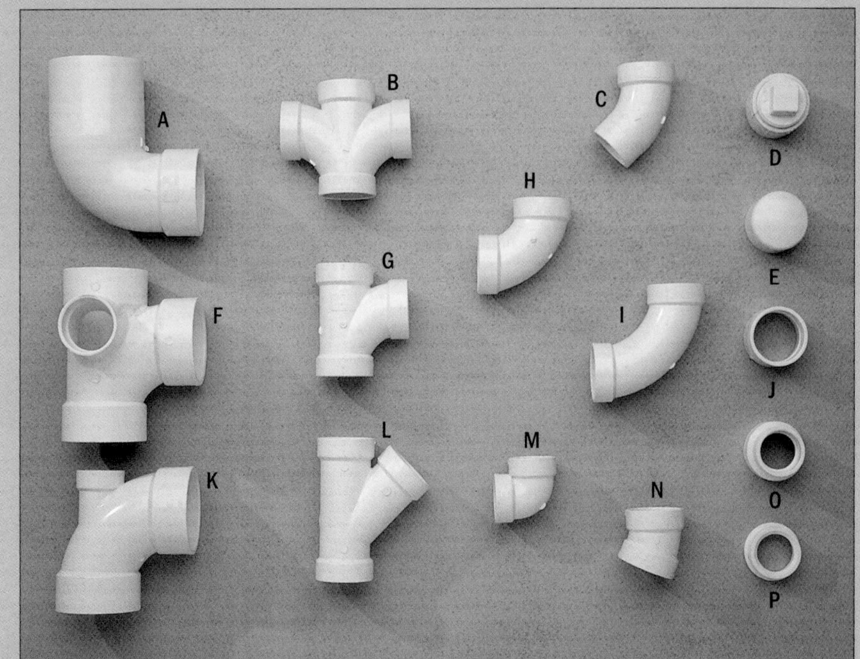

(A) closet bend; (B) waste cross; (C) 45° reducing elbow; (D) cleanout plug; (E) cap; (F) waste tee with side inlet; (G) waste/sanitary tee; (H) 90° elbow; (I) long-sweep 90° elbow; (J) coupling; (K) 90° elbow with side inlet; (L) wye fitting; (M) vent elbow; (N) 22° elbow; (O) reducer; (P) reducing bushing.

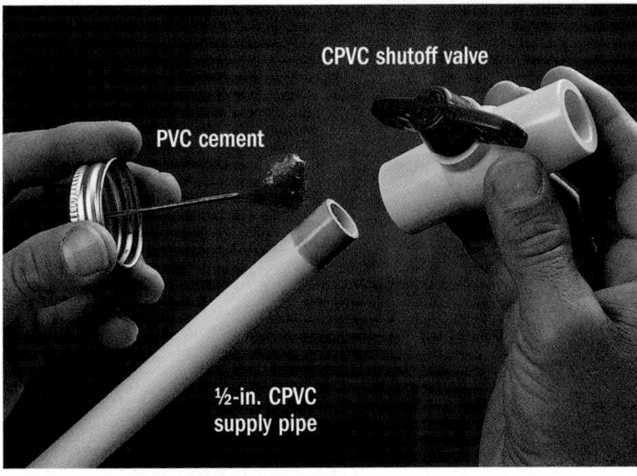

CPVC supply pipe growing in code acceptance

Most water supply pipe used to hook up plumbing fixtures has been copper. CPVC (chlorinated polyvinyl chloride) supply pipe has been around for some time, but many local codemakers have been reluctant to accept it. CPVC has been found to be a reliable supply pipe material that's easy to work and also has better insulating power than other materials. It's installed using the same solvent welding process as PVC (see page 120). Check with your local building inspection department to find out if CPVC supply pipe is allowed in your area.

Materials for chemically welding PVC

When working with PVC pipe, make certain you use the correct materials. Solvent and primer should be labeled for PVC pipe. Colored solvent and primer allow you to inspect more easily to make sure all parts are coated. Sandcloth or emery paper is used to smooth rough edges. Primer helps degloss the pipe's slick surface, ensuring a good seal. Solvents and primers are toxic and flammable. Provide good ventilation and keep these products away from heat.

OPTIONS FOR CUTTING PLASTIC PIPE

Plastic tubing cutters

A PVC ratchet cutter will make short work of smaller PVC pipes. This tool is especially useful if you have a large variety of plastic pipes to cut.

Power miter saw

If you have a lot of plastic pipe to cut—and you want to make neat cuts very quickly—use a power miter saw fitted with a blade that has a high number of teeth per inch (see pages 30 to 31).

PVC pipe saw

To cut PVC pipe by hand, a PVC pipe saw will give you better results than an ordinary hacksaw. Make certain to hold the pipe securely in a vise and keep the saw blade straight while cutting.

PREPARING PLASTIC PIPE FOR SOLVENT-GLUING

Trim away burrs created by cutting

PVC pipe must be smooth and free of burrs to ensure a watertight connection. Use a utility knife to slice off burrs from the edges of cuts.

Scuff and degloss mating surfaces of pipes

It's a good idea to lightly sand the outside of the pipe and the inside of the connection hub using sandcloth or emery paper before applying primer. Surfaces that are to be glued together should have a dull finish.

HOW TO SOLVENT-GLUE PLASTIC PIPE

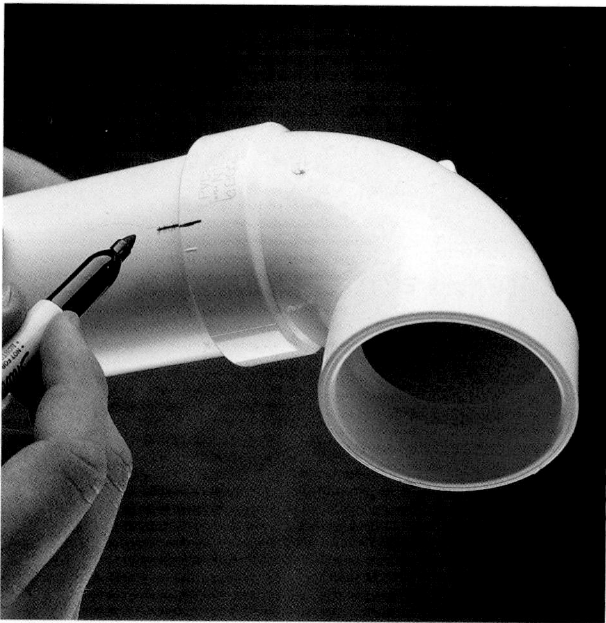

1 Cut the pipes to length and prepare the mating surfaces (see previous page). Fit the pipes and fittings together in the desired layout. Draw an alignment mark across each joint with a permanent marker.

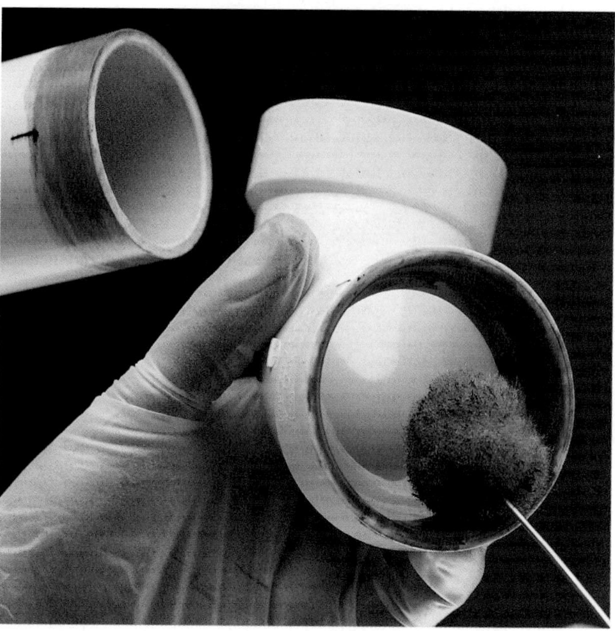

2 Apply PVC primer to the outside of the pipe and the inside of the connection hub or fitting. The primer is colored so you can see when full coverage has been achieved. Wear disposable gloves, and make sure the work area is adequately ventilated. Also be sure to read the directions and safety precautions on the labels of all products you'll be using.

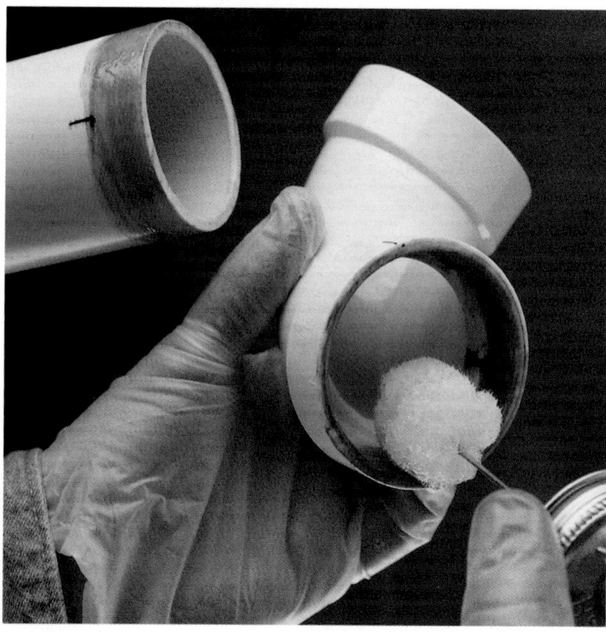

3 Apply a thick coat of solvent glue to the outside of the pipe and a thin coat on the inside of the connection hub.

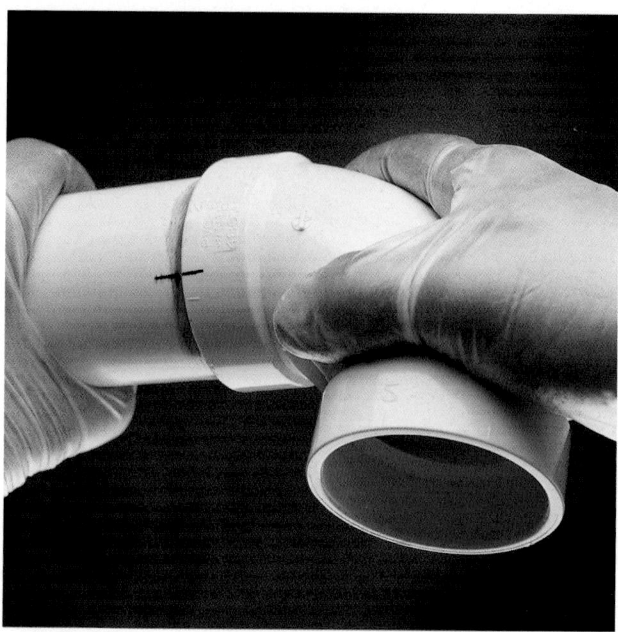

4 Quickly slip the pipes and fittings together so the alignment mark you drew across the joint is about 2 in. off center, then twist the pipes into alignment. This will ensure the solvent is spread evenly. The solvent will set in about 30 seconds, so don't waste time. Hold the pipes steady for another 20 seconds, then wipe away excess solvent with a rag. Don't disturb the joint for 30 minutes.

Cast Iron Drain Stack

Most older houses, and even some newer ones, have a main stack made out of cast iron. Cutting into the stack to add an auxiliary drain or vent line can be difficult and dangerous. This sequence shows the correct way to support the main stack, cut out a section, and insert a drain or vent connector fitting. Cast iron cutters can be rented at most rental centers.

1 Cast iron drain stacks must be braced with a riser clamp at each floor the stack passes through. Make sure the bracing exists, then mark the location for the new connector—the cutout should be sized to the height of the connector, plus 4 to 6 in. of pipe that should be solvent-welded to each end of the connector so it's the same diameter as the stack. Install a riser clamp about 6 in. above the top of the cutout area. Attach cleats to the wall studs to support the riser clamp.

2 Cut out the section of the main stack with a cast iron cutter (sometimes called a pipe breaker). The tool, equipped with cutting wheels on a heavy-linked chain, wraps around the pipe. Ratcheting the cutter wrench handle up and down tightens the chain until the pipe snaps. For safety, it's not a bad idea to support the section to be removed with a riser clamp before cutting it. Make the upper cut first. Remove the waste section carefully.

3 Slip a banded coupling onto each end of the stack. Slip a neoprene sleeve over the pipe ends. Fold the sleeve out of the way.

4 Insert the connector into the opening, making sure the inlets are oriented exactly as you want them to be.

5 Fold the sleeves over the connector, making sure the ridge inside each sleeve is flush with the joint. Tighten the screw clamps.

Plumbing Illustrations

TOILETS

Float ball flush & fill mechanism

Most older toilets in use today employ this familiar system for flushing and filling the toilet tank. A float ball is connected to a plunger with a metal arm. When the toilet is flushed, the float ball sinks down to the lower water level, then gradually returns upward as the water level rises. When the tank is full, the float arm depresses a plunger on top of the ballcock, causing the inlet valve to close when the tank is full of water.

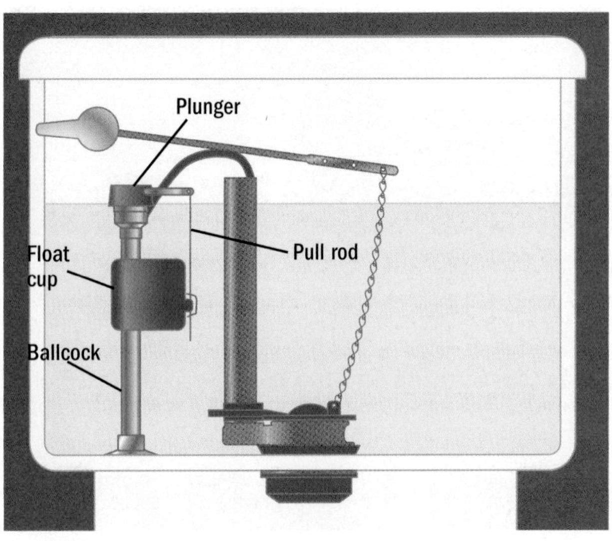

Float cup flush & fill mechanism

This variation of the float ball mechanism is becoming increasingly popular because it's more reliable than the float ball system. The basic principle is the same, but instead of a detached float, a plastic float cup mounted on the shank of the ballcock moves up and down with the tank water level. A pull rod connected directly to the plunger controls the flow of water into the tank. It also comes with an anti-siphon valve, which is now required by code for new construction toilet installations.

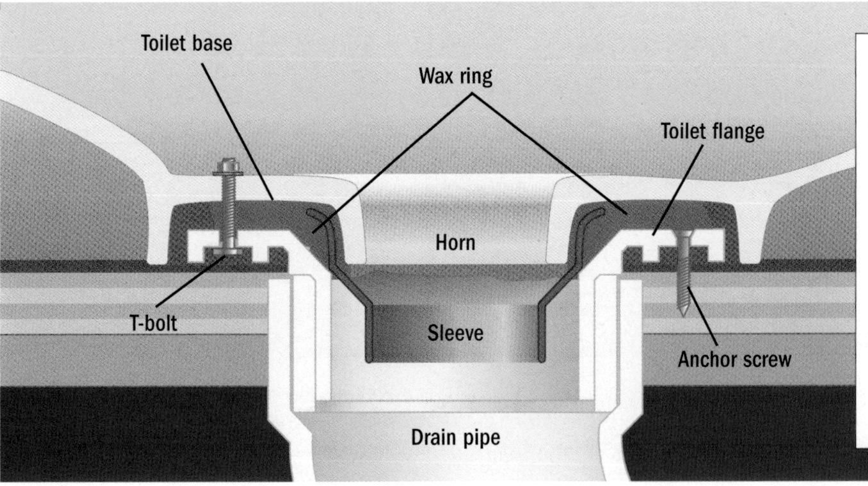

Cross-section of toilet mounting system

The toilet is bolted down to the floor so the "horn" where waste exits is directly over the floor drain opening. A compressible wax ring seals the joint between the base of the toilet and the floor drain opening.

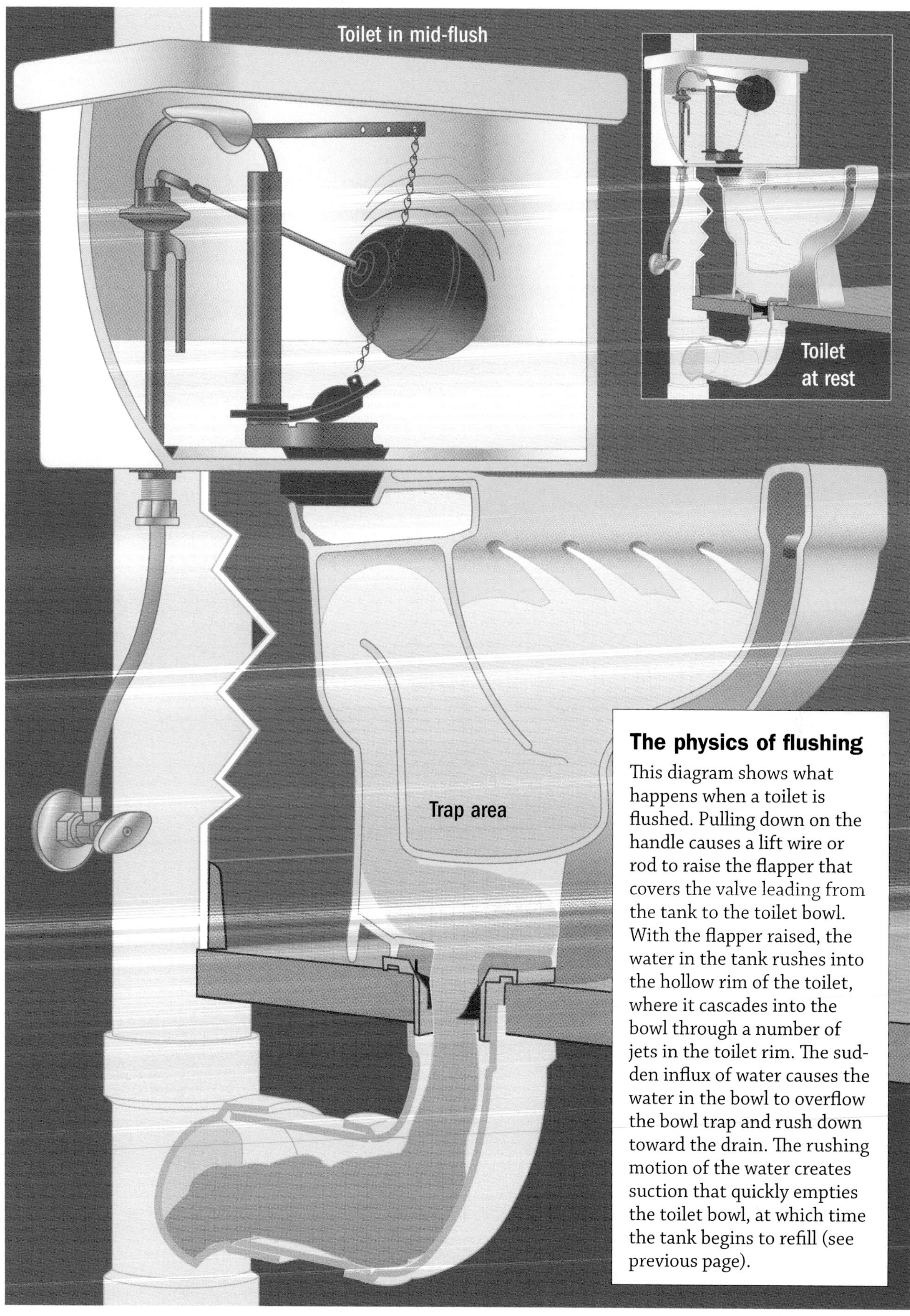

The physics of flushing

This diagram shows what happens when a toilet is flushed. Pulling down on the handle causes a lift wire or rod to raise the flapper that covers the valve leading from the tank to the toilet bowl. With the flapper raised, the water in the tank rushes into the hollow rim of the toilet, where it cascades into the bowl through a number of jets in the toilet rim. The sudden influx of water causes the water in the bowl to overflow the bowl trap and rush down toward the drain. The rushing motion of the water creates suction that quickly empties the toilet bowl, at which time the tank begins to refill (see previous page).

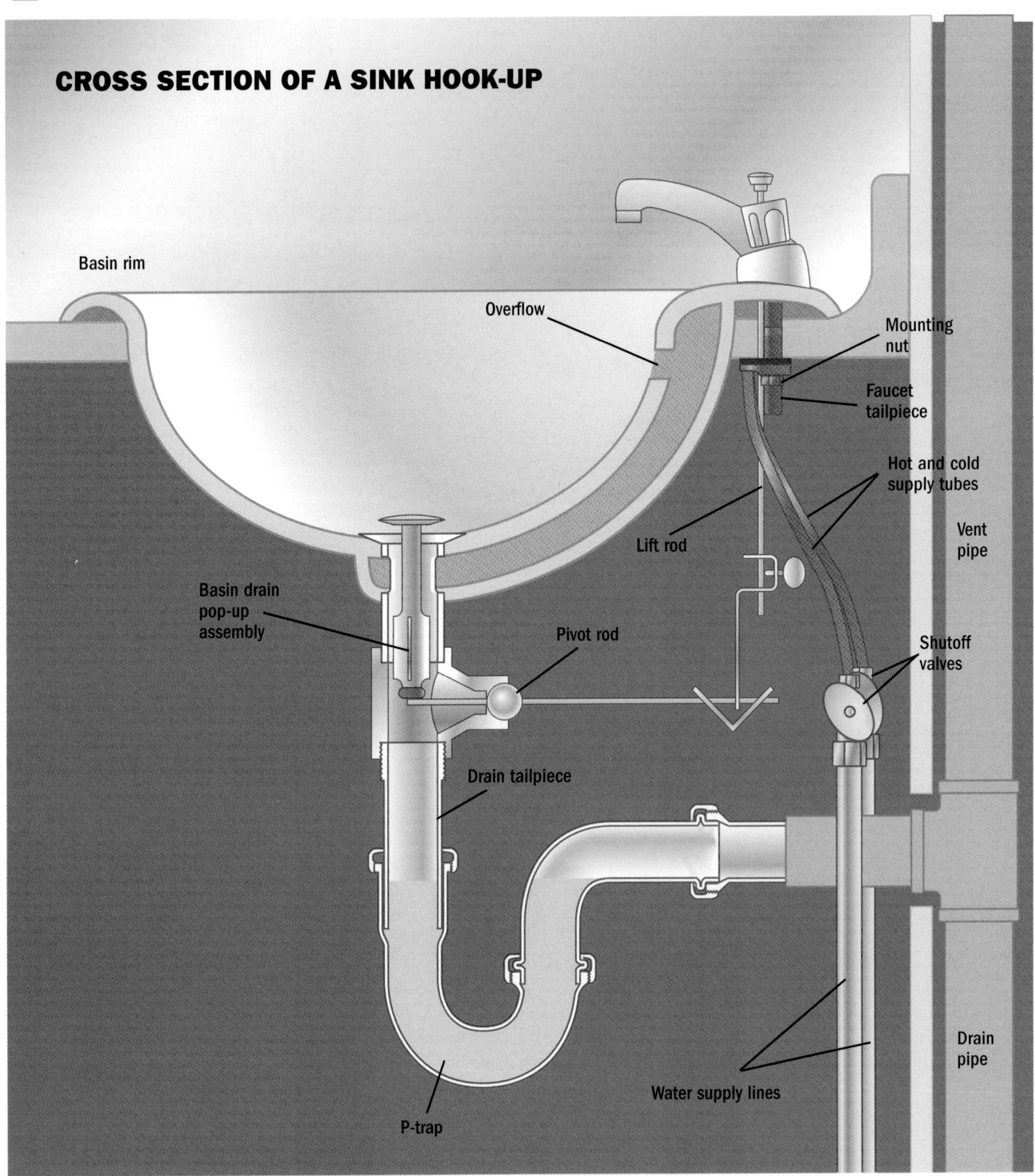
CROSS SECTION OF A SINK HOOK-UP
Basin rim
Overflow
Mounting nut
Faucet tailpiece
Hot and cold supply tubes
Vent pipe
Lift rod
Basin drain pop-up assembly
Pivot rod
Shutoff valves
Drain tailpiece
Drain pipe
Water supply lines
P-trap

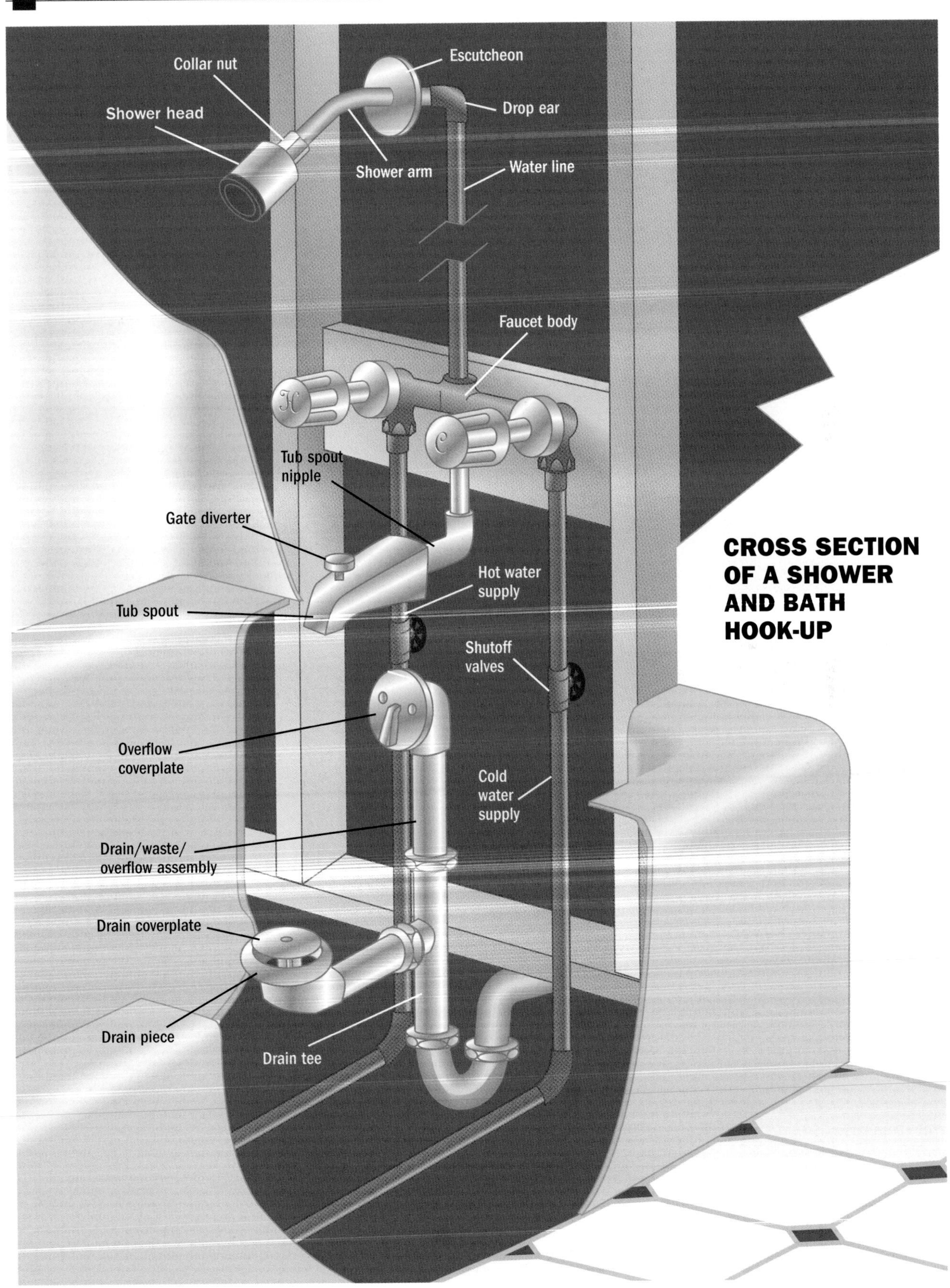

CROSS SECTION OF A SHOWER AND BATH HOOK-UP

Vacuum breaker required on sillcocks

Vacuum breakers should be installed on all outdoor hose bibs to prevent cross-contamination of your home drinking supply. Cross-contamination can occur if the water pressure drops suddenly, creating negative pressure. A broken water main, for example, can sometimes produce backflow. If an outdoor hose is turned on and submerged into a muddy pool, the backflow can suck the contaminated water into your home plumbing system. A vacuum breaker prevents backflows. Most Building Codes now require vacuum breakers in new construction.

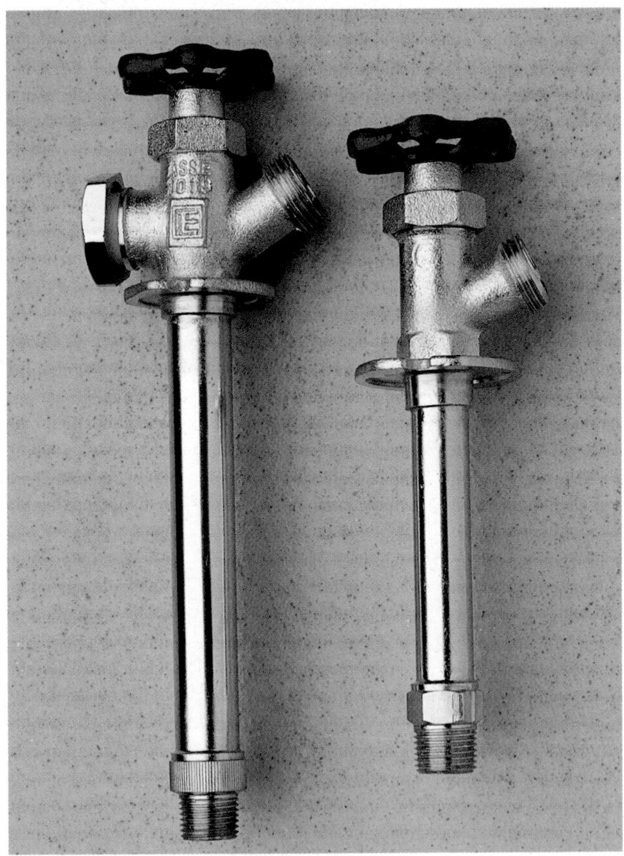

Frost-proof sillcocks

To prevent the water supply leads for sillcocks from freezing and bursting, homeowners in colder climates should install a frost-proof sillcock. These devices are equipped with shutoff gates that are located far enough back into the supply lead that they stop he water flow inside the house. Some are equipped with vacuum breakers.

Wiring

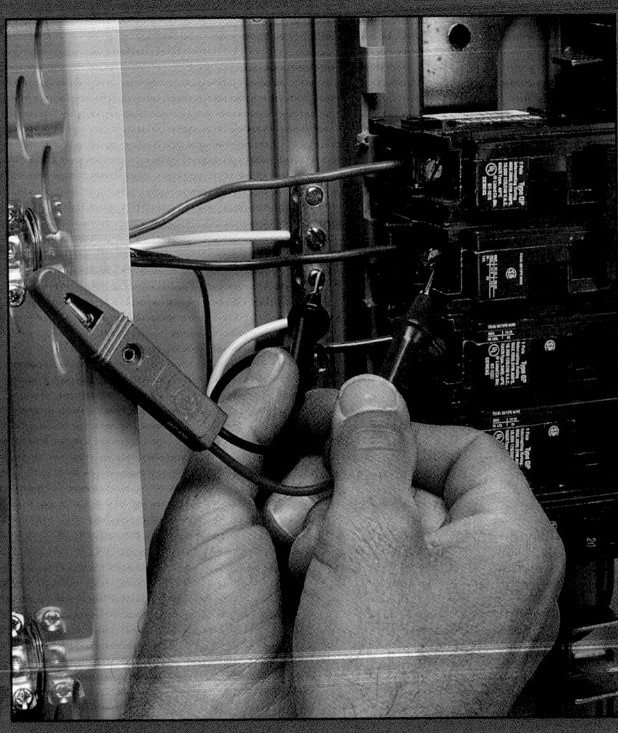

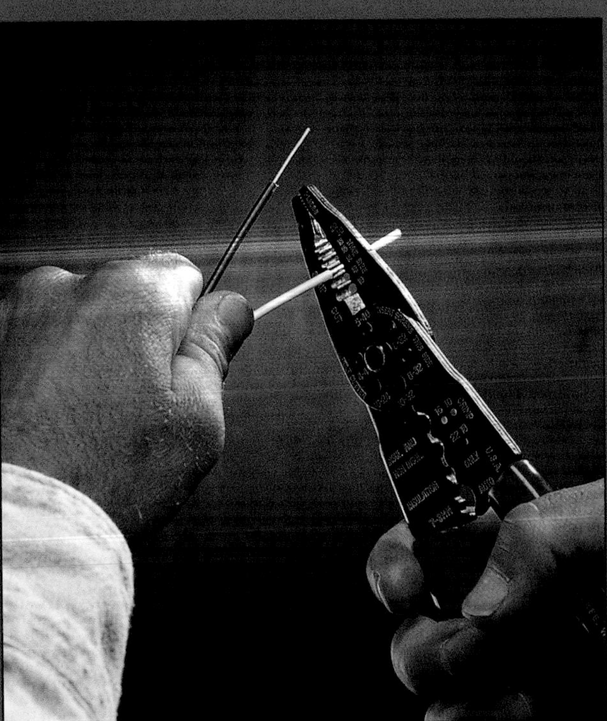

Wiring Basics

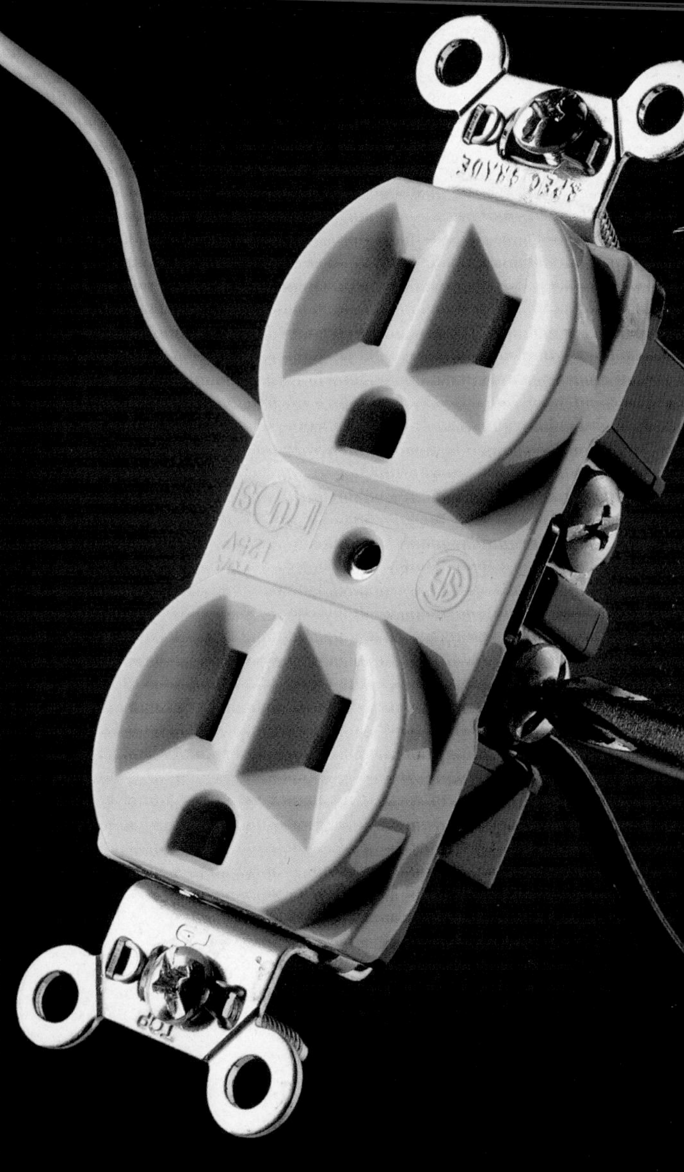

Installing wiring is not difficult. If you can use a tape measure, swing a hammer and operate a portable drill, you're halfway there. But there are professional techniques for working with wiring tools and materials that will simplify your work. It also is important to know proper installation requirements so your wiring project meets electrical code requirements.

The tools and skills information in this section shows you techniques and installation requirements for working with wiring materials used in the most common wiring projects. You see which types of electrical boxes to use and where to place them. Then you see how to install plastic sheathed cable, metal or plastic conduit, or armored cable. The best methods for connecting wires to switches, receptacles and fixtures also are demonstrated.

Tips are shown for installing wiring within existing rooms. You learn how to use a fishtape and run cable within a finished wall. You see how to create a wiring path behind baseboard and other trim. A basic ceiling fixture installation is shown, as well as how to replace a ceiling unit within a recessed fixture. Installing a vent fan and the special requirements for installing a ceiling fan also are shown. Plus, see how to work with three-way switches, GFCI receptacles, and how to install a new circuit breaker in the main service panel.

This information will help you do wiring projects that keep your home comfortable and functional. And you will save money doing the the work yourself.

ELECTRICAL CODES

The information found on these pages conforms to the National Electrical Code requirements. These requirements ensure safe, durable wiring installations that will best serve your needs. But your wiring project may have additional requirements not covered by the Code. Also, the Code requirements in your community may differ from those in the National Code. Local Code always takes precedence in these situations. Always check with your local electrical inspector to make certain your project will comply with local standards. If your wiring project is part of a larger remodeling or building project that includes plumbing work, remember that plumbing has the right-of-way. Always do the plumbing installation before beginning any wiring work in that area.

ELECTRICAL EQUATIONS & DATA

- Wattage divided by voltage = Amperage
- Kilowatts × 1000 = Wattage

- Here is a sample calculation of circuit load:
  Circuit #3 (non-dedicated)
  Circuit Information: Voltage = 120, Amperage = 20

APPLIANCE	WATTAGE/VOLTAGE	AMPERAGE
Microwave	800/120	= 6.7
Toaster	1050/120	= 8.75
Exhaust Fan	100/120	= .83
Total Load on Circuit #3	**= 16.28 Amps**	

- Typical watt/amp ratings for household appliances:

Toaster: 1050/8.75	**Microwave: 800/6.7**
Refrigerator: 600/5	**Dishwasher:1500/12.5**
Air conditioner: 2000/8.3	**Computer: 600/6**
Circular saw: 1200/10	**Table saw : 2160/18**

CODE SPECIFICATIONS FOR ROOM WIRING

Code for general living areas

Always check with your local electrical inspector for regulations applying to your work.

One 15-amp or 20-amp basic lighting and receptacle circuit should supply every 600 sq. ft. of living space. Every room should have at least one light fixture controlled by a switch located at the entryway. Receptacles should be spaced no more than 12 ft. apart, though closer spacing may be more useful. Any separate wall surface more than 24 in. wide, such as a wall between doorways, must have a receptacle.

Receptacle boxes should be installed 12 in. above the finished floor surface, and switch boxes are typically at 48 in. Special situations, such as making switches wheelchair accessible, are allowed; check with your inspector. Route cable to the receptacles at 20 in.

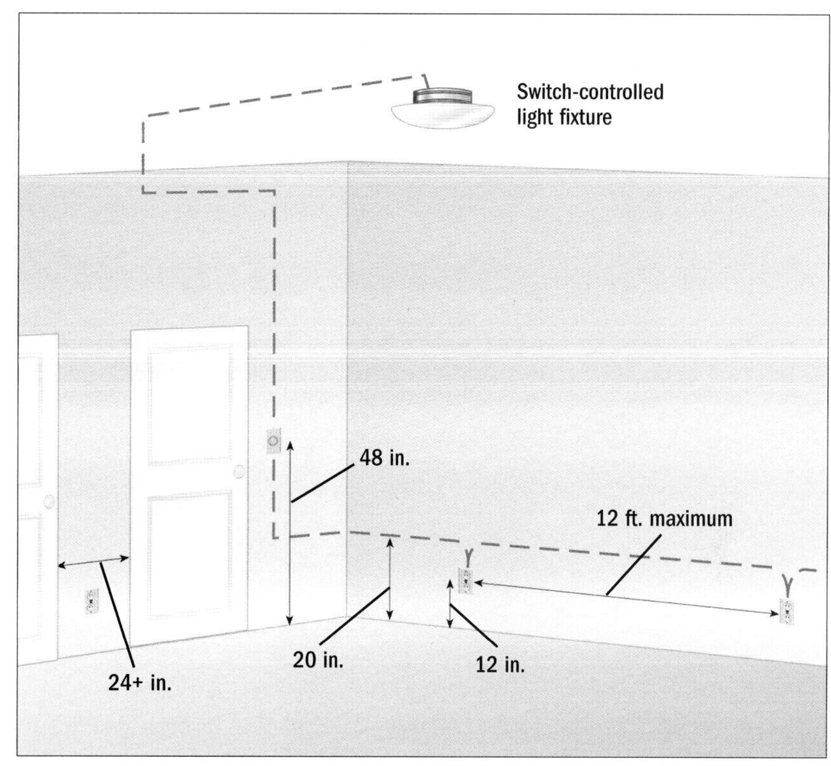

Code for kitchens & baths

Basic Code requirements for general living areas (above) apply to the kitchen and bath, but these rooms also have special requirements. Check with your local inspector regarding regulations applying to your work.

The switch-controlled light fixture must be ceiling-mounted. The switch should be on the latch side of the entryway. In the bathroom, no switch should be within 3 ft. of a bathtub or shower.

All accessible receptacles must be GFCI-protected. Receptacles installed above countertops should be no more than 4 ft. apart, though closer spacing in high-use areas may be helpful. Any separate countertop space more than 24 in. wide, such as countertop between a stove and refrigerator, must have a receptacle.

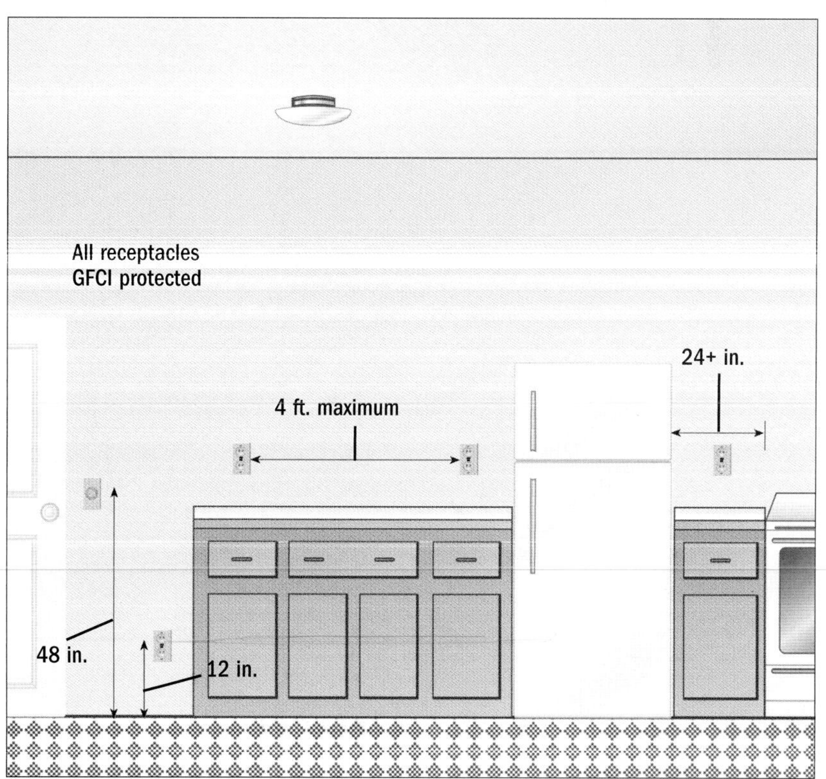

SAFETY NOTES:

- When unscrewing a fuse to remove power from a circuit, never loosen the fuse and leave it in the screw-in holder. It is possible for the fuse to vibrate back in and make contact, re-energizing the circuit. Instead, remove the fuse completely from its holder and set it aside (photo, left).
- If you have thrown the breaker off to work on a circuit and are afraid that someone might accidentally throw the circuit back on again, lock-outs (using a padlock) are available to lock the breaker in the OFF position. Lockouts can be found at most large electrical distributors.

THE POWER OF LISTENING

You can save yourself a few trips up and down stairs to see if the breaker you tripped was the right one for the circuit you're trying to shut off. Simply plug a radio into one of the receptacles in the circuit and set it to fairly high volume. Go to the service panel and flip breakers until you hear the radio stop playing. Then, record the information on your panel index so you don't have to test again.

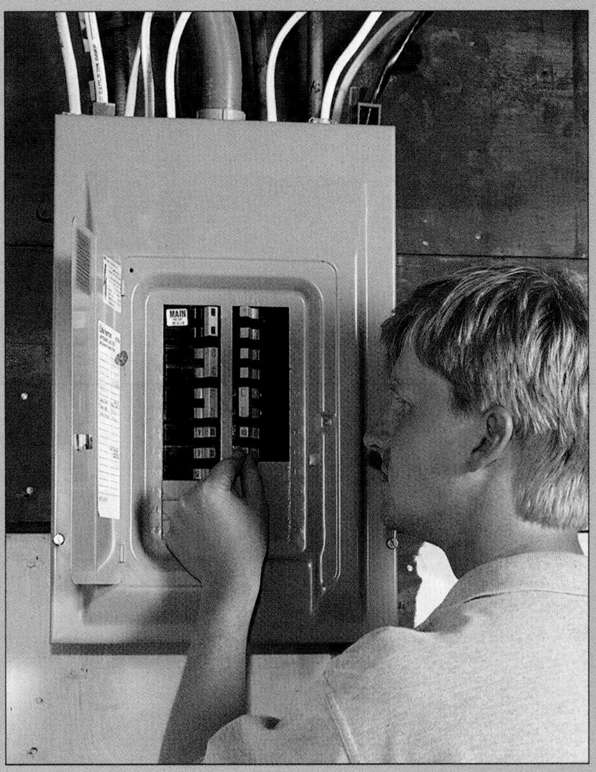

HOW TO TEST FOR ELECTRICAL CURRENT

At a receptacle: Turn off power at the main panel. Insert the circuit tester probes into the receptacle slots. Check both halves of the receptacle. If the tester glows, power is still present. Turn off the appropriate circuit and test again.

At a switch: Turn off power at the main panel. Carefully pull the switch out of the box, touching only the mounting strap. Touch one circuit tester probe to the grounded metal box or bare copper grounding wire. Touch the other probe to each screw terminal. If tester glows, power is present. Turn off another circuit and test again.

At the main panel: Turn off the main breaker but leave all other breakers on. Touch one circuit tester probe to the neutral bus bar. Touch the other probe to each terminal on a double-pole breaker (but not the main breaker). If tester glows, power is still present. Make sure main breaker is off and test again. NOTE: Wires to the main breaker terminal are always 'hot', even when the main breaker is shut off. Use care when working near them.

At wire connections: Turn off power at the main panel. Remember that more than one circuit may pass through a box. Remove the box cover. Insert one circuit tester probe into the wire connector for the black wires and the other probe into the wire connector for the white wires. If the tester glows, power is still present. Turn off the appropriate circuit and test again.

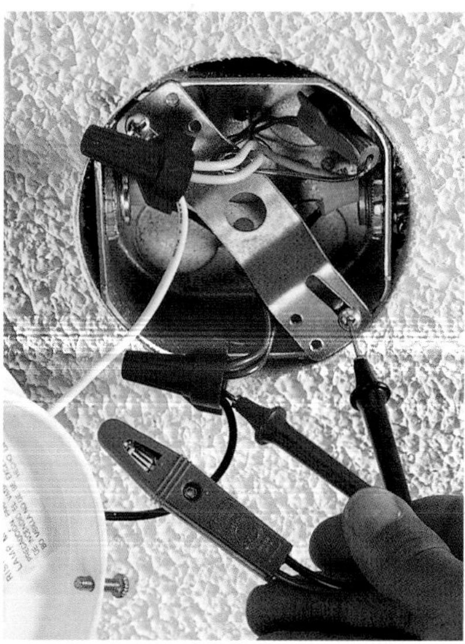

At a light fixture: Turn off power at the main panel. Remove the globe, light bulb and fixture mounting screws and pull the fixture away from the box. Touch one circuit tester probe to the green grounding screw or bare copper grounding wire. Insert the other probe into each fixture wire connector. If the tester glows, power is still present. Turn off the appropriate circuit and test again.

IS A RECEPTACLE WIRED CORRECTLY?

Use a receptacle tester to check that a receptacle is correctly wired. Insert the tester prongs into each half of the receptacle. Glowing lights indicate whether the receptacle is properly grounded and if the hot and neutral wires are attached to the correct terminals.

Working with Cable

CHOOSING ELECTRICAL CABLE

CABLE TYPE	APPLICATIONS
NM (nonmetallic)	The primary type of cable used for most non-exposed interior installations. It features two or three vinyl insulated wires as well as a bare ground wire. Modern NM features vinyl outer sheathing, which provides better durability than the previously rubberized fabric sheathed version.
UF (underground feeder)	Designed for underground use, the vinyl sheathing of this cable is molded directly to the insulated wires as well as a bare ground.
Armored cable	Generally used for short exposed runs in interior situations such as basements. There is no separate ground wire because the flexible metal sheathing not only protects the wires but also acts as the ground. A bonding strip ensures a good grounding path.
Metal conduit	Provides excellent protection in exposed wiring situations. Conduit must be cut, bent and connected with specific fittings before the wiring is pulled through.

Select the proper type of cable for the task

Vinyl-sheathed cable is classified as either NM (nonmetallic) or UF (underground feeder). NM cable can be used only for indoor projects in dry locations. UF cable is intended for damp or wet locations and can be buried directly in the ground. Both types of cable are identified by the gauge (size) and number of insulated wires they contain. The bare copper grounding wire is not counted, but is included in the labeling as "with ground", or "G". For example, a cable labeled 14/3 G contains three insulated 14-gauge wires plus the bare grounding wire. The gauge indicates what level of current (ampacity) the wire can safely carry, which determines its use in a wiring project.

HOW TO STRIP NM (NONMETALLIC) CABLE

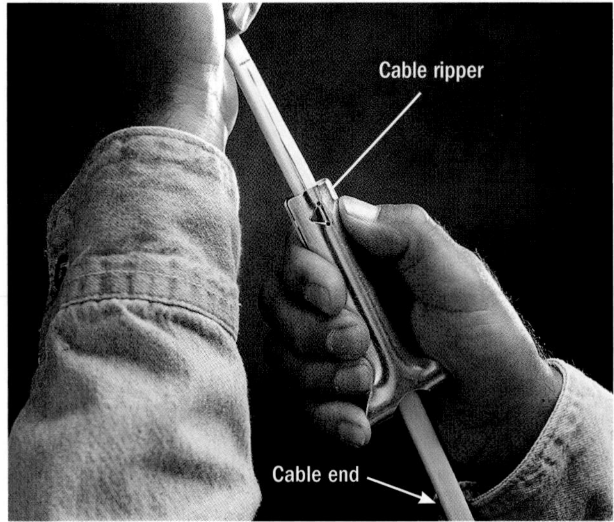

1 Use a cable ripper to cut through the cable sheathing without damaging the wires inside. This works best on cable containing two wires with ground. Insert the cable through the ripper, then firmly press the arms together, forcing the cutting tip into the sheathing. Pull the ripper to the end of the cable to cut through the sheathing.

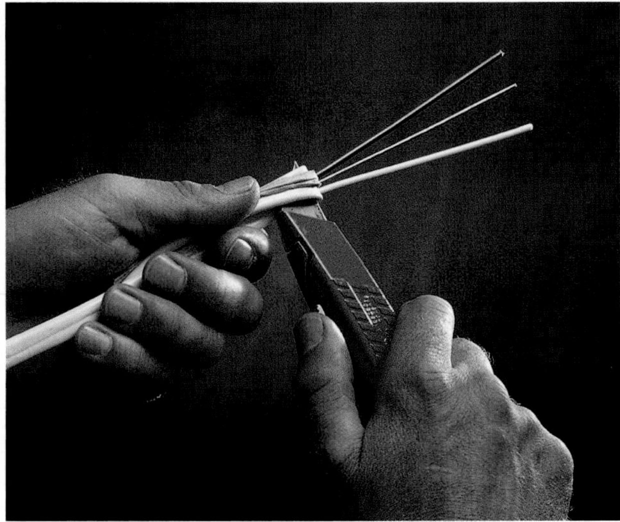

2 After cutting through the cable sheathing, peel the sheathing and the paper wrapper back, then cut them off with a utility knife or wire cutters. Be careful that you don't nick the wire insulation as you do this.

WORKING WITH 3-WIRE CABLE

Three-wire cable, because it's heavier and stiffer, can be more difficult to install than 2-wire cable, particularly if it contains wires larger than 14-gauge. A helper will make pulling the cable over longer distances much easier. Where possible, drill larger holes in the framing members, but only as large as necessary. For example, a ¾-in. hole is adequate for 12-gauge, 3-wire with ground cable.

One 3-wire cable can carry two circuits from a double-pole breaker in the main service panel to a location some distance from the panel, such as a basement, attic or detached garage. This saves the time and cost of running two 2-wire cables to accomplish the same thing. At the first electrical box in this location the circuits can branch out from the 3-wire cable, using 2-wire cable.

Three-wire cable is used when creating two circuits with alternating receptacles. Use 3-wire cable between three-way switches to make connections to the three terminals found on each switch. Three-wire cable also is used for installation of 120/240 volt circuits.

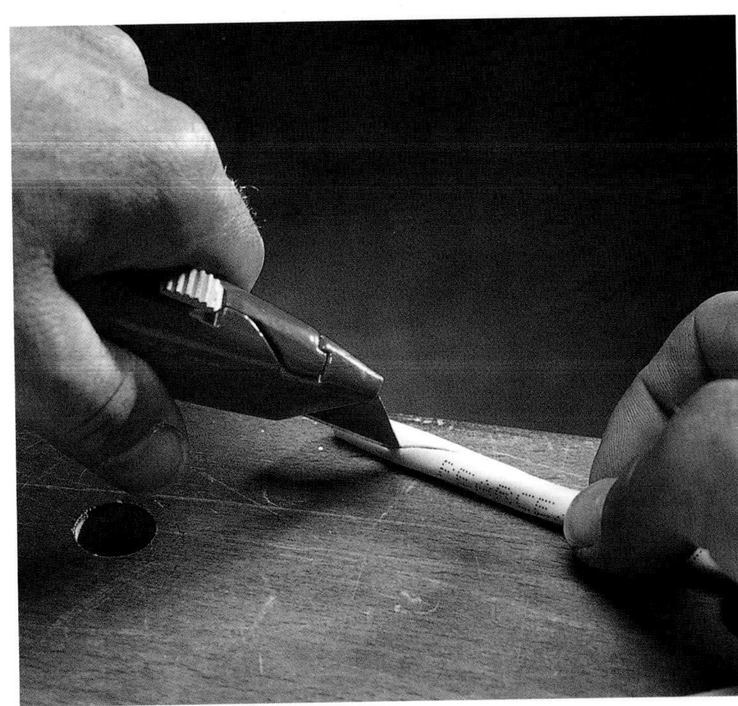

Cutting through sheathing on 3-wire cable with ground is more difficult because the wires spiral inside the sheathing. A utility knife may work better than a cable ripper to do this. You must follow the twist of the wires carefully with the knife so you don't damage the insulation on the individual wires. Once the sheathing is ripped, peel it and the paper wrappers back, then cut them off with a utility knife.

HOW TO STRIP UF (UNDERGROUND FEEDER) CABLE

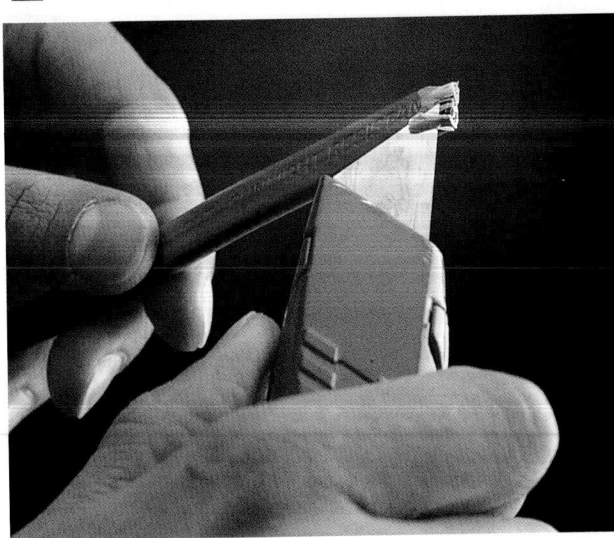

1 Use a utility knife to cut away about ½ in. of the solid sheathing from the wires at the cable tip. Don't worry if you cut into the insulation on the individual wires since these wire ends will be cut off later.

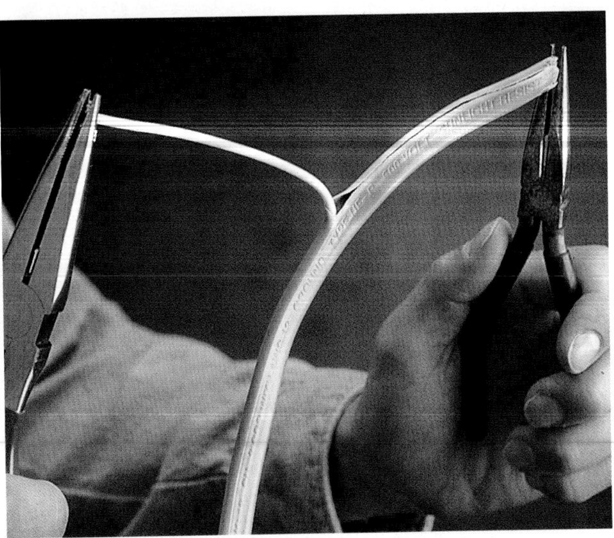

2 Grip one wire tip with a needlenose pliers and use another pliers to firmly hold the cable. Pull the pliers apart to rip the individual wire out of the solid sheathing until you have about 10 in. exposed. Repeat this action for the other individual wires. Cut off the empty sheathing with a utility knife or wire cutters.

STRIPPING INDIVIDUAL WIRES

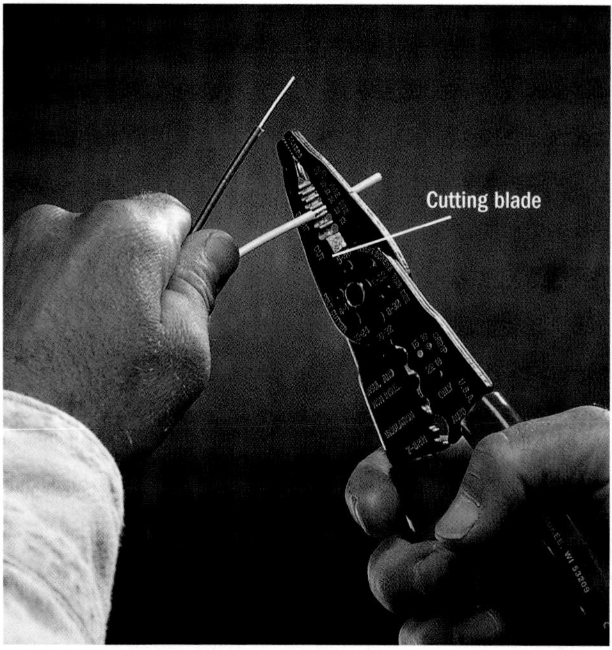

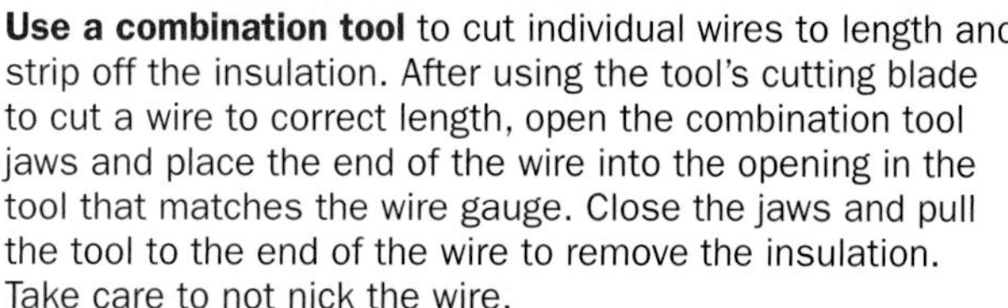

Use a combination tool to cut individual wires to length and strip off the insulation. After using the tool's cutting blade to cut a wire to correct length, open the combination tool jaws and place the end of the wire into the opening in the tool that matches the wire gauge. Close the jaws and pull the tool to the end of the wire to remove the insulation. Take care to not nick the wire.

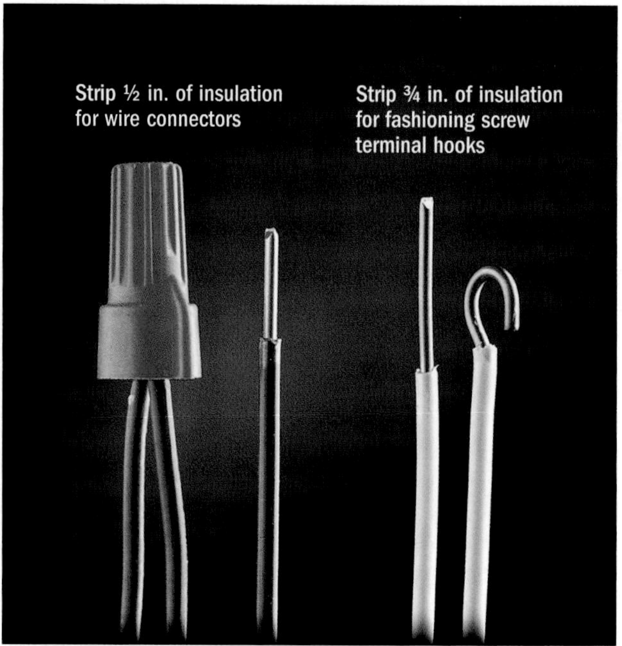

When stripping individual wires, remove ½ in. of insulation if using a wire connector (left) or ¾ in. of insulation when you will make a hook to attach to a screw terminal. No bare wire should show beyond the bottom of the wire connector, and insulation should end at the screw terminal.

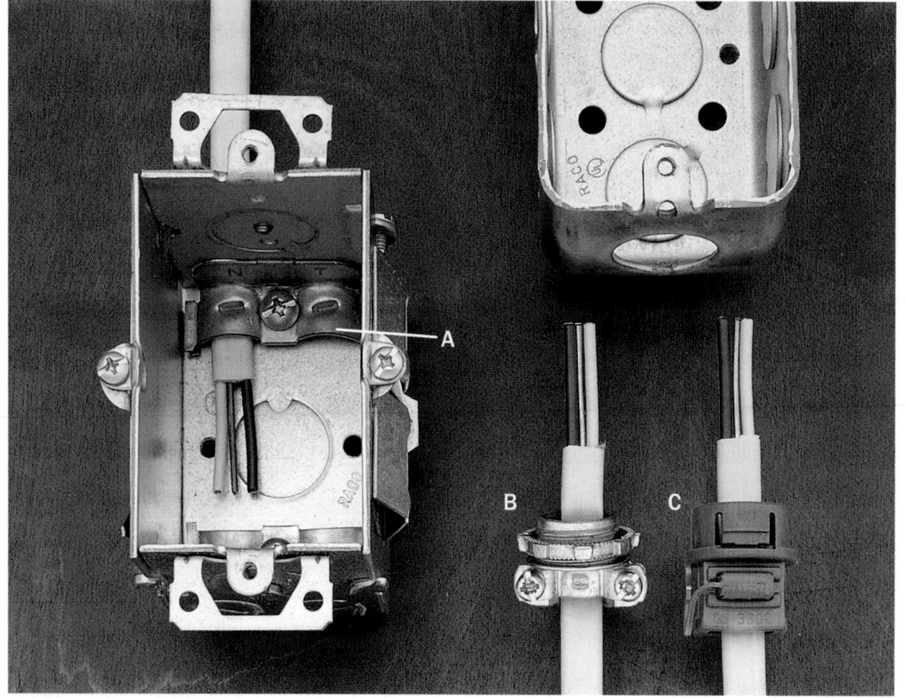

An internal cable clamp (A), shown on a metal remodeling box, makes connecting cable to a box in an existing wall surface much easier. External clamps are simple to use in new construction. Types available include a threaded metal clamp (B) and a plastic snap-fitting clamp (C). (Wires are shown cut short for photo clarity.)

Cable clamps secure cables to box

A cable clamp must be used to attach a cable to a metal electrical box. Any type may be used, as long as it is the correct size to fit the knockout opening in the box. Typically, one clamp is used for each cable entering the box. It is important to tighten the clamp so the cable is held securely, but not so the sheathing or wires are crushed or crimped.

Clamps for single-gang plastic boxes aren't necessary since the cable can be stapled within 8 in. of the box. Plastic boxes larger than 2 × 4 in. and all remodeling boxes, both metal and plastic, must contain internal cable clamps.

MAKING SCREW TERMINAL CONNECTIONS

To make a secure connection at a screw terminal on a switch, receptacle or fixture, first strip about ¾ in. of insulation off each conductor using a wire stripper. Then, with a long-nosed or needlenose pliers, grasp each conductor firmly, just short of the stripped end. Rotate the pliers while holding the conductor steady to form a loop. When you attach the wire, be sure to orient it so the loop is clockwise. Then, when you tighten the screw, the screw will work with the loop, not against it.

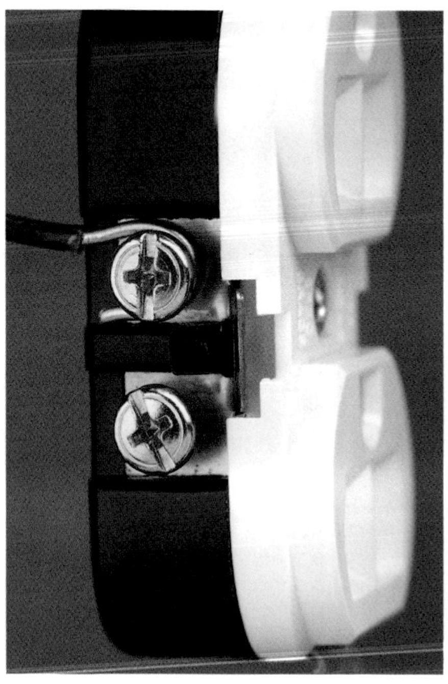

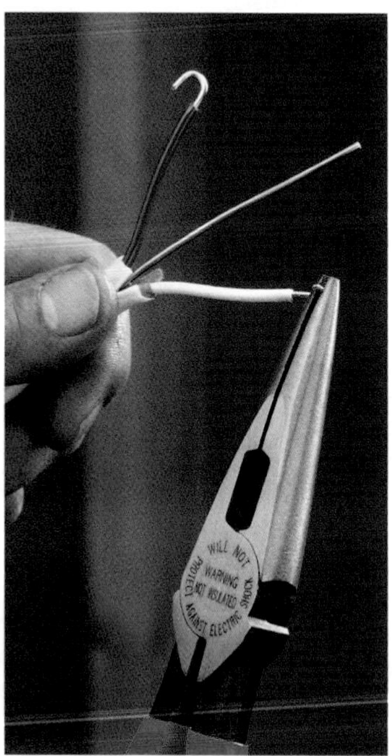

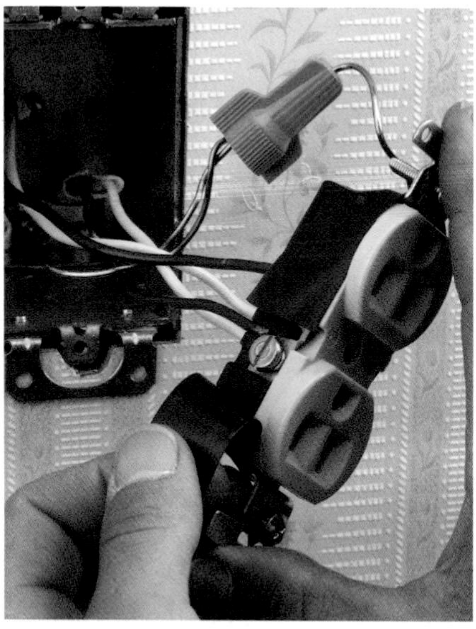

OPTION: Cover the screw terminals with electrical tape before mounting the receptacle or switch in a metal box.

COLOR-CODING HELPS YOU CHOOSE WIRE CONNECTORS AT A GLANCE

Wire connectors are color-coded to indicate the number of wires of various gauges they can connect. An orange connector handles up to two 14-gauge wires. Yellow accepts three 14-gauge or two to three 12-gauge wires. Red connects four to five 14-gauge or four 12-gauge wires. Gray connects six 14-gauge or five 12-gauge wires. Green wire connectors are used with grounding wires. They can handle two to four 14-gauge or 12-gauge wires. Some green connectors have a hole in the tip allowing one grounding wire to pass through and connect to a grounding screw terminal, so an extra pigtail isn't needed. Wire connector packages should list the maximum number of all wire gauge sizes and combinations they can safely connect.

PIGTAIL CONNECTIONS

Pigtails connect multiple wires to a single screw terminal

A *pigtail* is used to connect two or more wires to one screw terminal, since only one wire may be attached to a terminal. Cut a short length of wire of the same color as the wires that need connecting. (Keep excess cable pieces for this purpose.) Strip ½ in. of insulation off of one end, then strip ¾ in. off the other end and make a hook (see pages 134 to 135). Attach the hook end to the terminal, then connect the other end to the wires.

Use a wire connector when connecting wires together. Strip ½ in. of sheathing from the end of each wire. Hold the wires so the stripped ends are parallel, with their ends aligned. Place the wire connector over the wire ends and twist it onto the ends in a clockwise direction. Continue turning the connector until the sheathed portions of the wires begin to twist together. The photo at right illustrates how the wire connector twists the bare ends of the individual wires tightly together. No bare wire should extend past the bottom of the connector.

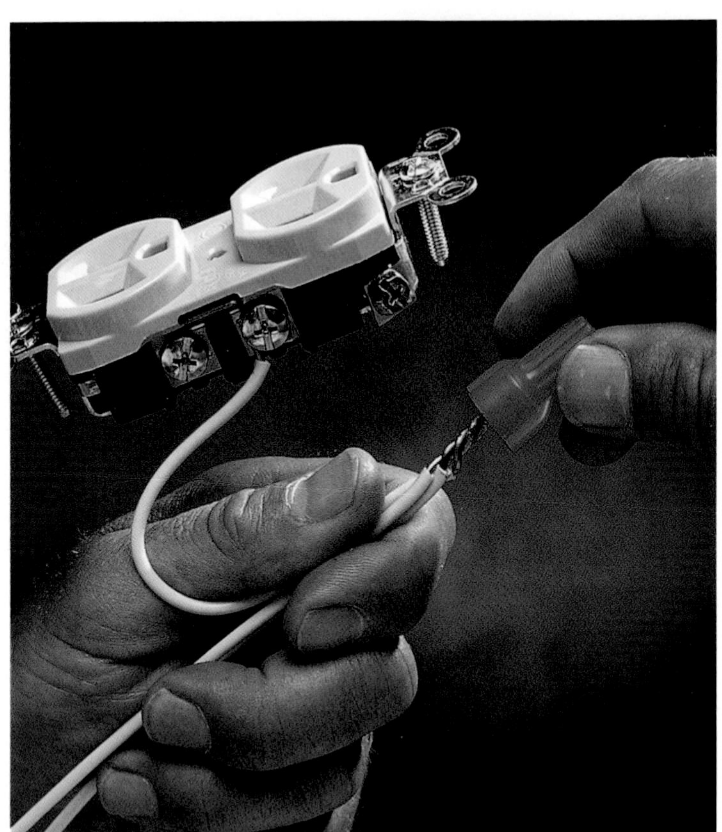

HOW TO GROUND METAL BOXES

Metal boxes must be connected to the circuit grounding system so they are safely grounded. A green wire connector should connect one end of a green insulated pigtail to the cable grounding wires and to the fixture grounding wires or to the grounding terminal on a receptacle or switch. The other end of the insulated pigtail is attached to a green grounding screw (photo left) or to a grounding clip (photo right) if the box doesn't have a grounding screw. In a conduit installation, Code allows the conduit to be the grounding conductor, but most electricians use the grounding pigtail to ensure that the system is properly grounded.

Armored cable can be an easy-to-install substitute for conduit

Armored cable is a flexible galvanized metal tubing containing wires. It can be installed in the same dry, interior locations as plastic-sheathed cable. It is installed in locations where wires need greater protection than sheathed cable can provide.

Because of its flexibility armored cable is easier to install than conduit (see pages 140-141). Installation methods are similar to those used with sheathed cable. Use galvanized metal staples and cable connectors (see photo, below right) designated for use with armored cable. Another advantage armored cable has over conduit is that no wire-pulling is required. This will save a significant amount of time, though you must cut armored cable carefully see photo, right). Check with your local electrical inspector for appropriate applications where you use this material.

Cut through armored cable with a hacksaw. Hold the blade at a right angle to a ridge in the cable and cut through the raised center of the ridge and slightly into the edges. Make sure you do not cut into the wires or the bonding strip. Bend the cable at the cut and then twist sharply to break and remove the short end. You may want to make practice cuts on scrap pieces before beginning your project.

HOW TO MAKE CONNECTIONS WITH ARMORED CABLE

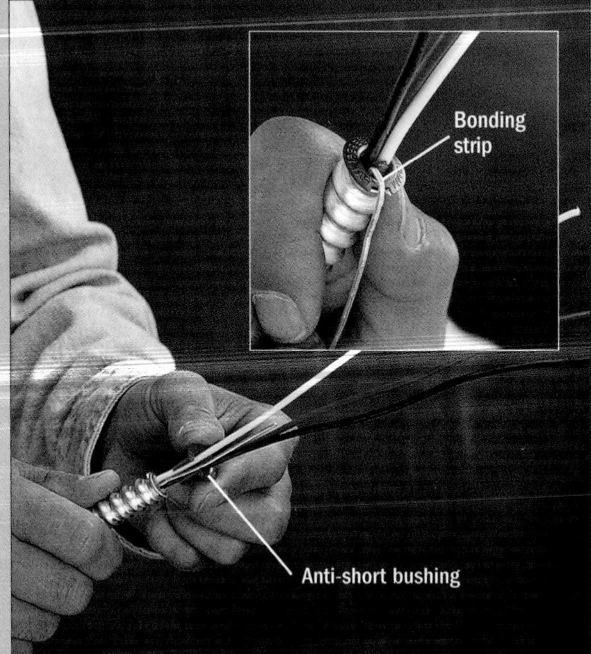

1 An anti-short bushing must protect the wires in armored cable from the rough edge of the cut cable. Slide the bushing over the wires and into the end of the cable. Push the bushing firmly into the end of the cable. Cut the bonding strip so there is about 2 in. remaining, then bend the strip over the bushing to hold it in place (See inset photo).

2 Attach the cable to a metal box with an armored cable connector. The holes in the end of the connector show that the bushing is properly in position.

ELECTRICAL BOXES

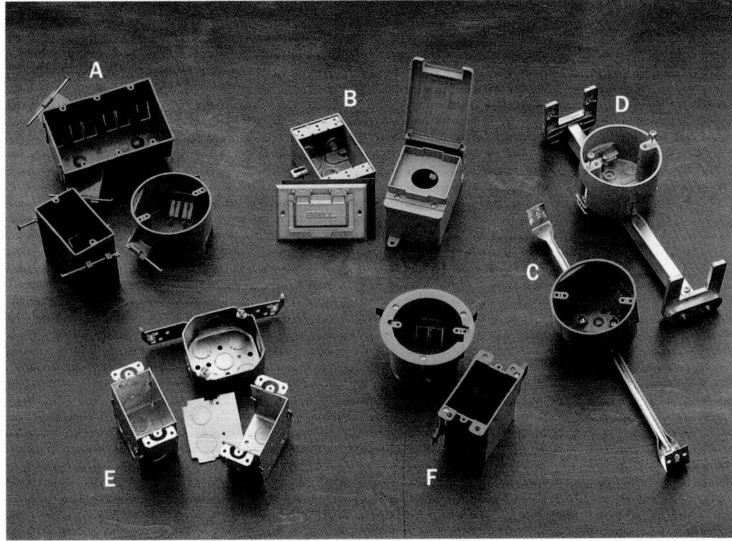

Types of boxes: (A) plastic boxes with preattached mounting nails for indoor construction installations, (B) weatherproof cast aluminum and plastic boxes for exterior installations, (C) brace and fixture box for fixture installation between framing members, (D) heavy-duty brace and box for ceiling fan or heavy light fixture installation, (E) metal boxes for conduit or interior cable installations, (F) plastic remodeling boxes, also called retrofit boxes, for installations in existing ceiling and wall surfaces (metal remodeling boxes also are available).

ELECTRICAL BOX WIRE CAPACITIES

OUTLET BOX		MAX. WIRES		
Box size	Box shape	#14	#12	#10
4 × 1¼	Round/oct.	6	5	5
4 × 1½	Round/oct.	7	6	6
4 × 2⅛	Round/oct.	10	9	8
4 × 1¼	Square	9	8	7
4 × 1½	Square	10	9	8
4 × 2⅛	Square	15	13	12
4 11/16 × 1¼	Square	12	11	10
4 11/16 × 1½	Square	14	13	11
4 11/16 × 2⅛	Square	21	18	16
Switch/Receptacle Box		#14	#12	#10
10.3 cu. in.		3	3	3
16 cu. in.		8	7	6
18 cu. in.		9	8	7
20.0 cu. in.		10	8	8
21.1 cu. in.		10	9	8
22.5 cu. in.		11	10	9

TYPICAL ELECTRICAL BOX HOOK-UP

Attach a plastic box to a framing member so the box face will be flush with the finished wall surface. Guidelines for common wall depths are on the sides of most boxes. Remove a knockout for each cable that will enter the box, using a hammer and screwdriver. Strip cable sheathing so 8-in. lengths of wire extend past the box face and at least ½ in. of sheathed cable extends past the cable clamping device. Anchor cable with cable staples within 8 in. of each box and also every 4 ft. where it runs along framing members.

Do not route cable diagonally between framing members. Cable should cross framing members at right angles. If you need more than one hole in a framing member, drill the holes along the length of the wood. Keep holes as close to the center of the wood as possible, with at least 1 in. of wood between them. Do not drill holes across the framing member's width, which can weaken it.

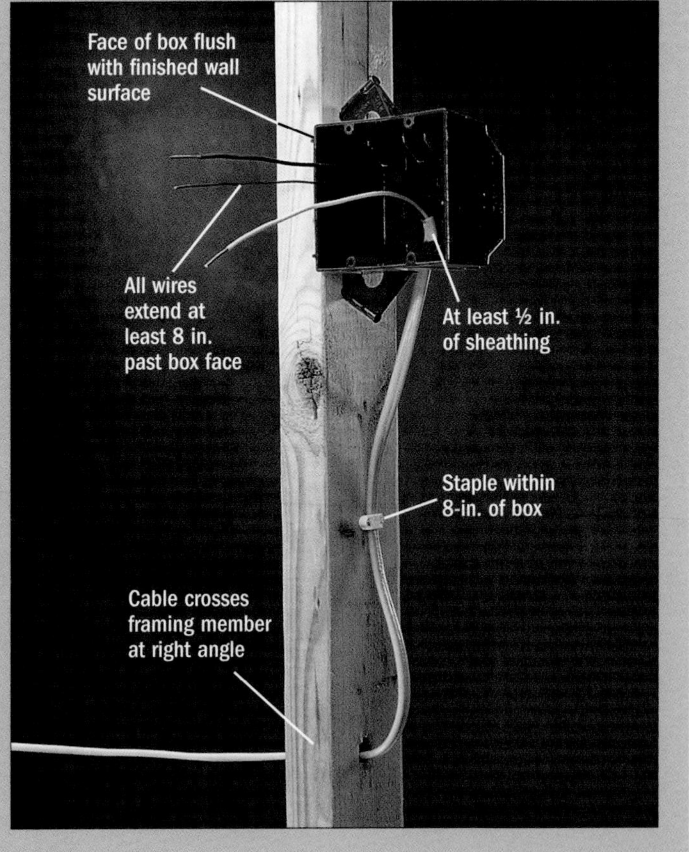

SPLICING CABLE IN A JUNCTION BOX

1 Any time a run of cable is interrupted, you can splice new cable to the old to lengthen the run. But the splice must be made with wire connectors and sealed in a junction box. Attach the junction box to a joist or wall stud and knock out entry holes for both cables (if using a metal junction box). Feed both cables into the box, securing them at the knockouts with cable clamps. You'll need a good 6 to 10 in. of cable entering the box from each side. Strip the cable sheathing and wire insulation then connect the like-colored wires with wire connectors. Fold the wires into the box, starting with the ground wires.

2 Check to make sure all the connections are intact and secure, then cover the junction box with a box cover plate.

WORKING WITH CABLE

CUT-IN BOX TYPES

Most boxes designed for retrofit, called cut-in boxes, employ a system of toggles or wings that are drawn in tightly against the interior of the wall to hold the box in place. They are designed to be "free-floating" in that they mount anywhere on the wall surface; many will not work properly if installed next to a wall framing member where the operation of the wings will be impeded. The types shown above include: (A) Thermoset box with metal tension straps; (B) PVC box with metal flip-out wings; (C) PVC fixture box with plastic flip-out wings; and (D) metal box with screw-tightened compression tabs.

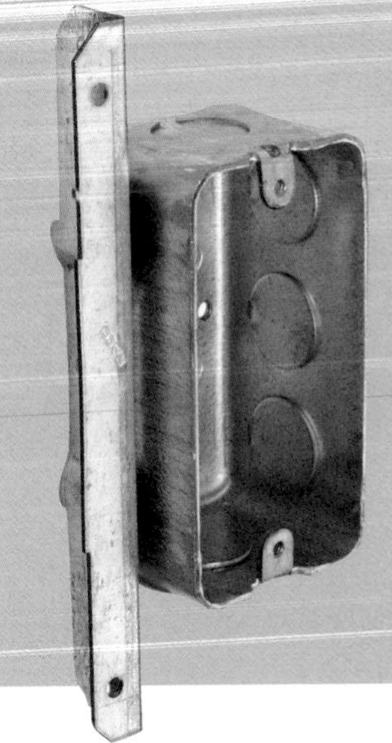

CAUTION: HANDY BOXES CAN BE A HAZARD

The most inexpensive (and, consequently, popular) outlet box is known in the trade as the "handy box." Although they're readily available, cheap and easier to fit into tight spaces than more generously-proportioned boxes, they are responsible for many of the problems that afflict a home wiring system. With as little as 10.3 cubic inches of volume, they're just too small to hold more than a single light-gauge wire and an outlet. The only way to get the cabling for most hookups into them is to force them in, usually by using the receptacle or switch mounting screws to press the wires back with the outlet as the screws are tightened. This can cause connections to fail, insulation to strip off and wires to short out against the metal box. Avoid the handy box. See Electrical Box Wire Capacities chart (page 138) for minimum box volume recommendations.

Working with Conduit

Conduit is used to protect wires in exposed locations, such as on masonry surfaces in a basement. Conduit rated for exterior use can be used to install circuits outdoors. Check with your local electrical inspector to determine the type of conduit your project requires.

Metal conduit is available in three types. *EMT* (Electrical Metallic Tubing) is lightweight and easy to work with, but because of its thinner tubing, shouldn't be installed where it could easily be damaged. *IMC* (Intermediate Metallic Conduit) has thicker, galvanized walls to withstand rougher treatment. It also is a good choice for outdoor installations when used with weatherproof fittings. *Rigid metal* conduit provides heavy-duty protection, but is the most expensive and also requires threaded fittings. IMC or EMT should be adequate for most of your projects.

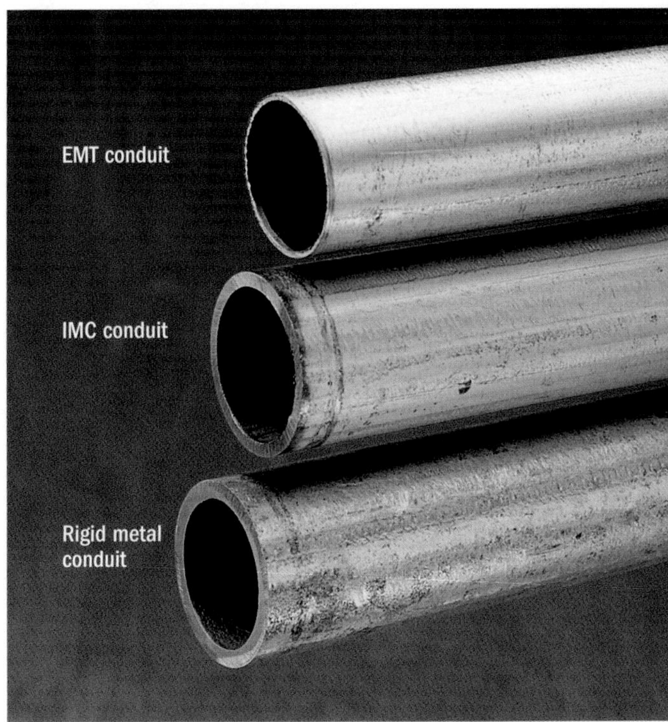

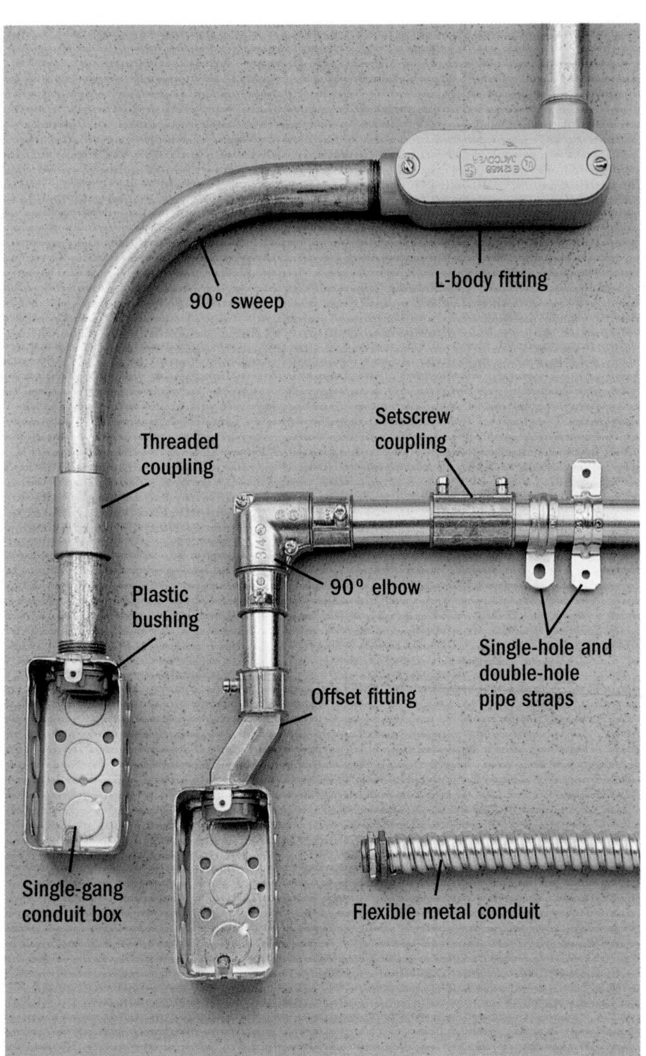

Metal conduit fittings

Metal fittings are available to make the installation of metal conduit quite easy. Rather than bend the conduit yourself with special tools, you can purchase these connectors pre-made to create the conduit layout your project requires.

Threaded couplings, connectors and sweeps are used to install rigid metal conduit.

Setscrew fittings are used with EMT and IMC. The removable cover on the *90° elbow* makes it easy to pull wires around the corner (see page 144). An *offset fitting* connects conduit, anchored flush against a wall, to the knockout on a metal electrical box.

The same metal electrical conduit boxes are used with all conduit types. An *L-body fitting* is used as a transition between vertical and horizontal lengths of conduit, such as when underground wires must enter a building. The cover can be removed, making pulling wires easier. Plastic bushings cover exposed conduit ends, protecting wires from damage by the rough metal edges. Metal pipe straps anchor conduit against masonry surfaces or wood framing members. Conduit should be supported within 3 ft. of each electrical box and fitting, and every 10 ft. otherwise.

Flexible metal conduit bends easily and can be used for short unsupported distances where rigid conduit is difficult to install. It is frequently used to connect appliances that are permanently wired, such as a water heater. Wires are pulled through flexible metal conduit in the same manner as with other conduit.

WORKING WITH METAL CONDUIT

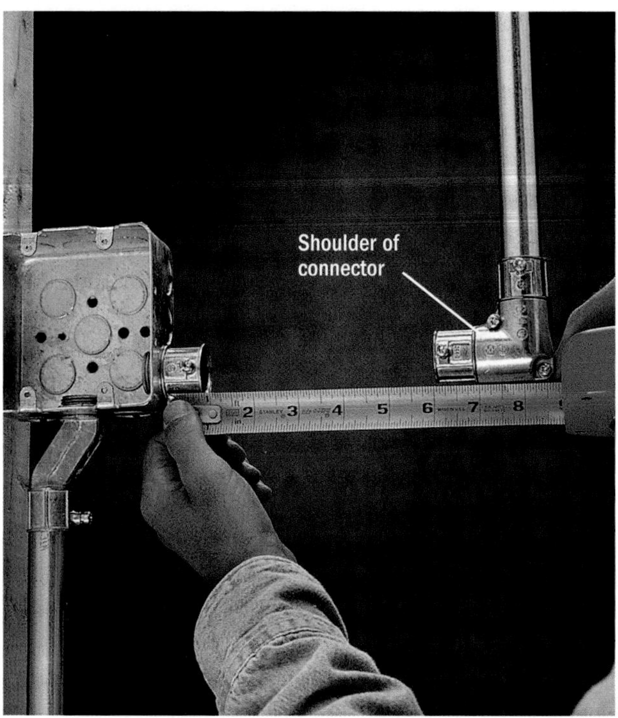

Measure from shoulder to shoulder

Use a tape measure to determine the length of conduit needed between locations. Measure to the shoulders of connectors to allow for the distance the conduit will require.

Attaching hangers to masonry

Anchor conduit to masonry surfaces with self-tapping masonry screws and galvanized metal pipe straps. Conduit must be anchored within 3 ft. of each box or fitting and every 10 ft. otherwise. See page 61 for more information on anchoring to masonry.

PLASTIC CONDUIT

A simple alternative to metal

Most local codes allow the use of PVC plastic conduit in installations requiring wire protection. Plastic conduit and fittings are lightweight and very easy to install. It is cut and assembled with solvent glue just like PVC plumbing pipe. Plastic conduit is usually connected to plastic electrical boxes and fittings similar to those for metal conduit, but it can be attached to a metal box by welding a threaded male coupling onto the end and securing the coupling in the metal box with a cable clamp nut. Run a green insulated grounding wire when using plastic conduit, as the conduit doesn't provide a grounding path.

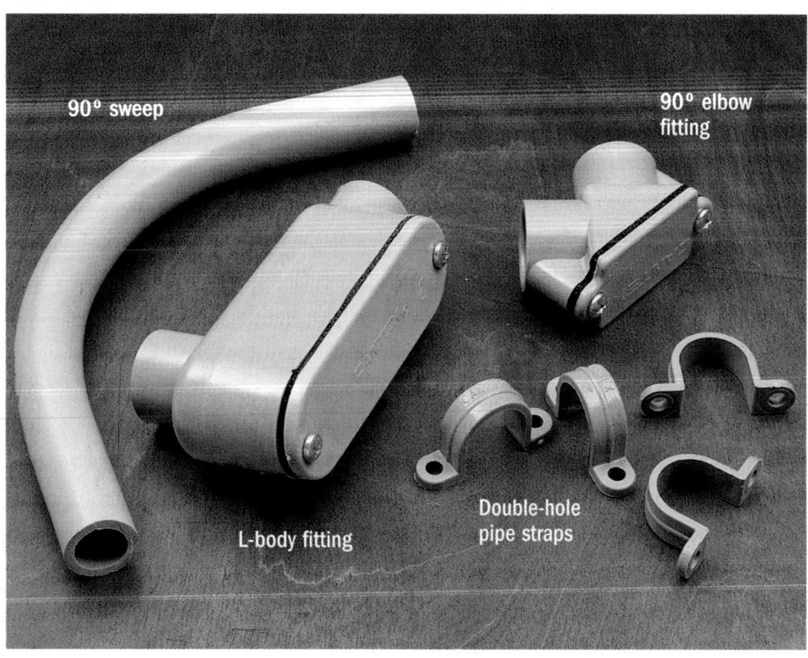

HOW TO PREPARE A FISHTAPE FOR RUNNING CABLE

1 Remove about 3 in. of sheathing from the end of the cable. Insert the wires through the hook at the end of the fishtape, then bend them back onto the cable. Begin wrapping electrical tape on the fishtape above the hook.

2 Continue wrapping electrical tape tightly around the fishtape and wires and onto at least 2 in. of cable past the connection. The junction should be as thin and smooth as possible.

HELPFUL TIPS FOR RUNNING CABLE

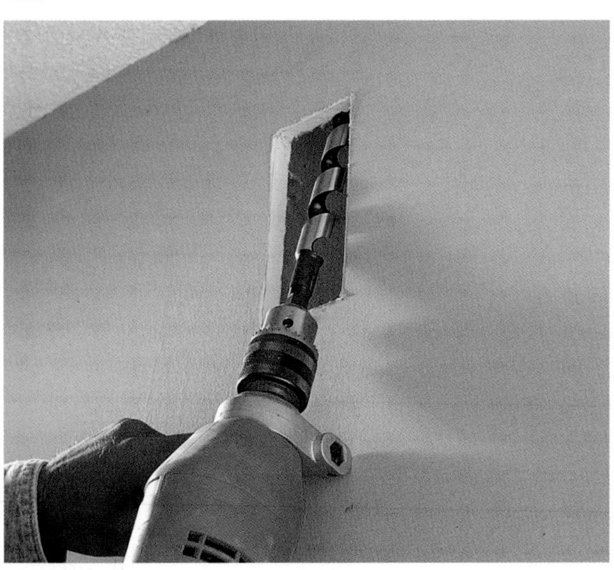

Cut out for wall-to-ceiling access

To route cable from one finished room to the room above, cut a 3 × 5-in. opening in the wall surface near the ceiling. Drill through the top plate using a long auger bit at as steep an angle as possible. If you need to route the cable into the ceiling, cut another 3 × 5-in. opening in the ceiling near the wall. You may need to drill another hole to make a path for the cable into the joist cavity. Patch the wall and ceiling with wallboard.

Creating wall-to-floor access

To route cable from one finished room to the room below, cut a 3 × 5-in. hole in the wall surface near the floor, behind the baseboard if possible. Drill through the bottom plate using a long auger bit at as steep an angle as possible.

HOW TO RUN CABLE WITH A FISHTAPE

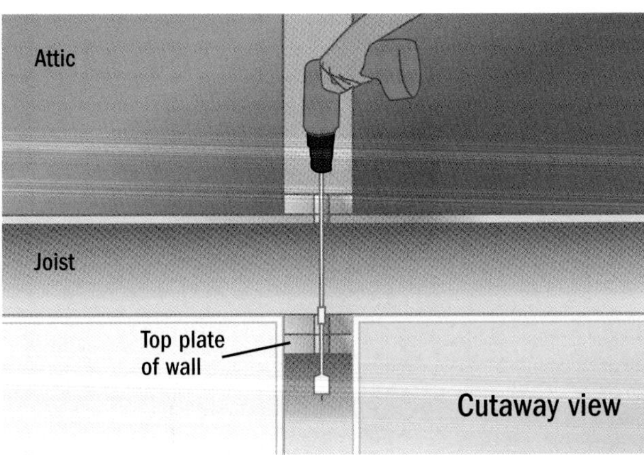

Drilling from above a wall

Routing cable through a wall is much easier if you have access to the attic space above the wall. Measure carefully from a structural member common to both levels to determine where to drill. This same method is used when drilling up into the wall cavity from the basement below the wall.

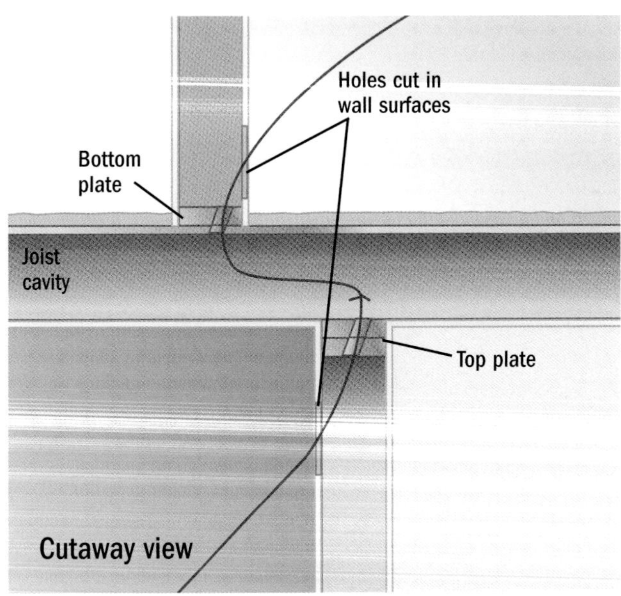

Routing cable through offset walls

Routing cable through offset walls in finished rooms is difficult. You will need two fishtapes and a helper. Cut holes in appropriate wall surfaces and drill holes in the bottom and top plates of the walls (See page 142). Have your helper run one fishtape down through the holes in the room above. Push the other fishtape up through the holes in the lower room and catch the first fishtape with the hook on yours. Pull your fishtape until the hook from the other fishtape emerges from the holes. Attach cable to the fishtape and have your helper pull it to the room above.

Fishing alternative

You can use mason's string and a lead weight to fish cable through a wall. You must have access to the space above and below the wall to do this. After drilling holes in the bottom and top plates, have a helper lower the weighted string from above. Bend a hook in the end of a piece of stiff wire and push it through the lower hole to snag the string. Attach the string to the cable as if it were a fishtape (see page 142).

Cut a baseboard channel

Routing cable behind baseboard and door casing is a simple method for adding new cable within a finished room. Carefully remove the baseboard or casing so it can be re-installed. Remove enough wall surface behind the trim pieces so you can work but make sure the trim will cover the work area. You won't need to patch holes in the wall surfaces that are covered by trim pieces. Create a route for the cable, cutting notches in the wall studs that the cable must cross. Once the cable is in place, cover each notch with a metal protective plate. Re-install the trim pieces. You may need to fill gaps between the trim pieces and framing members caused by wall surface removal, using scrap lumber spacers.

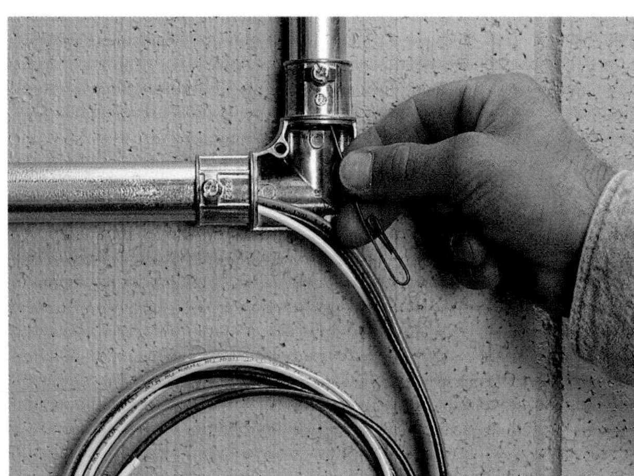

Fishing through conduit

Push a fishtape through the conduit until the hook appears at the end of the conduit where the wires need to enter. Connect the wires to the fishtape (see page 142). Pull all wires through the conduit together. At 90° corners, remove the fitting cover and use the fishtape to pull through each length of conduit rather than trying to make one pull around the tight corner.

HOW TO CREATE AN OPENING TO RUN CABLE DOWN FROM THE ATTIC

1 Drill a ⅜-in.-dia. access hole in each end of the length of floor board you need to remove, at the inside face of the joists. Cut across the board along the edge of the joist, using a jig saw.

2 Cut 1 × 2-in. cleats and attach them with screws. When the electrical work is finished, re-attach the piece of floor board to the cleats.

Making Connections

CONNECTING A LIGHT FIXTURE

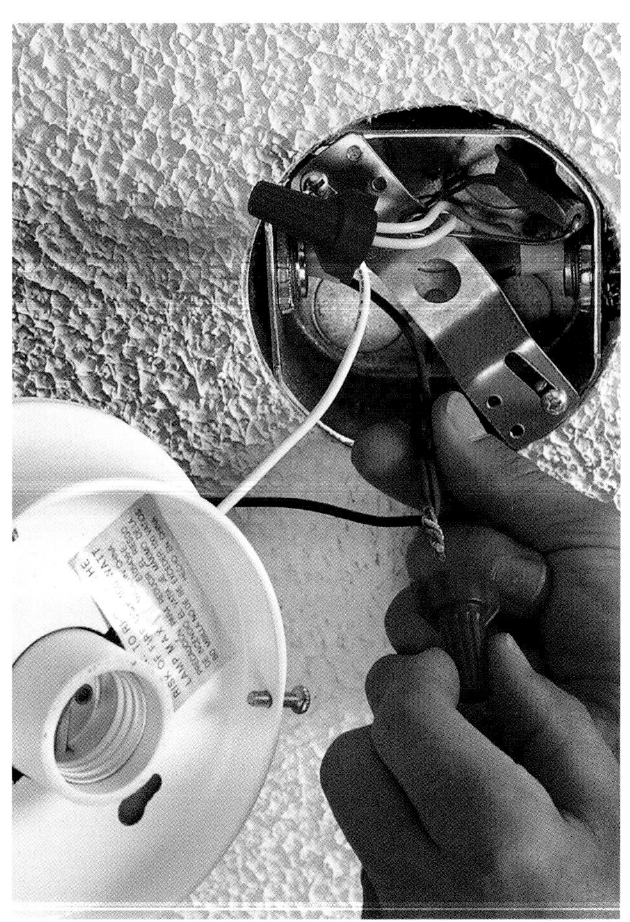

All standard light fixtures are attached to the electrical box and the cable wires in a similar fashion, whether they are ceiling or wall mounted. To replace a light fixture, remove the globe, light bulb and mounting screws and carefully pull the old fixture away from the electrical box. Turn off the power and test with a circuit tester (see page 131). Disconnect the wire connections. Attach the mounting strap that came with the new light fixture, if the electrical box does not already have one. Connect the black lead from the new fixture to the black cable wire. Connect the white lead to the white cable wire and the cable grounding wire to the green grounding screw on the mounting strap. Tuck the wires into the box. Position the new fixture and attach it to the mounting strap with the mounting screws.

A ceiling fan requires more support than a standard light fixture. When replacing a light fixture with a fan, the electrical box must be attached to a framing member or to a heavy-duty brace. This brace comes with an electrical box with special mounting hardware.

TIPS FOR INSTALLING & CONNECTING A CEILING FAN

Install a mounting bar between ceiling joists

Turn off the power and check with a circuit tester (see page 131). After removing the light fixture and existing electrical box, insert the brace through the hole in the ceiling. Use an adjustable wrench to extend the ends of the brace until they are firmly seated against the joists.

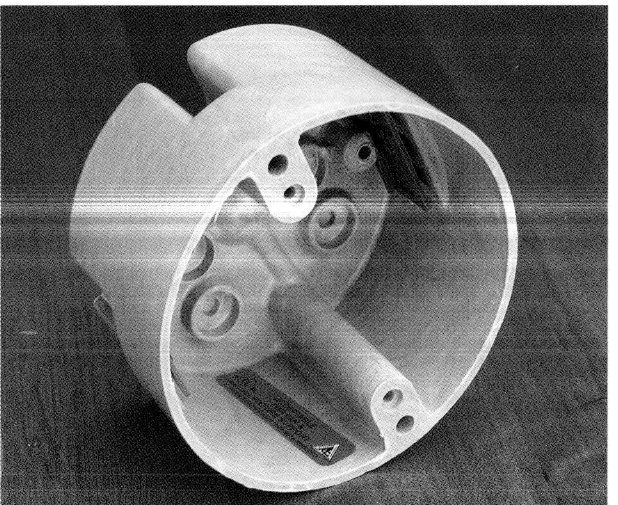

Ceiling fan-rated boxes

Ceiling fans and fixtures that are very heavy (in excess of 50 pounds) require heavier-duty ceiling boxes that are directly supported by a joist or crosspiece. These boxes are labeled "Approved for use with ceiling fans."

Installing canister-style recessed light fixtures

You can replace a standard light fixture with a recessed light fixture. Recessed fixtures have a self-contained electrical box. Retrofit units are designed to fit through an opening in the ceiling; other units must be installed from above. Make sure you purchase a unit designed for contact with insulation if your project requires it. Note: If you don't have access to the ceiling from above, you must attach the cable to the electrical box and make all wire connections before you insert the unit through the hole in the ceiling.

1 If the ceiling joists in the installation area are accessible from above, make a cutout in the ceiling for the light, then position the unit over the hole and attach it to the joists with support braces. When working on uncovered ceiling joists, lay a large plywood scrap across the joists to create a kneeling surface and prevent you from stepping or falling through the ceiling.

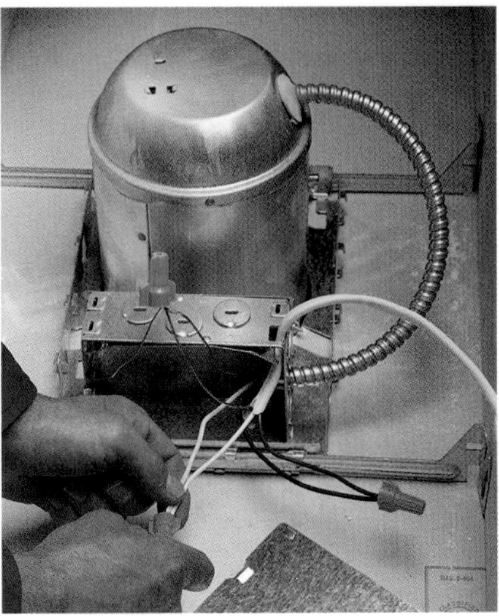

2 Run the feeder cable into the fixture box, securing it with a cable clamp. Make sure the installation of the circuit cable conforms to your local codes: in many cases, conduit or armored cable are required for attic installations. Make the wiring hook-ups, then install the trim kit from below.

INSULATION CONTACT (I.C.) RATINGS

Non-I.C.-rated (or "T" type) canister lights need at least 3 in. of free air space on all sides, or heat build-up will cause the fixture to shut off. Fiberglass insulation can simply be cut back, but if you have loose insulation you'll need to create an insulation dam by tacking a board into the joist cavity on each side of the unit.

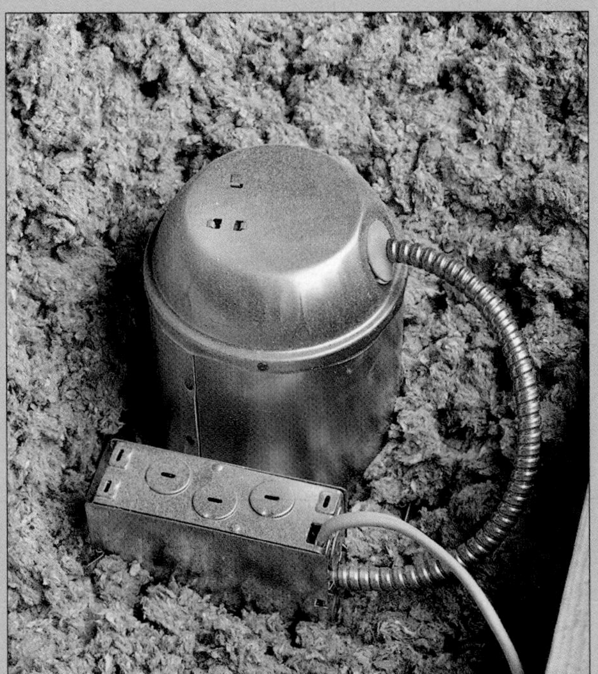

I.C.-rated (or "ICT" type) canister lights have an internal thermal protection feature so you can insulate up and around the light fixture canister without creating heat buildup issues.

Electrical Illustrations & Diagrams

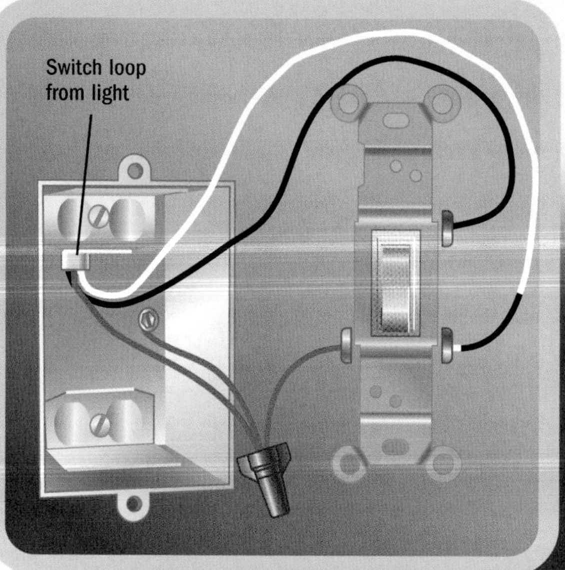

Switch connections

Wires from either one or two cables will be connected to a single-pole switch. More cables may be present in the electrical box containing the switch but will not have any wires connected to the switch.

One cable connected to switch (above) means that current is first routed to the light fixture electrical box and then a cable brings current to the switch box for the switch to control. This is often called a switch loop. The neutral white wire serves as a hot wire and must be tagged with black electrical tape.

Two cables connected to switch indicate that current comes to the switch box before being routed to the light fixture.

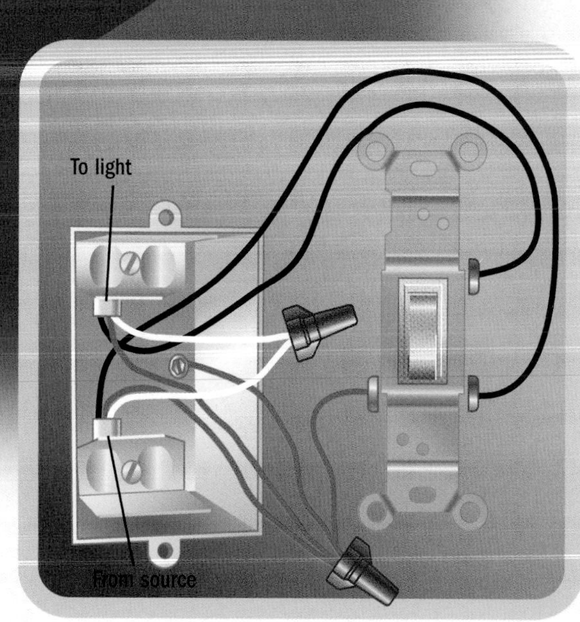

Receptacle connections

There are four basic receptacle wiring patterns. Always connect neutral wires to silver terminals and hot wires to brass terminals.

One 2-wire cable connected to the receptacle (above left) indicates the receptacle is at the end of the circuit run.

Two 2-wire cables connected to the receptacle (below left) mean the receptacle is in the middle of the run.

One 3-wire cable attached to the receptacle (above right) indicates a split receptacle, with each half of the unit serving a separate circuit or use, such as when one half is controlled by a switch. Note: The connecting tab between the brass terminals must be removed on a split receptacle.

A two-slot receptacle (below right) is often found in older homes. There is no grounding screw on the unit. Do not replace a two-slot receptacle with a 3-slot receptacle unless a grounding path is created.

Standard single ceiling fixture

Wires from either one or two cables in a light fixture box will connect to the light fixture. Cables from other circuits may be present in the box but will not connect to the fixture.

One cable connected to the light fixture indicates that current is routed to the switch box before coming to the light fixture.

Two cables connected to the light fixture indicate that current is routed to the fixture's electrical box through one cable and is then routed to the switch through the other cable, often called a switch loop (see page 147). The white wire in the switch loop must be tagged with black electrical tape because it serves as a hot wire.

If your project has two or more light fixtures controlled by one switch, see page 152 for wiring connections.

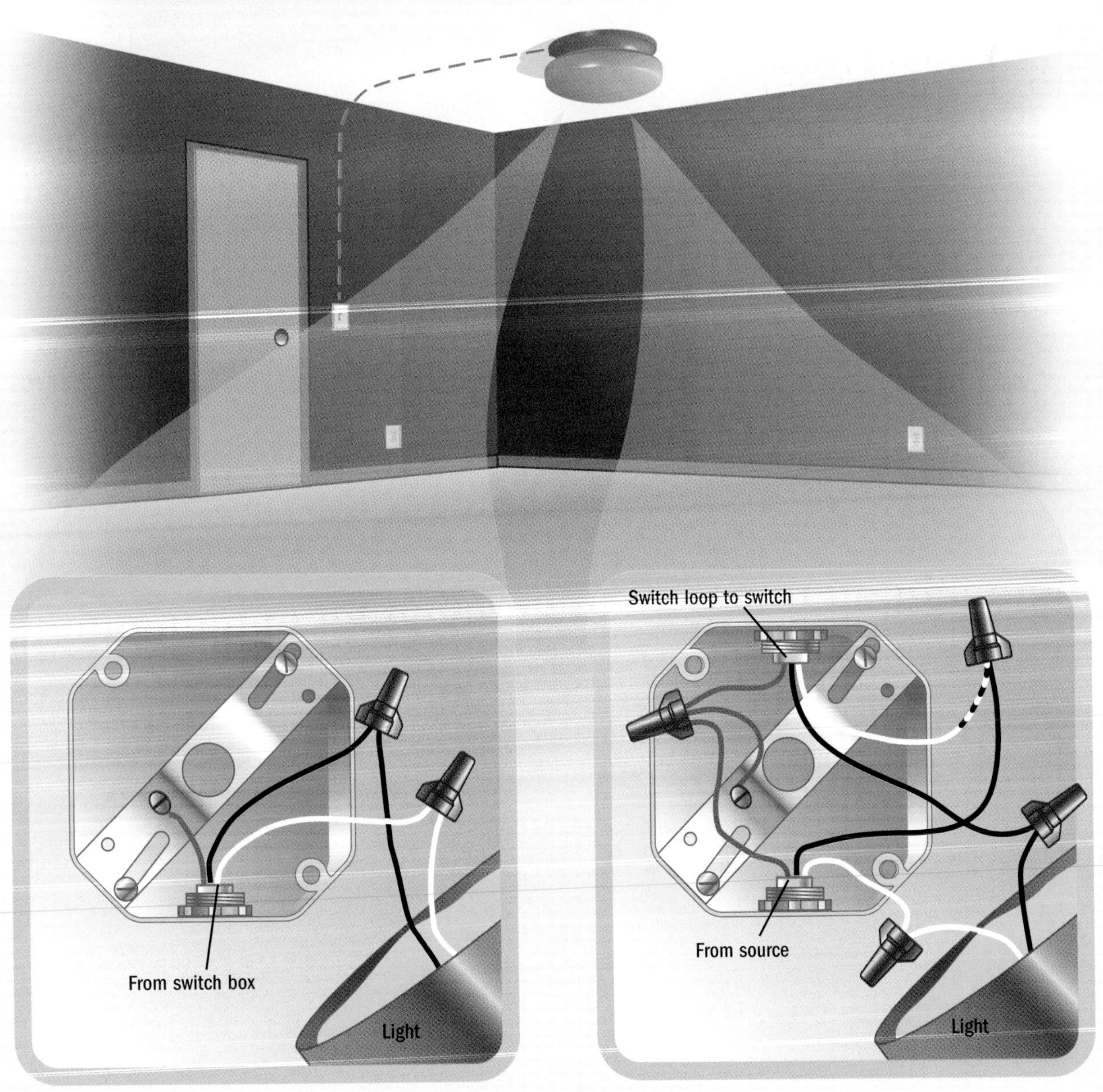

ELECTRICAL ILLUSTRATIONS & DIAGRAMS

Adding a new receptacle

When adding a new receptacle, it is usually easiest to access power from an existing receptacle. An existing receptacle will be in the middle of the circuit run or at its end (see page 148). This illustration shows obtaining power from a receptacle at the end of the circuit. If you need to access power from a middle-of-run receptacle, use the wiring diagram on page 148 as a guide.

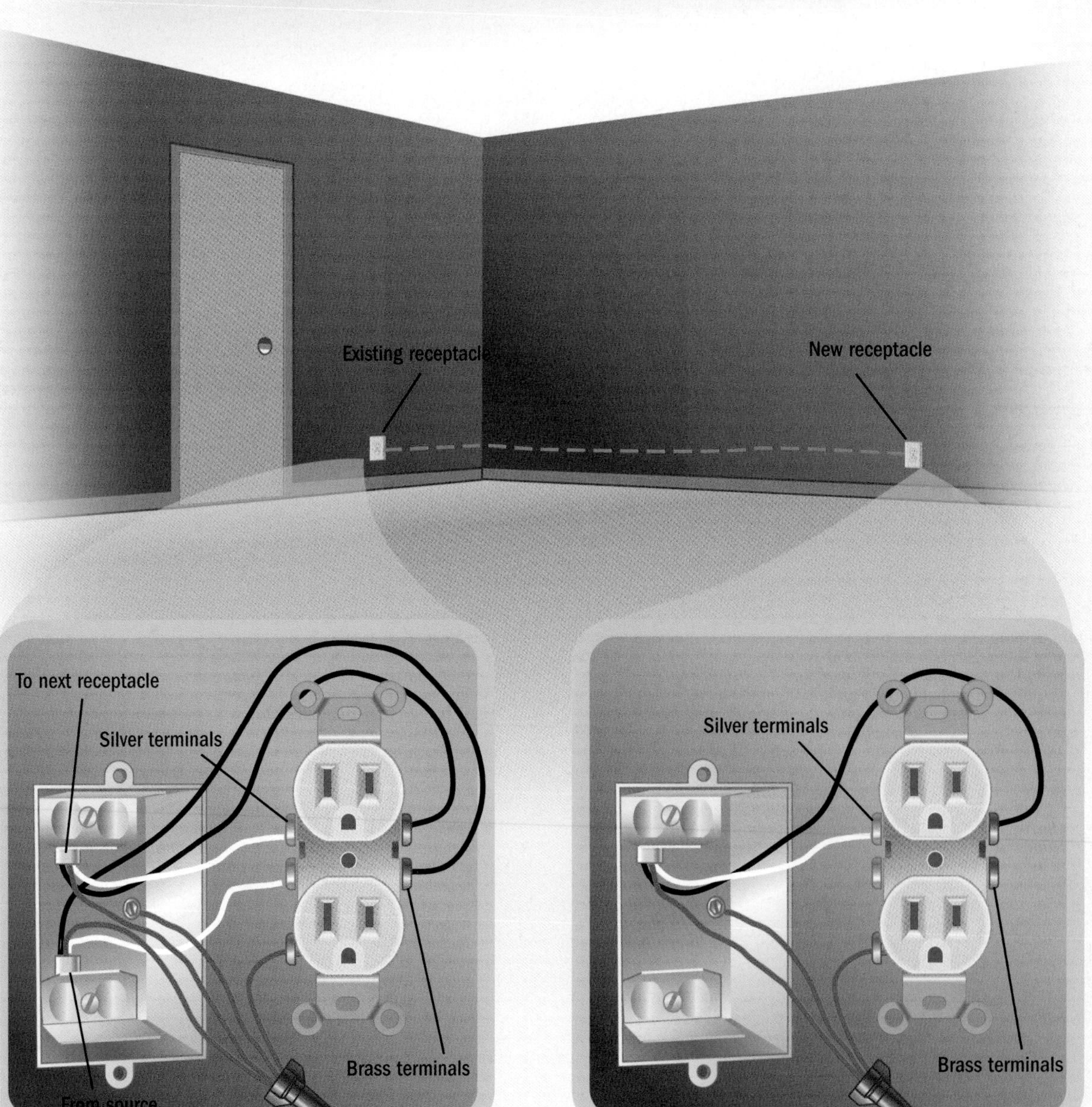

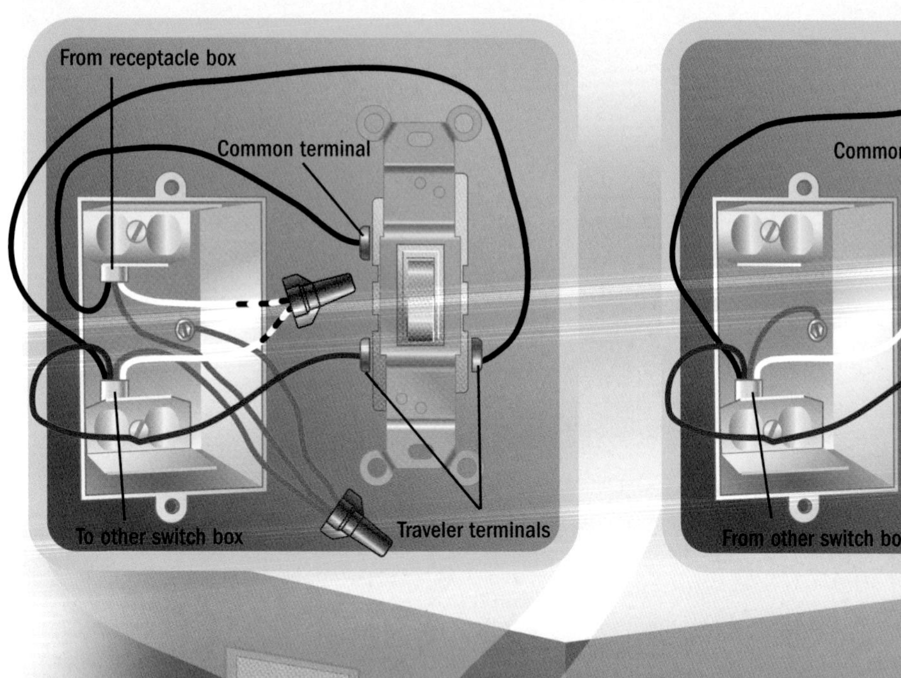

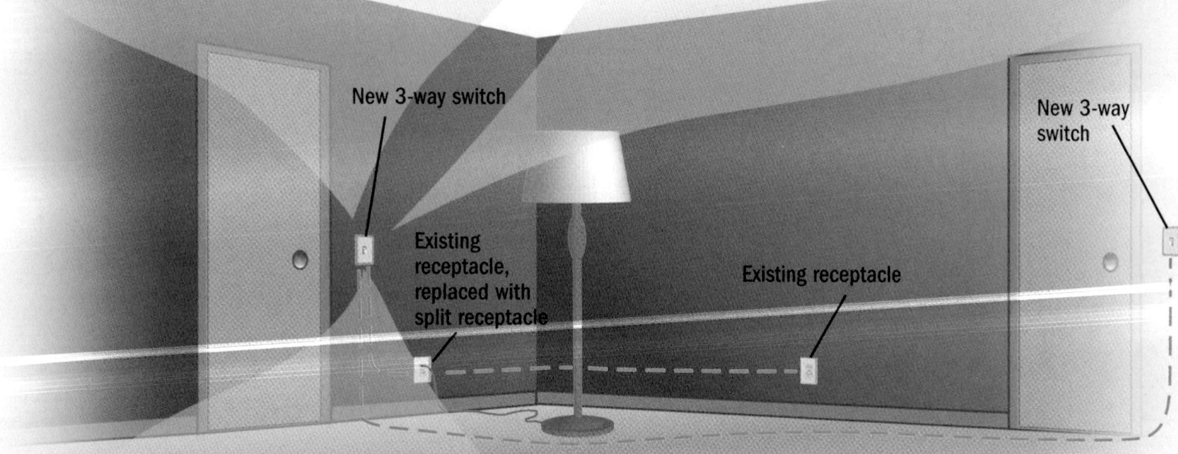

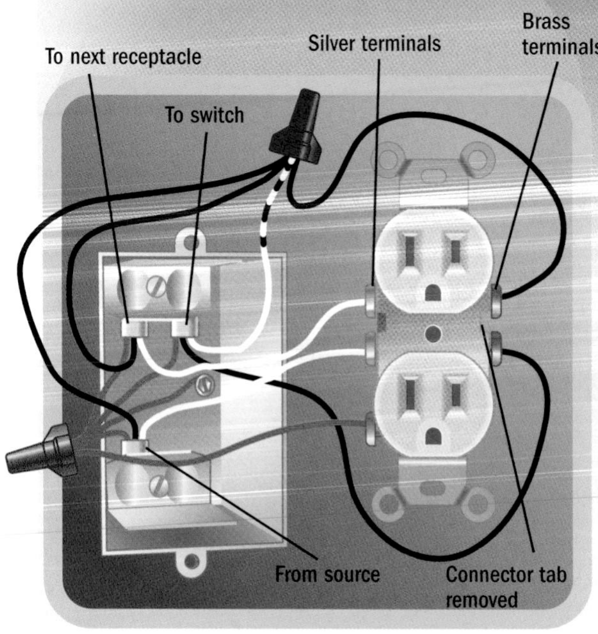

Switched outlet controlled by 3-way switches

Adding a switched light fixture to a finished room can be done by replacing an existing receptacle with a split receptacle where one half is controlled by a switch. A light fixture, such as a floor lamp, is plugged into this half of the receptacle. This is a good method for rooms where access above the ceiling isn't available to install a ceiling fixture.

In this illustration, 3-way switches are installed at both entryways. One type of 3-way switch installation is shown. Every 3-way installation must follow this pattern: The common terminal on one switch is connected to the power source, the common terminal on the other switch is connected to the hot lead of the fixture (in this case the hot terminal on the receptacle), and the traveler terminals on both switches are connected together. All neutral wires connected to switches must be tagged with black electrical tape to indicate they are serving as hot wires.

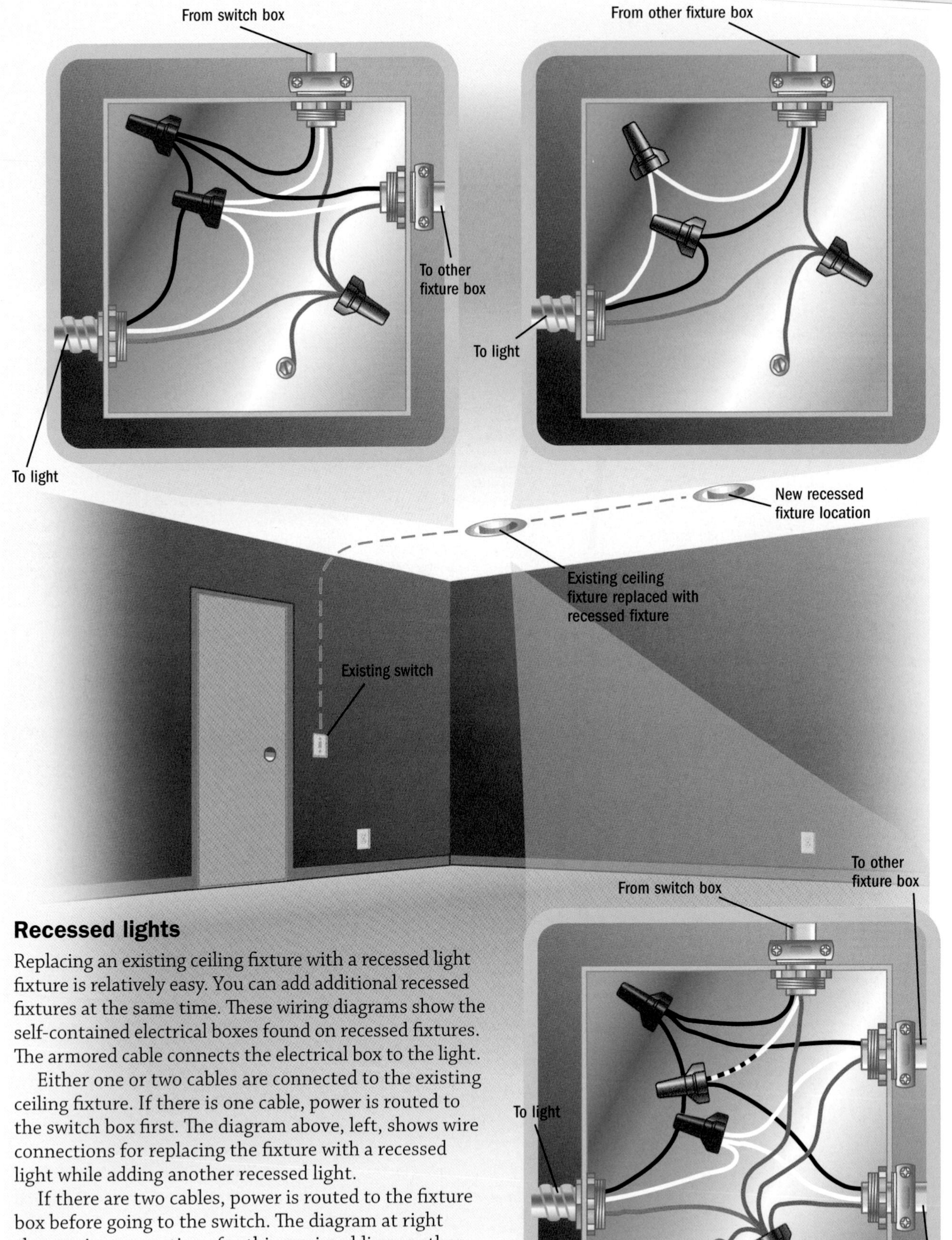

Recessed lights

Replacing an existing ceiling fixture with a recessed light fixture is relatively easy. You can add additional recessed fixtures at the same time. These wiring diagrams show the self-contained electrical boxes found on recessed fixtures. The armored cable connects the electrical box to the light.

Either one or two cables are connected to the existing ceiling fixture. If there is one cable, power is routed to the switch box first. The diagram above, left, shows wire connections for replacing the fixture with a recessed light while adding another recessed light.

If there are two cables, power is routed to the fixture box before going to the switch. The diagram at right shows wire connections for this, again adding another recessed light.

The diagram above, right, shows wire connections for the additional recessed fixture in either situation.

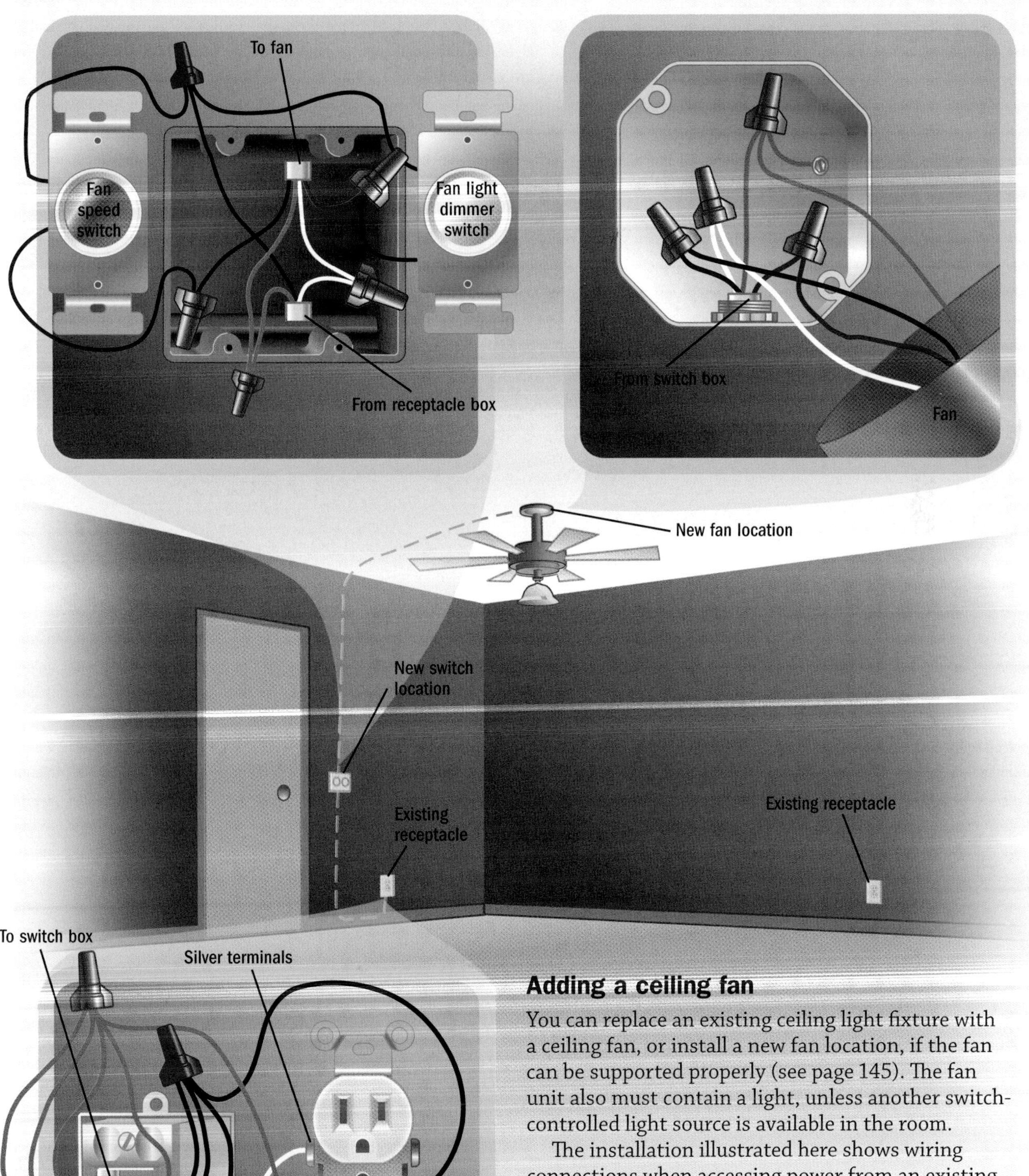

Adding a ceiling fan

You can replace an existing ceiling light fixture with a ceiling fan, or install a new fan location, if the fan can be supported properly (see page 145). The fan unit also must contain a light, unless another switch-controlled light source is available in the room.

The installation illustrated here shows wiring connections when accessing power from an existing receptacle. You must have a 3-wire cable between the switch box and the fan location if you wish to control the light and fan speed with wall switches. Otherwise, you must control the light with a wall switch. Fan speed is controlled by a pull chain at the fan.

Bathroom vent fan

You need access to the attic above the bathroom to easily install a vent fan. Purchase a unit containing a light if a switch-controlled ceiling light fixture isn't already present. The illustration at left shows the connections for a fan unit. The diagrams below show connections when the fixture has both a fan and a light. Then the wire connector box on the fan unit would have one more lead, usually red. If ceramic tile covers the walls, it can be difficult to cut a new box opening. The option shown below, right, uses an existing single-gang opening with a double-switch device. However, you can't use a fan timer switch when using this method.

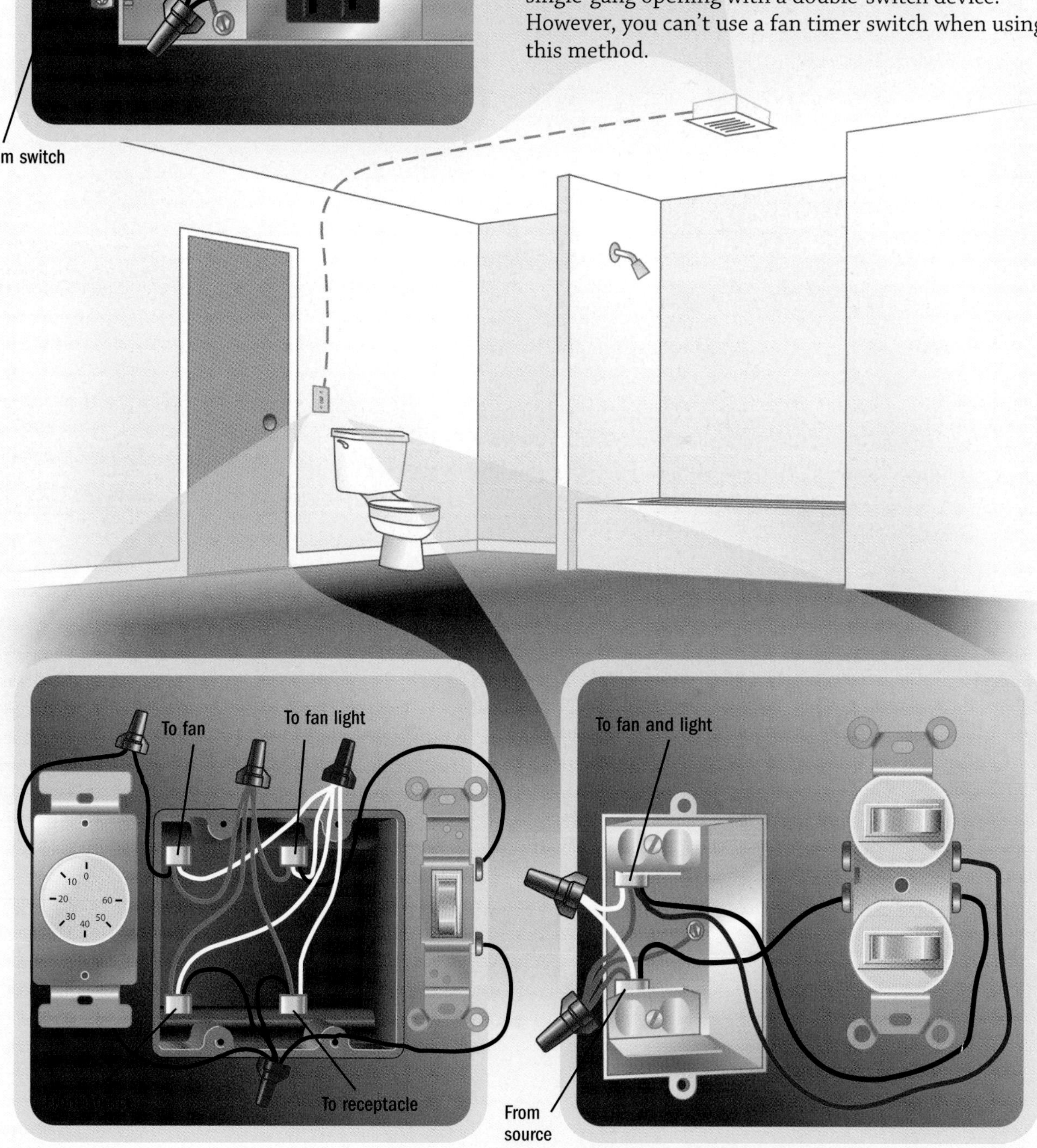

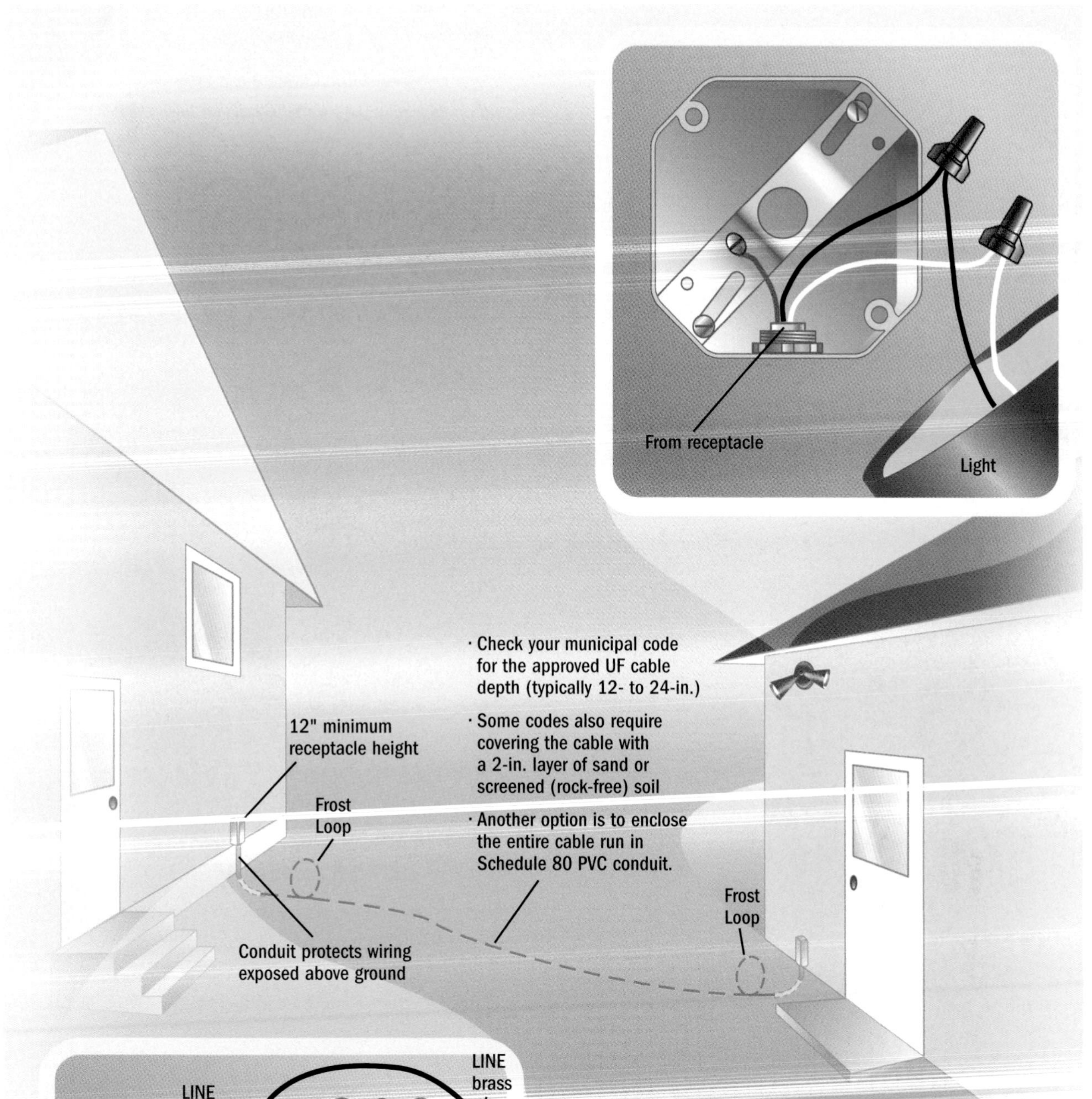

From receptacle
Light
12" minimum
receptacle height
Frost
Loop
· Check your municipal code
for the approved UF cable
depth (typically 12- to 24-in.)
· Some codes also require
covering the cable with
a 2-in. layer of sand or
screened (rock-free) soil
· Another option is to enclose
the entire cable run in
Schedule 80 PVC conduit.
Frost
Loop
Conduit protects wiring
exposed above ground

LINE
silver
LINE
brass
From source
To garage
LOAD
silver
LOAD
brass

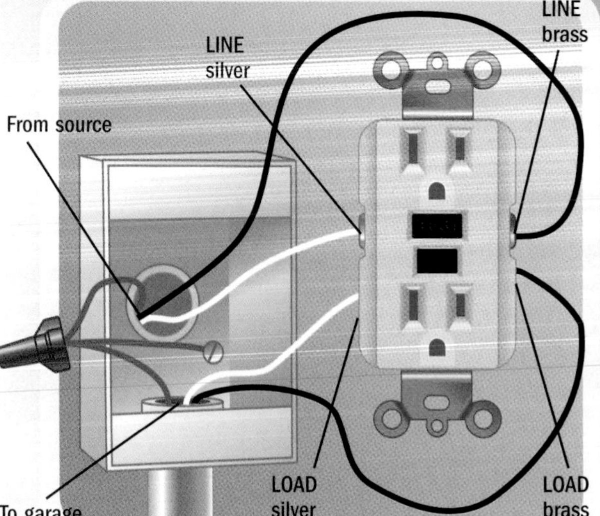

Outdoor circuits

All outdoor receptacles should be GFCI-protected devices. The terminals on these receptacles are marked LINE and LOAD. The LINE terminals are connected to the power source and to the rest of the circuit if it doesn't require GFCI protection. Connecting to the LOAD side of the GFCI receptacle provides GFCI protection for the circuit from that point on. Check with your local electrical inspector to determine your project requirements. The security light installed on the garage in this illustration would contain light and motion sensors. You could also install a switch to manually control the fixture.

Index

St Francis of Assisi

also by Pascale Allamand

THE ANIMALS WHO CHANGED THEIR COLORS

by Pascale Allamand and Nina Bawden

WILLIAM TELL

First published in Great Britain in 1983 by Jonathan Cape Ltd

Printed in Italy by New Interlitho, SpA, Milan

First U.S. Edition
1 2 3 4 5 6 7 8 9 10

Library of Congress Cataloging in Publication Data

Bawden, Nina (date)
St. Francis of Assisi.

SUMMARY: A biography of the young Italian who gave up his wealth in order to devote his life to preaching God's word and caring for the poor.
1. Francis, of Assisi, Saint, 1182–1226 – Juvenile literature.
2. Christian saints – Italy – Assisi – Biography – Juvenile literature.
3. Assisi (Italy) – Biography – Juvenile literature.
[1. Francis, of Assisi, Saint, 1182–1226. 2. Saints]
I. Allamand, Pascale, ill. II. Title. III. Title: Saint Francis of Assisi.

BX4700.F69B38 1983 271′.3′024 [B] [92] 82-13105
ISBN 0-688-01649-9
ISBN 0-688-01653-7 (lib. bdg.)

St Francis of Assisi

Story told by Nina Bawden, 1925-
Pictures by Pascale Allamand

LOTHROP, LEE & SHEPARD BOOKS NEW YORK

Eight hundred years ago, when knights charged into battle in heavy armor and troubadours wandered from castle to castle, singing songs about true love and brave deeds, a young man called Francis lived in the little town of Assisi, in Italy. His father was a merchant who sold fine cloth woven in glowing colors. He expected his son to be a merchant, too. But although Francis was happy to be rich and wear beautiful clothes, he didn't want to make money. He had heard the songs the troubadours sang. He wanted to be a good knight, not a shopkeeper.

He was proud when his father sent him off to the wars in a new suit of bright armor. "I shall come home a great prince," he cried as he rode from the town, his head full of dreams. But along the way he met a poor knight whose clothes were threadbare and whose armor was rusty. They traveled together, and Francis was saddened to see his shabby companion watching him jealously. He sprang from his horse, gave the knight all his costly equipment, his lance, and his shining shield, and turned back to work in his father's shop in Assisi.

One day a beggar came to the shop, asking for alms. Francis was serving a customer, and, by the time he was free, the beggar had gone. Ashamed, Francis raced after him, searching the narrow streets, the crooked, dark alleys. When he found the beggar, he emptied his pockets of gold and silver.

The beggar was bewildered to receive so much money, and Francis's father was furious. Assisi was crawling with thieves, and Francis had left the shop unattended! Francis said he was sorry. He was afraid of his father. But he was soon to make him angrier still.

Outside Assisi was a small, ruined church. The priest was too poor to repair it. Francis sold a bale of his father's best silk and gave the money to the priest, who was as astonished as the beggar had been. And Francis's father exploded with rage. He dragged Francis into the marketplace of Assisi and accused him of being a thief. He said that Francis was a wicked son to steal from his father, who had given him everything!

Francis said, "You are no longer my father." He tore off his clothes and stood, naked, in front of the townspeople. He said, "Here are the clothes you have given me. From now on, I will obey only my Father in Heaven."

Francis dressed in a peasant's brown tunic with a rope for a girdle. He sang a troubadour's song as he walked barefoot like a beggar. When people offered him bread, he asked them for stones. He wanted to help the priest rebuild his church.

He grew thin and pale, but he was glad to be poor. He had dreamed of being a knight, a rich prince. Now that he owned nothing, he felt rich in a different way. The earth belonged to him. The sun and the moon were his brother and sister.

Francis had a friend called Clare. She was to become a saint as famous as Francis, but at this time she was only a girl who loved to talk to him. On Friday, after they had walked the whole day in the mountains, they came to an inn and asked the innkeeper for supper.

The innkeeper was a sour, evil man. He knew that religious people were not allowed to eat meat on Friday. So to spite them, he set a roast chicken before them.

He was amazed by what happened. Francis blessed the chicken, and it turned into a plump fish. The innkeeper shook with anger and fear, and slunk away to his kitchen.

Other young men came to join Francis in the hills around Assisi. Francis called them his Brothers. Unlike the monks, who were snug in their monasteries, Francis and his friends lived like tramps, never knowing when they would eat, or where they would sleep, even in the winter snow.

Once, at a crossroads, a Brother asked Francis which way to go. Francis said, "Remember what children do? Spin like a top." The Brother whirled around until he was giddy. Francis said, "The road you are facing is the right road. God has shown you."

XI
VII

Nobody washed much in those days, and the Brothers hardly at all. When they traveled to Rome to ask the Pope for his blessing, the Pope was disgusted. "Go roll with the pigs," he said. "That is all you are fit for."

Francis found a pigsty. He said, "Brother Pig, may I join you?" He wallowed in dung and went back to the Pope even dirtier. The Pope held his nose, but he blessed Francis. The Brothers were living as the Gospels had taught them to – in peace and in poverty.

Francis was always polite. If he kicked a stone, he apologized to it. He spoke courteously to everyone and everything. When he came upon a host of birds in a harvest field, squabbling over the corn, he stopped them by saying, "Little Sisters, it is my turn to be heard."

The birds were silent while Francis spoke to them, telling them to praise their Creator, who had given them wings for flight and feathers for clothing. And when he finished, they rose in a fluttering cloud, praising God with their singing.

The Brothers preached to the citizens of the bustling towns, to the farmers in the hill villages. And, as Francis had taught them, they preached to the animals, even to the fishes in the swift rivers and in the deep seas.

When a Brother stood on the shore and called to the fish, they came in great shoals, the little fish at the front, the bigger fish behind them, and at the back, the sea mammals, the whales and the dolphins. They listened respectfully, opening their mouths and bowing their heads, to show that they honored the holy man who had summoned them.

Even dangerous beasts trusted Francis. The town of Gubbio was plagued by a wolf that was killing the sheep. Francis found the wolf in his lair and spoke to him kindly. The wolf snarled once or twice, as a savage wolf should, and then came meekly to Francis.

When the people of Gubbio saw Francis and the wolf at the gate of the town, they were frightened. But Francis held the wolf's paw and said, "Here is Brother Wolf, who has come to say he is sorry." The people came forward to greet him, and for the rest of his life the wolf lived in Gubbio, and everyone fed him.

The Brothers were poor, refusing all presents. But when a nobleman who had great estates offered Francis a mountain, he was pleased to accept it. He wanted a place to be private.

Alone on this mountain one morning, he saw an angel, a seraph with six wings, filling the sky. It stayed only a moment and, as it faded and vanished, like a dream in the sunrise, Francis felt a sudden grief in his heart and sharp pains in his hands and his feet. And when he looked, he saw the marks of nails on them.

The wounds would not heal. Francis said, “My Brother Body is weary,” and went home to Assisi. He was near death now, and as his mind drifted, half asleep, dreaming, he remembered a rich lady in Rome who had once made some almond cakes for him.

The Brothers decided to send for her. But before they could call a messenger, the lady appeared with her servants, tired and dusty after the rough ride from the city. She had brought the cakes. She had also brought a linen shroud for his burial.

Francis ate the cakes. But he refused the shroud. It was too fine a garment for a poor man. He asked his friends to lay him, in his shirt, on the cold ground. They stood around in their brown tunics, watching and waiting. And others crept close and watched, too. Rats and mice, rabbits and foxes – all the timid, wild creatures, saying good-bye to their special saint, their Brother Francis, who loved them.